W9-CEB-002

Religion and Immigration

Christian, Jewish, and Muslim Experiences in the United States

EDITED BY
YVONNE YAZBECK HADDAD
JANE I. SMITH
JOHN L. ESPOSITO

ALTAMIRA
PRESS

A Division of
ROWMAN & LITTLEFIELD PUBLISHERS, INC.
Walnut Creek • *Lanham* • *New York* • *Oxford*

ALTAMIRA PRESS
A Division of Rowman & Littlefield Publishers, Inc.
1630 North Main Street, #367
Walnut Creek, CA 94596
www.altamirapress.com

Rowman & Littlefield Publishers, Inc.
A Member of the Rowman & Littlefield Publishing Group
4720 Boston Way
Lanham, MD 20706

PO Box 317
Oxford
OX2 9RU, UK

Copyright © 2003 by ALTAMIRA PRESS

All rights reserved. No part of this publication may be reproduced, stored in a retrieval system, or transmitted in any form or by any means, electronic, mechanical, photocopying, recording, or otherwise, without the prior permission of the publisher.

British Library Cataloguing in Publication Information Available

Library of Congress Cataloging-in-Publication Data

Religion and immigration : Christian, Jewish, and Muslim experiences in the United States / edited by Yvonne Yazbeck Haddad, Jane I. Smith, John L. Esposito.
    p. cm.
    Includes bibliographical references and index.
    ISBN 0-7591-0351-8 (alk. paper) — ISBN 0-7591-0352-6 (pbk. : alk. paper)
    1. Immigrants—Religious life—United States—Congresses. 2. United States—Religion—Congresses. I. Haddad, Yvonne Yazbeck, 1935–. II. Smith, Jane I. III. Esposito, John L.
    BL2525.R456 2002
    305.6'0973—dc21
                                        2002009973

Printed in the United States of America

∞™ The paper used in this publication meets the minimum requirements of American National Standard for Information Sciences—Permanence of Paper for Printed Library Materials, ANSI/NISO Z39.48-1992.

KIRAN CUNNINGHAM

Religion and Immigration

Contents

Acknowledgments

This volume brings together studies on Christian, Jewish, and Muslim immigrant communities in America. For the most part, the chapters represent the contributions of the authors to a conference titled "Becoming American: Immigration and Religious Life in the United States" sponsored by the Center for Muslim Christian Understanding at Georgetown University May 11–12, 2000. The conference was cosponsored by the Macdonald Center for the Study of Islam and Muslim-Christian Relations at Hartford Seminary and the Maurice Greenberg Center for Judaic Studies at the University of Hartford. The chapters by M. A. Muqtedar Khan and Amina McCloud were specifically solicited for this volume.

The editors would like to give special thanks for the financial support for the conference to the following officers of Georgetown University: Dorothy M. Brown, provost; Jane Dammen McAuliffe, dean of Georgetown College; Robert Gallucci, dean of the Edmund C. Walsh School of Foreign Service; Susan F. Martin, director of the Institute for the Study of International Migration; and Jo Ann Moran Cruz, chair of the Department of History. We also want to acknowledge the important contribution of Professor Charles B. Keely, Hertzberg Professor of International Migration, Georgetown University, in helping to conceptualize and give structure to the deliberations of the conference. Special thanks are also due to Kim Harrington, Thea Ewing, and Rajae Nami for help in the organizational oversight of the manuscript and the preparation of the bibliography.

Introduction: Becoming American— Religion, Identity, and Institution Building in the American Mosaic

For most of its history, America has been a Christian nation. Today, however, the reality is an America that is far more religiously diverse and dynamic. While followers of many other religions, such as Hindus, Buddhists, Sikhs, Jains, and Bahais, have emigrated in significant numbers since the 1960s, it is Christianity, Judaism, and Islam that account for the vast majority of Americans. The American religious landscape of the twenty-first century is dominated by the churches, synagogues, and mosques of its three largest faiths.

With the immigration of new ethnic groups, issues of faith, identity, and institution building become critical for immigrant communities seeking to establish themselves as part of the American mosaic. American Muslims today struggle with many of the same kinds of concerns that immigrant Christians and Jews faced earlier in American history. This volume provides a comparative perspective on the religious history and experiences of Catholics, Protestants, Jews, and Muslims.

America remains a country in which religion is a dynamic part of life and society. Religion has been a central and often defining force throughout the history of the United States. From the time of the early pilgrims, who fled religious persecution in their homelands and came to America seeking religious freedom, America has been promoted as a haven for men and women from every part of the world escaping religious and political persecution or seeking economic opportunities and a better life.

The same pilgrims who established a colony in Massachusetts where people could practice their religion as they chose were also, it must be acknowledged, prejudiced against Catholics and Jews and intolerant toward other Protestant sects, such as Presbyterians and Baptists. Yet the founding fathers of the United States were men who believed in the separation of religion and state and who wrote into the Constitution the principle of freedom of religion. These tensions continue to characterize American society, often exacerbated as immigrants bring with them a great variety of ethnic, national, and religious identities.

During the early part of the twentieth century, it became popular to define the United States as a "melting pot" where all nationalities and ethnicities could, at least in theory, blend together in one heterogeneous but unified whole. Roman Catholics were in the process of achieving recognition as a legitimate part of the American religious constituency. Jews, whose struggle initially may have been harder, eventually became full participants in redefining America. As the century played out, however, it became increasingly clear that some groups were missing from the melting pot, such as African Americans and Latino Americans, for whom full assimilation never seemed a realizable possibility. After the revocation of the Asia Exclusion Act of 1965, successive waves of immigrants arrived, with the result that the religious demography of the United States changed. A definition of America as Protestant, Catholic, and Jewish was promoted as an alternative to the melting-pot metaphor. Immigrant Muslims, for the most part latecomers to the American scene, have actively sought recognition, some even calling for a definition of America as Judeo-Christian-Muslim. Nonetheless, they find themselves still in the process of discovering whether it is possible for them to be full partners in American society and whether they are willing to pay the price of belonging.

The chapters in this volume are the product of a conference held in Washington, D.C., that attempted to document the relationship between immigration and religion in the United States, focusing on movements in Christianity, Judaism, and Islam. At the time it was held, before the trauma of the September 11, 2001, attacks on the World Trade Center and the Pentagon, it appeared that Muslims were on a trajectory to create a place for themselves in the American kaleidoscope. They were ready to shed some of their own cultural distinctions in the process of becoming American and were also seeking parity in recognition, representation, and influence with other religious communities

in the United States. They had pondered their options, and the majority appeared to have agreed that they would follow the Jewish model of negotiating
for full participation in the American system.

The attacks of 9/11, which led to a significant backlash on the Muslim community, seem to have put a damper on the process. Not only has there been an
increase in racial profiling, but in some sectors it has become acceptable to demonize Islam and to blame the religion and its American adherents for the
acts of violence perpetrated on the country. In the post-9/11 period, the Muslim community increasingly has come to see Islam vilified by some Christian
and Jewish public officials and the press, and see themselves targeted as a potential security risk. It seems to many that no matter how often they denounce
and renounce violence, the press and the public demand more such renunci-
ation. Some Muslims are seeing parallels between the kind of American mind-
set that fostered the abuse of German citizens during World War I, Japanese
internment during World War II, and the anti-Communist fever of Mc-
Carthyism. Regardless of the insistence of the government that the current
war is only on terrorism, some Muslims are beginning to wonder whether in
fact Americans have not really declared war on Islam itself.

A number of themes surface throughout the chapters of this volume.
Among them are the following:

1. Discrimination on the part of those who are already citizens of the United
   States toward newcomers representing new religions and new cultures.
2. The heritage of Western colonialism and its effects on the ways in which
   those who were formerly colonized choose to adapt to American society.
   This theme plays itself out in the experiences of Hispanics, African Americans, Jewish victims of the Holocaust, and Muslims.
3. The challenge of moral equivalency, that is, the tension over whether one
   group's ethnicity, culture, or religious expression is more acceptable than
   another in the fabric of religious America.
4. The expectation that immigrants should assimilate as quickly as possible,
   shedding their cultures and ideologies, at the same time that they themselves are blamed when assimilation is not immediately achieved.

Thus, the following chapters serve as the backdrop for considering what current patterns of immigration mean for the American religious context and

how new religious communities are responding to the reality of living and practicing in America.

A defining characteristic of Western and certainly American culture is an emphasis on individualism, which often contrasts with the more communal orientation of the traditional societies from which many immigrants come. The experiences of members of immigrant communities in America demonstrate the often-difficult balance between the needs of the individual and expectations of the community. In chapter 1, David J. O'Brien examines several pairs of concepts that inform current thinking about religion and society. He notes that individualism is probably the single most important aspect of American religious culture. Surveys consistently confirm a sturdy independence, personal faith and piety, and suspicion of religious institutions in general as characteristic of immigrants as well as of the American middle class. The quest for community is especially evident among virtually all immigrant groups as people look for others who share their experience and/or convictions and with whom they can find a sense of belonging based on a common faith.

Another major challenge facing most religious groups has been balancing the diversity of believers within the uniformity of faith. The issue, as O'Brien notes, is how to preserve the integrity of the faith in the midst of the bewildering pluralism that characterizes the American religious milieu. Local congregations and national denominations struggle to welcome newcomers, attempting to be sensitive to their distinct needs while ensuring a sense of common fellowship with more established members. This process can be seen in recent years in the example of the Catholic Church's incorporation of the Latino/Hispanic community in the United States. O'Brien maintains that while labels such as liberal and conservative, modernist and fundamentalist, have been defining orientations in the past, today more and more people within particular congregations, especially among the younger generation, are eschewing these traditional divisions and trying to capture the best of both extremes. At the denominational level, such divisions serve to deepen the chasm between congregations and the transcongregational life of religious denominations, with serious consequences for the unity, integrity, and cultural impact of religion. O'Brien questions whether denominations will even have a place in the future of American religion, especially if they are unable to unite people around shared beliefs and a common mission.

A third issue of concern to religious communities today is the balance between the public and the private. It is commonly noted that Americans tend to restrict religion to private life, leaving a barren public square without religious meaning or moral guidance. O'Brien believes that many communities continue to reflect this high degree of privatization. Nonetheless, there are signals of the effort to maintain the unity and coherence of particular religious groups within American pluralism. Catholicism presents an interesting example in the American context. On the one hand, it is still organized, or at least portends to be, as a single entity. The Church is unified by the bishops who represent some blend of common belief, doctrine, morality, and discipline. To some real extent, that unity was facilitated precisely because of the anti-Catholicism that has prevailed for much of the history of America. Now, perhaps because the religious basis of anti-Catholicism has all but disappeared with the decline of the organizational strength of so-called mainstream Protestantism and the diffusion of resurgent evangelical Christianity, Catholic leaders are having difficulty maintaining the former unity and integrity of the Church. Recent scandals within the priesthood itself have made the task of Catholic unity even more difficult.

SOME CHRISTIAN IMMIGRANT COMMUNITIES IN AMERICA

American Catholics provide a full-blown example of an immigrant church and community that after a long struggle has moved from the margins of American society to its center as both a religious and an economic presence. Yet, as Chester Gillis demonstrates in chapter 2, since colonial times Catholics have faced discrimination and exclusion. Prejudice did serve, however, to galvanize the Catholic community and encouraged members to form organizations designed to serve their particular social and professional needs. After decades of growth and development, the Catholic "ghetto," which served as a means of preserving religious identity while Catholics struggled to become part of the American melting pot, peaked in the 1950s and has gradually dissolved in the post–Vatican II (Second Vatican Council) period.

Gillis provides an overview of the development of American Catholicism as it moved from the periphery to the center. From 1940 to 1960, the Catholic population doubled, partly because of the postwar baby boom. The 1950s witnessed the largest expansion of Catholic schools and churches since the mid-nineteenth century. Catholic culture reached its apex, and Catholics began to establish themselves in the political sphere. Catholics were assimilating into American society, becoming wealthier, more educated, and more geographically diversified. Over the past forty years, this Catholic subculture—which provided security and identity for the immigrant community—has declined as Catholics have become increasingly assimilated. Vestiges of subculture remain (some still vibrant, others dwindling), now joined by a new crop of post–Vatican II Catholic organizations, including the Catholic League for Religious and Civil Rights, Catholics for Free Choice, and the Conference for Catholic Lesbians.

One component of the decline of Catholic subculture, Gillis notes, is the changing attitude toward Church authority since disobedience to Church practices is less costly now than a generation ago. For many Catholics today, compliance is seen as voluntary. The Church remains important but must compete with social, cultural, and economic forces that pull in other directions. In recent years, a significant Catholic minority has begun to voice discontent with the assimilation process that began with Vatican II, claiming that many Catholics too easily follow cultural trends that at their core represent values inconsistent with Catholic teaching and tradition. The price of assimilation, they say, is loss of identity.

Catholics of European ethnicity today no longer constitute a mainly immigrant community; their levels of education and economic status have risen significantly. However, some fear that as Catholics assimilate, they will suffer a fate similar to mainline Protestant churches that have been losing members steadily since the second half of the twentieth century. Traditionalists and conservatives mounting a campaign to revive the Catholic subculture are rebelling against Vatican II reforms. Many conservative Catholic groups now support a return to traditional Catholic practices and liturgy and are clear in their opposition to such innovations as the ordination of women and recognition of gay marriages.

This conservative mood is also reflected in the growth of evangelical Protestantism both domestically and internationally. Despite the significant decrease in proselytization among mainline churches, Christianity continues to spread through the global activities of its missionaries. As Randall Balmer notes in chapter 3, the patterns of the late twentieth century reveal the extent to which evangelicals enjoy the level of success once achieved by Catholic missionaries. The initial evangelical invasion of Latin America was caricatured as

American cultural imperialism, fueled by massive amounts of money and conveyed by "anglo" missionaries. Today, evangelicalism, especially Pentecostalism, has become an indigenous Latin American movement with enormous popular appeal, primarily among the poor and marginalized. Despite the efforts of liberation theologians, for many Latin Americans, Roman Catholicism is still associated with elite Latin culture, which for them implies their own poverty and colonization by the Spaniards.

Evangelical Christians, missionized in Latin America, Africa, India, and Southeast Asia, began arriving in the United States in the late twentieth century and have been welcomed by the evangelical churches. Part of the appeal of these churches in America is their theological emphasis on egalitarianism and spiritual upward mobility and the assistance they provide to new immigrants in such mundane matters as finding affordable housing, employment, and day care facilities. They also offer access to the evangelical "subculture," including church congregations, publishing houses, seminaries, mission and relief societies, and Bible camps. The function of the evangelical subculture is essentially the same as that traditionally offered by the Catholic Church: shelter, nurture, and the safety of a like-minded community. Nonetheless, two-thirds of Hispanics identify themselves as Roman Catholic.

For the majority of Hispanic Americans, as Ana María Díaz-Stevens observes in chapter 4, culture, language, and religion continue to be the mainstays of Hispanic identity. More Hispanics identify themselves as being religious than any other groups (only 5 percent say they are nonreligious). However, as Díaz-Stevens reminds us, not all Hispanics/Latinos are immigrants. Indeed, including Puerto Ricans, nearly 70 percent of all Hispanics have been born as U.S. citizens.

Common language, shared cultural traits, the history of Spanish colonization, and in most cases shared religious tradition have facilitated the fostering of a common identity as members of a larger Latin American community inclusive of different national groups. Unlike most European immigrants, Latinos have been distinguished from the English-speaking population through the continued use of Spanish, facilitated by churches that operate bilingually. Marriage within the community, language, culture, and certain commonalties in the history of Latin American and the Hispanic Caribbean have made it possible for this pan-identity to be stronger for Hispanics/Latinos than for most other immigrant groups. Religion has aided in the maintenance of Latino ethnic identity.

The fact that Hispanics have not integrated as quickly as many other immigrant groups has been blamed on the Hispanics themselves. Díaz-Stevens, however, maintains that the history of U.S. colonization and the invasion in Mexico and Puerto Rico rendered Hispanics strangers in their own land, depriving them of social progress and economic prosperity. The subsequent encounters that Mexicans and Puerto Ricans have had with America in their own homeland and their identification of religious, cultural, and social traits in America that they feel are undesirable or detrimental to their own identity have been the real reasons for their lack of integration in America. Increased Latino/Hispanic immigration since the 1965 reform of immigration laws has added to the enclaves of U.S.-born Latinos, nearly doubling the population between 1970 and 1990, and along with it the number of Hispanic churches and associations. Hispanics are projected to make up 15 percent of the total U.S. population by 2020.

Another major constituent group of the American religious mosaic is the African American community. In chapter 5, Anthony B. Pinn explores the religious ramifications of migration as they relate to the development of a complex sense of African American religious identity. Pinn observes that the religious diversity in African American communities is mainly the result of three major movements: the slave trade, the Great Migration, and late twentieth-century immigration from the Caribbean. Although many English colonists saw slavery as an opportunity to convert Africans, he says, testimonies of slaves and former slaves speak to alternate forms of religious expression. Many enslaved Africans maintained rich ties to African religious thought and rituals. When these could not be explored openly, they were celebrated and remembered in more subtle ways, such as through the decorative arts, such as quilting.

Expressions of black religious diversity continued through the twentieth century. Following the Great Migration, many migrants were not welcomed into the established black churches. While some did assimilate into existing black denominations, others became members of black branches of mainly white denominations or joined Pentecostal churches. This period also witnessed the growth of "extrachurch" religious organizations, such as the Moorish Science Temple. This push away from the Christian church, which was seen as the symbol of black enslavement, often entailed a movement into African-based forms of religious practice.

Pinn maintains that despite strong evidence supporting a plethora of religious forms within African American communities, the vast majority of scholarly attention has been biased toward the black Christian church. It treats the Christian faith as the true center of black religious experience and anything non-Christian as simply external. He feels that this is too narrow a depiction of African American religious identity and that the religious experience and the religious identity it fosters cannot be adequately described through attention to doctrine and other elements that are bound to a particular tradition.

JEWS IN THE AMERICAN CONTEXT

The American Jewish experience highlights many of the issues faced by a non-Christian community trying to establish itself in an overwhelmingly Christian majority context and culture. In chapter 6, Jacob Neusner traces patterns of religious identification and practice over successive waves of Jewish immigration, using his own story as an example.

Early small groups of Sephardic communities (Jews from North Africa) did not last in America, perhaps because their numbers were too small to start rabbinical schools. Sizable numbers of German Jews migrated in the middle of the nineteenth century. With their presence came the organization of Judaism in many American cities through the establishment of synagogues. Neusner rejects as simplistic the popular theory that the orthodox first generation gave way to conservative Judaism in the second generation and to reform in the third, with a final stage of de-Judaizing especially through intermarriage with non-Jews. He maintains that in reality, Jewish immigrants undertook the task of acculturation by adjusting the received faith to the requirements of American life and that their children have continued the process. The second generation of Jews, wanting their children to become American and believing that society was hostile to difference, thought it best to blend in. The third generation came to consciousness during and after World War II, determined both to accept what cannot be changed (anti-Semitism) and to reconnect with practices of the first generation that the second generation had tried to forget.

This reversion to religious life could be measured by the extensive building of new synagogues and a vast increase in institutions of faith. Religion became the medium of ethnic assertion. It resulted in the idealization of immigrants

and especially their places of origin, a process that Neusner calls the "sentimentalization" of Jewish existence. The third generation turned an otherworldly religious culture into an ethnic identity, making the survival of the
Jews as a group an end in itself. Ethnic Judaism then built on what came before and focused on a Judaism of the Holocaust and Redemption, an effort
that turned a catastrophe into the defining moment of history and center of
life for many in the Jewish community.

As Neusner looks at the twenty-first century, he projects four major characteristics of American Judaism: 1) renewed interest in religious observance,
such as reform Jews adopting traditional practices; 2) paradoxically, more
Jews marrying outside the faith; 3) the increased influence of feminist movements that have led, for example, to the opening up of the rabbinate to
women; and 4) continued engagement with the state of Israel as an important
medium of Jewish self-expression in the United States and Canada. Despite
differences in religious practices, Neusner believes that all American Jews find
their identity first and foremost as Americans.

In chapter 7, Jonathan D. Sarna also sees American Judaism at a crossroads and identifies some of the major characteristics or transformations
that he believes will affect American Jewry in the twenty-first century. De-
mographically, the American Jewish community will shrink both absolutely
and relative to the population as a whole, continuing the decline that has
been evident for half a century. As a result, he says, it is likely that American Jewry will shrink in significance both nationally and internationally.
The decline in the American Jewish population means a decline in its status as an American religion. Where it was once viewed as the "third American faith," Judaism is quickly becoming one of many American "minority
faiths."

Sarna also believes that Jews will come to view the diaspora differently than
they view it today. The combined forces of persecution and Zionism have redrawn the map of world Jewry. The diaspora has shrunk by more than 40 percent since 1939. Jews are more concentrated than ever before, with more than
95 percent living in just fourteen countries. At the same time, however, Jews
now occupy more economically affluent, politically stable, and socially attractive environments than ever before. Sarna predicts that American Judaism is
likely to come to resemble the Protestant denominational structure even more
closely, with burgeoning pluralism, greater focus on the individual than the

group, more permeable denominational and even interfaith boundaries, and greater emphasis on the value of consent.

Significant questions about the future of American Jews persist. Will assimilation or revitalization mark the twenty-first century? As Sarna observes, signs of assimilation abound: intermarriage, disaffiliation, and ritual laxity. Yet at the same time, there are also strong elements of revitalization and renewal within the community. Jewish educational institutions and programs are flourishing, synagogue attendance is increasing, and there is a perceptible return to religion among youth. A critical question in the years ahead is whether most Jews will become increasingly religiously polarized or whether they will return to the "vital center" in Jewish life, isolating extremists on both sides. Although conflicts between orthodox and reform Jews make schism seem a possibility, there are also signs of movement back to the center, especially at the lay level.

The great causes that once energized American Jewry—immigrant absorption, saving European Jewry, creating and sustaining a Jewish state, and rescuing Soviet, Arab, and Ethiopian Jews—have now been successfully completed. Today, for the first time in historical memory, no large community of persecuted Jews exists anywhere in the world. Thus, Sarna's final question is whether American Jews in the twenty-first century will be able to identify a mission compelling enough for the community to embrace with passion.

Judaism and Catholicism in America have shared some similarities as minority communities seeking to assimilate and yet preserve their distinctive identity. One of the ways in which both communities have attempted to do this is through the process of institution building, including hospitals. In chapter 8, Alan M. Kraut reminds us that there is a long tradition, dating back to the earliest Jewish immigrants to America, of Jews "taking care of their own," fulfilling spiritual needs, and providing economic support. Until the early twentieth century, hospitals in the United States were seen mainly as charitable institutions where those who had no families could receive care from strangers or where poor people went to die. In the early and mid-nineteenth century, hospitals became fertile grounds for evangelical Protestants seeking Jewish as well as Catholic converts on their deathbeds. Both Catholics and Jews responded by building hospitals of their own, and this played a central role in the assimilation of newcomers to the United States.

During the peak period of Jewish immigration at the turn of the twentieth century, Jewish hospitals allowed patients to continue religious observance in traditional ways as they negotiated the transition from alien to American. Many Jews also felt that they needed separate hospitals as places of training and practice for Jewish physicians facing discrimination by the American medical establishment. In the 1960s, the barriers in medical schools and hospital residencies began to fall, with the result that Jewish hospitals lost one of their reasons for being. Today the number of Jewish hospitals is dwindling, and those that still exist serve primarily inner-city patients, many African American or Latino, and far fewer Jews.

MUSLIMS AS CITIZENS OF AMERICA

Of the three major monotheistic religions, Islam has experienced the most accelerated growth in America in recent decades and is fast becoming the religion with the second-largest representation in the United States. Although Islam is often portrayed as a recent addition to America's religious landscape and primarily the product of immigration, the reality of Islam in America is far more complex.

The formation of the Muslim community in the United States began with early Muslims who were African slaves brought to the United States in the seventeenth and eighteenth centuries. It picked up again with the arrival of immigrant Muslims in the mid- to late nineteenth century who were mainly Arabs from greater Syria, Lebanon, Jordan, and Palestine hoping to earn money and return home. Arab immigrants were joined in the latter half of the twentieth century by Muslims from virtually all over the world, the largest numbers coming from the Indian subcontinent, Iran, Afghanistan, and Africa and a smattering from Southeast Asia. The Muslim community in the United States is unique in the world both by virtue of its heterogeneity in representing every Muslim country in the world and because a major part of its constituency is made up of African Americans, some of whom are orthodox (Sunni and Shiite) and others sectarian.

As Aminah McCloud observes in chapter 9, actual community building began in the twentieth century within two major and distinct groups: immigrants and converts. The small Arab immigrant community in the early twentieth century practiced their faith in private if at all, downplaying any affiliation with what would be perceived as a "non-American" religion.

Many sought complete assimilation. After the opening up of immigration in 1965, many Muslim students and professionals, especially in the sciences, medicine, and engineering, came seeking employment. They were better educated, better off financially, and more competent in English than earlier Muslim immigrants, and they fairly quickly joined the American middle and upper middle classes. Arabs and South Asian Muslims began to build mosques, schools, and community centers in suburbs and major urban areas. Meanwhile, the various ethnic divisions within Muslim American communities, whether cultural, racial, or sectarian, had to face the reality of different kinds of stereotyping on the part of American citizens.

Muslims who wanted permanent residence assimilated by adopting Anglicized names and marrying non-Muslims. Many have felt torn by trying to hold on to their Islamic culture at the same time that they wanted the "American Dream" of the educational and financial opportunities that America provides. Second-generation Muslims, schooled in America and acculturated to a significant degree, generally accept American values, though they are keenly aware of their Islamic heritage and often experience extreme tensions when they feel that aspects of American culture or policy are at odds with that heritage.

Interaction between indigenous and immigrant Muslims has always been a sensitive issue. McCloud argues that for the most part, the immigrant community, proportionately far wealthier and with access to greater resources than African Americans, has focused on Muslims overseas and that little or no attention has been paid to the racism or financial problems faced by African American Muslim communities. In addition, she says, immigrants often do not consult African Americans about their political preferences, as, for example, in the 2000 presidential election, when immigrants projected the image that the entire Muslim community favored the election of George W. Bush.

Regardless of the challenges, McCloud sees hopeful signs for the future. One clear marker of the extent to which a group has successfully "Americanized" is the number and quality of institutions that it has been able to establish. The Muslim community has built mosques, Islamic centers, schools, and other institutions, including facilities for immigrant refugees, each with its own ethnic flavor and Islamic overlay. She notes that as second- and third-generation Muslims increasingly find their identity as Americans, ties to home countries weaken. The result is that many Muslim youths are rejecting their parents' and grandparents' efforts to define Islam in culture-specific terms and are working to create an American Islam that meets the challenges of its own egalitarian ideology.

In chapter 10, M. A. Muqtedar Khan argues that the classification of American Muslims into two main communities—immigrants, who tend to see themselves as "Muslims in America," and indigenous, whom he says can usually be described as Americans who are Muslim without prejudice toward either American or Muslim identity—is being challenged by a rapidly emerging third identity, that of American Muslim per se. The interplay between American values and Islamic values and the mutual reconstitution of each are leading to a liberal understanding of Islam more in tune with dominant American values, such as religious tolerance, pluralism, multiculturalism, and multireligious coexistence.

Khan feels that to participate in American life, Muslims have been forced to develop a conception of what it means to be an American. Two clear images of America seem to characterize (and divide) Muslim attitudes: "America the democracy" and "America the colonial power." That is, some see America primarily as liberal, democratic, tolerant, and multicultural, while others perceive it as an evil force, using its power to dominate foreign nations, stealing resources, and depriving other countries of their right to self-determination. Those who adopt the latter view often continue to look to their country of origin as home, tend to be more focused on U.S. foreign policy, and are resentful and distrustful of America. Those who view the United States as their home are more concerned with establishing Islam in America.

Muslims who wish to make America their home are prominent among the American Muslim leadership and have been successful in establishing their view as the prevailing norm. Consequently, those in the United States who take the "America as colonial power" viewpoint have become marginalized. The fact that immigrants since the mid-1960s were mainly better educated and intellectually sophisticated has provided the community with a Muslim leadership capable of articulating enlightened self-interest and formulating a far-reaching vision for the revival of Islam and Islamic values. Muslim leaders have created a variety of social, political, and educational organizations to promote this agenda. These groups hold in common the single most important goal: that Muslims are not to assimilate but rather are to defend and consolidate Islamic identity. Their secondary goal is developing intellectual and

political resources capable of making significant social and political changes
in the Muslim world.

Key challenges to these goals exist. Among the more important is prejudice
against Islam in the American mainstream and resistance to adjustment
within the community itself that would pose a major barrier to engagement
with the American mainstream. Because of discrimination, pressure to assimilate remains high. Among the major developments of the 1990s are the
growth and success of CAIR (Council on American Islamic Relations), the
outward focus of the MSA (Muslim Student Association), and the explosion
of Islamic media on the Internet. Three social forces can be identified as having shaped the American Muslim identity. First is the shift in the understanding of America from a melting pot to a multicultural milieu, which has helped
American Muslims maintain their particularities. Second is the historical
force of Islamic resurgence, which has energized American Muslims to build
mosques, Islamic centers, and schools. Third is the creative thought and activism of the American Muslim elite, who have educated the Muslim community in new ways to think about the West and Islam, helping construct a liberal Muslim self that affirms both its Islamic and its American identity.

In chapter 11, Ingrid Mattson agrees that many factors determine the ways
in which Muslims interpret and define America. Among them are level of education, proficiency in English, level of access to modern communication
technology, exposure to American military might in the home country, and
the different ways in which Muslims are influenced by the messages of their
home governments. Mattson proposes that Muslim views of the relationship
with America can be grouped into three general categories. First are "paradigms of resistance," which view the United States as a *jahili* (a polytheistic environment that existed in pre-Islamic Arabia) society—pagan, hedonistic, and
irreconcilably opposed to the Islamic premise that society should be based on
obedience to God's commands. This results in a strong sense of isolationism
and resistance to participation in American politics and society, which are
viewed as void of morality. Second are "paradigms of embrace," in which the
United States is perceived as the new home/adopted country. Advocates point
to stories in the Qur'an justifying Muslim participation in the ruling apparatus of a non-Muslim country. Such stories try to show that the constitutional
democratic structure of America is almost equivalent to the political structure
of an ideal Islamic state and that the American Constitution is concordant

with Islamic principles. Third are "paradigms of selective engagement," adopted by the majority of Muslims who are striving to define their place as religious minorities in a country that they acknowledge does in fact allow great religious freedom.

The main issue facing American Muslims today, Mattson maintains, is how to correct wrongs within American society generally without compromising their beliefs and allegiance to Islam. The areas of engagement most comfortable for these Muslims are social causes, grassroots activism, and "alternative" forms of activism, such as environmentalism, social justice movements, and neighborhood associations. Although engagement in the American political system beyond the local level has, until recently, been considered undesirable by many Muslims, the past few years have witnessed increased political participation on a national level, due in part to the growth of organizations such as the Muslim Political Action Committee and the American Muslim Council.

Mattson believes that the Muslim community may be unique in demonstrating concern for articulating the religious justification for participation in national politics. Some Muslim leaders are now beginning to propose a fuller embrace of America, while at the same time other Muslims have become disillusioned and highly skeptical of their ability to bring about anything but superficial change in the American political system.

Immigration patterns in the twenty-first century reveal the extent to which change remains part of the American religious experience. For the first time, we have the results of a pioneering pilot study providing a random sampling of recent immigrants that includes their religious affiliation. We can now expect to have a more scientific way of determining how immigrations impact the overall religious scene in America. In chapter 12, Guillermina Jasso, Douglas S. Massey, Mark R. Rosenzweig, and James P. Smith discuss how the religious preferences of the new immigrants are changing the religious profile and ethnic landscape of America.

Only 65 percent of new immigrants are Christian, as compared to 82 percent of native-born Americans. Because the immigrant concentrations are from Mexico, Latin America, and the Philippines, most of them are Catholic. The largest single group of Roman Catholics, however, comes from Poland. The proportion of faiths outside the Judeo-Christian tradition represented in

the new arrivals is constantly growing. Muslims represent some 8 percent of
these immigrants, and together with Buddhists and Hindus make up 15 percent. The largest Muslim immigration (18 percent of the total) is Pakistani.
Most of the Jews and Eastern Orthodox coming to America are from the Soviet Union. Educational levels among immigrants vary remarkably, especially
among women. In general, Catholic and Protestant as well as Muslim women
have relatively low levels of schooling. Many of the most educated immigrants
are from newer religions—men representing Buddhist, Muslim, and other
Eastern religions and Hindu and Christian Orthodox women.

The next survey of the new immigrants according to their religious preferences will have to take into account the changes in government policies incurred as a result of the events of September 11, 2001. It is possible that new
figures will represent a decrease in the numbers of Muslims, reflecting the fact
that the Immigration and Naturalization Service is currently in the process of
tightening immigration procedures and restricting immigration from Muslim
countries as well as the number of Muslim students who are allowed to study
in the United States. At the end of chapter 1, David J. O'Brien concludes that
the two major questions facing religions in America today are the balance between deep commitment to one's faith and one's relationship to others in a
pluralistic society and how to reconcile differing religious beliefs with the
need for serious commitment to one another and our earth. For some immigrants today, including Arab Christians as well as Muslims, a third question
must be the extent to which they are able to survive in a society in which the
ramifications of a frontal attack on America are still unfolding.

Judaism, Christianity, and Islam have been religiously and politically inter-
twined throughout history. They represent a rich array of religious, ethnic, and
racial groups. Whatever the ensuing immigration restrictions, it is clear that in
the course of the twenty-first century, members of the three religious traditions
will continue to encounter one another not only in the Middle East but also in
America. The Muslim, Christian, and Jewish experiences presented here reflect
shared struggles of faith and identity (integration and assimilation), institution
building, and acculturation. In diverse ways, all represent minority experiences.
And in becoming American, all have faced the challenge of constructing an
identity that incorporates their faith and values within America's melting pot
or, more recently, its multicultural society. This transformation has challenged
everyone to face a new world in his or her own unique ways.

It is still too early to predict how the process of the Americanization of these new citizens will proceed. The answer, however, may have deep ramifications for the self-understanding of a society that has struggled to define itself as the model of religious inclusion and tolerance and as a welcoming venue for persons of all faiths and ethnic identities.

1

The Changing Contours of American Religion

David J. O'Brien

Robert Wuthnow, in *Christianity in the 21st Century*,[1] speaks of four pairs of concepts that shape our thinking about religion and society: individual and community, diversity and uniformity, liberal and conservative, and public and private. I examine each of these in this chapter.

INDIVIDUAL AND COMMUNITY

Individualism is probably the single most significant aspect of American religious culture. Isaac Hecker, a nineteenth-century Catholic convert evangelist, tried to persuade his fellow Catholics that they would do well to see Americans as "earnest seekers" who would respond to the religion that spoke most persuasively to the "aspirations of nature" and the "questions of the soul." Influenced by his youthful experience with the New England transcendentalists, Hecker developed a theology and spirituality anchored in the interior spiritual life. He was convinced that a bright future awaited his church if it could affirm the individualism spawned by personal freedom and the erosion of traditional loyalties amid America's bewildering pluralism.[2]

Most European Catholics found Hecker's vision incomprehensible. In 1899, years after Hecker's death, Pope Leo XIII condemned Americanism, which he described as a set of ideas associated with Isaac Hecker. Nor did American Catholics, mostly immigrants struggling to establish themselves, respond positively. Today, a century and a half after he formed his understanding of personal spiritual commitment as the pastoral prescription for American individualism, Hecker (and his transcendentalist friends) would be delighted with the majority of spiritual texts aimed at Generation X. Hecker was right, though not about everything all at once.

Individualism still dominates the religious trajectory in the United States. I use the word "trajectory" advisedly. Survey after survey reports a sturdy independence, personal faith and piety, suspicion of religious institutions, and fragility of social bonds, all qualities more notable among middle-class, no longer immigrant Americans than among newcomers but present, as far as we can tell, even among the newest arrivals, whose very presence often testifies to a loosening of traditional bonds in favor of new possibilities for individuals and families.

Mention of family comes easily when migrants are discussed, but family and community are as persistent themes in American religious experience as is individualism. One may stand alone before God, one may experience the necessity to choose, but people also seek out others. Individualism is almost always linked to community, arising from the desire to find others who share one's experience and/or one's convictions. Community is where people pray, worship, find a sense of belonging, and work toward objectives arising from shared faith.

The quest for community is perhaps even more universal among Americans than the individualism of Generation X. Immigrant Catholics, Protestants, and Jews, even the poorest, almost always experienced in migration a new sense of freedom, and almost always they chose to help form communities, often religious ones, with their own people. Recent newcomers undoubtedly share that experience of self-making and shared responsibility; they are forming a bewildering variety of communities, and in many of these, to use the wonderful phrase of Timothy L. Smith, "folk memories are brought to bear on new aspirations."[3]

I have always found that phrase helpful. Smith reoriented immigrant studies two decades ago by challenging an older view of ethnicity arising as a last-ditch, anachronistic holding action against modernization, an attitude still found among many contemporary students of "enclave" religions. Immigrants came across as victims and refugees, caught up in forces beyond their control, who almost automatically held fast to the old and familiar, to "folk memories." Smith, in contrast, found among many immigrants the historical agency that is now the familiar unifying theme of the new social history. People made choices (among these the decision to move) and then the deliberate, reasoned decisions to join together to form associations, often religious, to maintain group integrity, support family and communal values, and negotiate the demands of change. Thus "folk memories brought to bear on new aspirations."

"Folk" suggests peoplehood—with its complex of symbols and values, loyalty, and solidarity—and almost always stands in self-conscious opposition to the individualism of American culture. This is the theme sounded most forcefully by theologians speaking of Latino experience, and they are far from alone. Quite properly, scholars and community organizers of all sorts celebrate the sense of loyalty and solidarity that comes with identity as a distinct people.

"Memories" catches the people's determination to remain themselves and to express to others and pass on to the young the traditions and symbols, even the language, that gives meaning to their experience. But these communities are rarely ghettos or even enclaves. "Brought to bear" expresses the deliberation, the voluntary action that community building requires. However much church, synagogue, or mosque might look like one at home, each was, and is, different because these people constructed it. It is theirs, almost always in a way different from what that meant at home.

Finally, "new aspirations" suggests—and perhaps this is the most important point about the future—that ethnic associations arose from hope as well as memory. Their construction and maintenance, however conservative their appearance, were distinctly modern adventures. School texts spoke of citizenship, sermons spoke of duties incumbent on freedom, and American flags were everywhere. Pastors and politicians, editors and cultural advocates, all spent their lives mobilizing people for collective action to affirm their dignity, claim their rights, and participate in the decisions that affected their lives. Of course, part of the story was respect for who they had been and who they are. But part of the story is that better life, especially for the children. For those who made immigrant worlds—and they were and are not all immigrants— the future mattered as much as the past. And the very experience of group self-construction formed values and skills for that new adventure of family progress and public participation.

That the Smith portrait still helps is evident in at least some of the literature on congregational life among new groups. R. Stephen Warner writes that for immigrants the congregation is "the place in the United States where the standards you grew up with are still valorized and honored." But the cultural air in which you live is not yours, at least not yet, so that "if immigrants want to raise their children in their religious tradition, they really need to work at it and not take it for granted." That is why many people would claim in inter- views that they are "more religious here than they were at home."[4]

Warner and his colleagues echo another Smith theme when they report that in the congregation "people can exercise their talents, play roles and learn skills that may prepare them for the wider society—or perhaps compensate them for the losses they experience." This finding is echoed by Warner's colleague Nancy Ammerman, and similar judgments are built into the work of multiplying congregation-based community organizations around the country.[5]

But the hunger for community is at least equally intense among older groups, many now lacking in folk memories and unsure about new aspira- tions. Survey data show that Americans still yearn for community. When asked to measure the strength or weakness of their congregation, people re- spond with measures of community: sensitive leadership, a sense of feeling welcome and belonging, and help with the work of family, especially educa- tion. The nexus of individual and community is evident in the success of lo- cal independent congregations of all sorts and in the gap between stagnating rates of practice and persistent spiritual activity in the mainline churches. So one basic contour of the changing landscape of American religion remains the dynamic of personal conviction and voluntary community; the huge differ- ence is not between "mainstream" and independent congregation, I suspect, but between those that retain a sense of distinct peoplehood and those that do not. How those groups relate to one another will surely determine the fate of the U.S. Catholic Church in many parts of the country.

One more Catholic comment: The more one learns of the immigrant churches of the past and the congregations taking shape among new groups, the more the clerically dominated, school-centered, sacramental Catholic parish service stations of the postwar years seem an aberration. As people make churches for themselves across the landscape, middle-class Catholics are challenged by the decline of priests and the collapse of religious life. Once more they have to construct community, and many are doing so. A recent study of parish life documents the impact of lay leadership. Sociologist Eu- gene Hemrick concludes that "the change in parish staffing that everyone talks about is happening; the future is already here." But looking at the experience of Protestant denominations, one wonders about the long-range strength of parish life in the absence of either distinct peoplehood or a renewed sense of mission. (One recalls Sydney Mead's definition of a denomination as a people united on the basis of common belief for the purpose of accomplishing tangible and defined objectives.)

A final word for individualism, or at least for the wonderfully fruitful religious imagination of ordinary Americans. When Isaac Hecker was a seeker, he could consult Ralph Waldo Emerson and Orestes Brownson, George Ripley and Bronson Alcott, and even a few Shakers in the Boston neighborhood. Back home in New York, he could call on Oxford movement Episcopalians, Methodist perfectionists, followers of Joseph Smith, and even a wandering atheist. He had a lot of options. Yet later, when he was a Catholic leader, he still worried about the transcendentalists and hardly noticed the evangelical revivals sweeping American cities.

What about us? I spend a lot of time worrying about political divisions in my church and have joined some of the ideological trench warfare. While I was busy with such things, I missed out on charismatic renewal, the spread of populist papalism, the interesting evangelical converts, and most of the recent appearances of the Blessed Virgin Mary. Andrew Greely called it a new "do-it-yourself Catholicism." He should have called it "do-it-yourself religion," America at its most interesting. The presence of bottom-up religious diversity gives substance to religious liberty, enriches the culture, and provides a social ground for the practice of freedom. The more religious difference—real religious difference—the better the chances that democratic culture will muddle through.

DIVERSITY AND UNIFORMITY

Another American perennial: the chronic problem of seeking a degree of both unity and integrity amid persistent and bewildering pluralisms. Local congregations and national denominations struggle to welcome newcomers in ways that respond to their distinct needs while ensuring some degree of fellowship with more established members. They are not always successful. Bishop Joseph Fiorenza, leader of the U.S. hierarchy, celebrated the increasing diversity of American Catholicism, and *Encuentro* 2000 gathered Latino Catholics from across the country to help set a pastoral agenda. But the reality is harsh. Estimates are that up to 600,000 Hispanics leave the Catholic Church each year. A semiofficial survey reported by the bishops' documentary service noted that a number of practices make Hispanics feel unwelcome; the worst are administrative obstacles to reception of the sacraments. As newcomers are told to fill out forms, the researchers report, "Catholic ritual becomes almost commodified, subject to a kind of bureaucratization that blunts its spiritual power." Many are attracted instead to Protestant churches, by "powerful preaching that skillfully links the Scriptures with examples from everyday predicaments," and by the notion of church as "an extended family in Christ" where family is "equated with a strict ethos that provides clear orientation to its various members." Embedded in that assessment is a dynamic of memory and hope, of pastoral care and group solidarity that promises to sustain groups of Latinos through the next generation but not necessarily as churched Catholics.[6]

Reshaping contours is evident in the variety of forms of Latino Christianity, the report notices. Some form community outside Catholic boundaries, whereas others build vital communities within the church, sometimes in conflict with church leaders, helping to unite the community. Still others find genuine homes in the Catholic Church, in their own ethnic parishes, or in integrated parishes. And the Catholic leadership across the country consults the Latino community and claims to shape policy and ministry in response to community needs. Separatist, sometimes sectarian, impulses remain strong among new groups. But so does hope in the future. If memory pulls people toward separatism, hope pulls them toward forms of cooperation, if not integration. That dynamic tension has shaped American social history. I suspect that it will continue to shape the contours of American religion.

LIBERAL AND CONSERVATIVE

Wuthnow's third pair of concepts are icons of culture wars in which the terms were once modernism and fundamentalism. Parties with these names still fight for dominance in Christian denominations and in other shapes within Judaism. At times, all of us feel like lining up on one side or another, but I suspect that growing numbers of people want a little of what both sides have to offer. I particularly like Jonathan Rosen, reviewing Alan Dershowitz's book *The Vanishing American Jew*. Rosen was raised orthodox but later decided that many of its basic values, such as compassion, creativity, education, charity, and social responsibility, were supported more energetically at the opposite

end of the Jewish spectrum from orthodoxy. Looking back on his life, he admitted that he would like to mass-produce his own experience, a Jewish community that offered everyone an orthodox childhood and secular adulthood.[7]
Will deep differences about the meaning of historic faiths and their practice in the modern world continue to divide religious families? Certainly, survey data show that younger people are not very interested in the recent forms of these debates. All of us who visit local independent evangelical or charismatic congregations encounter evidence that stereotypical images of conservative churches are contradicted by local practice. We find multicultural cross-class congregations praying the Scriptures with gender-inclusive language while the sermon affirms family values that include respect for, even the leadership of, women. Even fundamentalist reliance on inerrant Scripture is modified by an enthusiastic ethic of love that seems to shatter all boundaries.

At the other end of the spectrum are so-called liberal congregations trying to restore a sense of the sacred to their ritual and praying the Scriptures with seriousness and apparent need. Young evangelicals are often university trained, committed to racial and sexual equality, and filled with anxiety about the destiny of their children: Fundamentalist fervor inevitably is tempered by such concerns. Liberal mainline Christians may at times look down their noses at evangelicals, but private anxieties lend a touch of envy to their relationship. Moreover, the radical distrust of authority, irreducible plurality and divisions in all of life, and profound ambiguity about truth undermine the self-assurance of liberal religion.

If liberal–conservative culture wars do not help at the pastoral level, they nevertheless continue to sap the energies of denominational works of mission and Christian intellectual life, as the experience of the Catholic Common Ground Initiative testifies. Large questions still need to be faced, and they almost always cause divisions. It is hard to see how such divisions can simply disappear, but it is easy to see how they can deepen the chasm between congregations and the transcongregational life of religious denominations, with serious consequences for the unity, integrity, and cultural impact of religion. In my own church, ideological polarization inhibits deliberate engagement with such problems as the status of women, the numbers and morale of the clergy, the collapse of religious orders, the mission and identity of Catholic institutions, and the spread of pieties that deny or ignore Catholic wisdom and intelligence. It is not clear that denominations have a large place in the future of American religion. They surely will not if they are unable to unite people around shared beliefs and common mission. If denominations and church-sponsored institutions continue to decline, responsibility will rest with church leaders, including intellectuals.

PUBLIC AND PRIVATE

Finally, there is the much-discussed pair of public and private, arising from convictions that we Americans restrict religion to private life, leaving a naked public square without religious meaning or moral guidance. Reflection on long-standing social gospels would lead to the conclusion that effective public religion needs to be rooted in and sustained by interior faith and distinct communities lest it end in accommodation. Similarly, private faith and separate community cannot long flourish without encountering the larger public life, which sets the pastoral agenda.

As individuals emerge from bounded communities, their experience often seems a liberation, but at the end of the journey it can be very lonely, and the common life may shrink. Sociologist Robert Bellah has long believed that exaggerated individualism remains the "flaw in the Protestant code." He still hopes that Catholics and other like-minded Christians with a sense of solidarity rooted in the Eucharist might help correct our culture's bias against shared responsibility and the common good. Wuthnow, Andrew Greely, most pollsters, and even Bellah's own findings leave us skeptical; high individualism and low solidarity continue to mark American religion. Our religions seem to reinforce rather than correct our individualism.

Still, there are signals of yearning for a center for our pluralism. One signal came in newspaper stories on the passing of New York's John Cardinal O'Connor. Surely I am not alone in wondering about the fascinated and respectful interest so many people in some large urban areas take in their (I use the word "their" inclusively) local Catholic bishop. I know that this connection of people and bishop is not true everywhere or all the time. But it is striking. In Boston, I was literally shocked by the compassionate media coverage of the death of Humberto Cardinal Medeiros, a leader in whom the press had never had much confidence. Immediately came almost rock-star treatment of the new Ozark bishop, Bernard Law. Then planeloads of highly competitive print reporters and television staff took off for Rome when Law became a cardinal. In Los Angeles, I noticed that Cardinal Roger

Mahoney has little trouble making the evening news, a phenomenon I am told is no accident. Perhaps most remarkable of all was the intense emotional response of the people of Chicago to the very public personal crisis, critical illness, and journey to death of Joseph Cardinal Bernardin. For those who knew Cardinal Bernardin's remarkable career, those days brought to mind biblical themes of authority and power following not on self-assertion but on humiliation, even crucifixion. In that short period, Bernardin was perhaps closer to being pastor to a whole large American city than any bishop before or since.

When we explore news accounts, the themes of unity and integrity that seem to me to mark the O'Connor stories show up in all these cases. Part of the fascination with Catholicism is that it is still organized: It is, or at least it seems to be, in some tangible sense, one thing. Even the appearance of unity is no mean achievement for any religious group. People in and out of the Church dispute what that one thing is; indeed, that is a large part of the media narrative about these bishops.

The story line is well known. The Catholic Church is unified by the authority of these bishops, who represent some blend of belief, doctrine, morality, and discipline that makes the Church one. These remarkable men spend their lives trying to keep the Church unified, to keep it one thing, and they try to ensure that unity is maintained not by latitudinarian accommodation of all views but with integrity—stubborn adherence to that which makes Catholicism one thing. I may have all kinds of differences with them about the content of that one thing and the way they run the Church, but the commitment to unity and integrity impresses people.

So here is one contour of American religion: the effort to maintain the unity and coherence of particular religious groups. The concept of denomination once emerged to distinguish American groups from established churches and dissenting sects, the one maintaining unity and integrity by partnership with governments and the other by rigid adherence to the doctrines and/or practices that distinguished it from a dominant establishment. Establishment and sectarian impulses have certainly not disappeared from American Christianity, as is evident in countercultural rhetoric that seems to penetrate almost all religious discourse. On exploration, it almost always turns out to be more about the unity and integrity of particular groups than serious construction of an alternative American culture.

There are three or four themes from this story that seem to me to invite general consideration. First, despite regular efforts to do so, church leaders have difficulty maintaining unity and integrity as they once did by reference to anti-Catholicism. For one thing, many of those who criticize the Church on some issues champion its cause on others. For another, the religious basis of anti-Catholicism has all but disappeared with the decline of the organizational strength of so-called mainstream Protestantism and the diffusion of resurgent evangelical Christianity. At times, the bishops have blamed the larger culture for their problems, hoping thereby to unite Catholics in a kind of countercultural modified sectarianism. In one remarkable passage of their most discussed pastoral letter of recent years, the bishops claimed that American society was increasingly estranged from Christian values, that real Christians live in an increasingly secularized, even neopagan, society, and they might even expect persecution and martyrdom. Blaming secularism and secularists for the problems of churches is a chronic temptation, but it ignores the way religious groups promote secularization, and it is remarkably self-serving. More broadly, it seems that for the mainline churches, blaming society for its hostility to one or another religion stumbles over the evident fact of assimilation. If society is the problem, we have met the enemy, and it is us. Countercultural rhetoric is built into group formation, but its capacity to underpin unity and integrity is limited.

Second, the interest the public takes in these Catholic personalities may well have to do with what Eugene Kennedy calls the hidden problem of authority. Erosion of respect for all institutions, the decline of ethnic solidarity (which always had its own sources of authority), and the pervasive influence of American individualism all weaken efforts to maintain group integrity: Witness the struggle of all American Christian groups with the status of women and homosexuals in the life of the church. For American Christian groups, the answer has always been reliance on the combination of the Bible, the people's book, and religious experience. For Jews, experience has always divided the people and eroded solidarity. One suspects that a similar struggle awaits other religious groups. Yet it is no easy matter to live a common life without a common authority, and the popularity of the bishops mentioned here may well reflect a deep cultural yearning for leadership, for a voice that deserves to be listened to in a more substantial way than the evening news allows.

Finally, so much depends on how we feel, genuinely feel, about our country. Peter Steinfels got it right in a column he wrote about the internal fights among American Jews; he could have been writing about any group:

> The conflict also involves different readings of the cultural forces enveloping religion in the United States. Is that envelope essentially positive and neutral, offering opportunities for religious traditions to reassert themselves inventively and creatively? Or are those forces essentially negative and disintegrative, calling for a wary eye and a strong defense of each tradition's integrity?[8]

It makes a huge difference; it always has, and I suspect that it will in the years to come. We all need to think honestly about newcomers and their descendents.

SPIRITUALITY, NOT RELIGION

Among those who work with the young, it is clear that Generation X is long on spirit and short on doctrine and ecclesiastical discipline. And they are not alone. In his book *Living Buddha, Living Christ*, Thich Nhat Hanh writes,

> Many of our young people are uprooted. They no longer believe in the traditions of their parents and grandparents, and they have not found anything else to replace them. Spiritual leaders need to address this very real issue, but most simply do not know what to do. They have not been able to transmit the deepest values of their traditions, perhaps because they themselves have not fully understood or experienced them. When a priest does not embody the living values of a tradition, he or she cannot transmit them to the next generation. He can only wear the outer garments and pass along superficial forms. When the living values are absent, ritual and dogmas are lifeless, rigid, and even oppressive.[9]

Some pastoral leaders think that this situation can be addressed by a strenuous reassertion of age-old Catholic doctrines and the retrieval of a sense of distinctive identity marked by distance from contemporary culture. Others, closer to ministry among the young, speak of basic cultural changes that will not be reversed by rebuilding Church structures. Instead, they think that changes go deeper, arising from pluralism, democracy, and individual personal choice. Those large cultural changes intersect with the erosion for many of the older formational culture of family, church, and school.

Robert Ludwig speaks of Catholicism as a spiritual path as "the direction in which Vatican II [Second Vatican Council], the hungers of today's young people, and cultural change all point." Catholicism becomes transforming experience grounded in Jesus' proclamations of the reign of God—communities of spiritual practice and moral discipline who walk in the way of Jesus and seek to live the life of compassion and justice. A new generation will use the resources of the tradition in the pursuit of personal self-transformation. "The ministry of monasteries, houses of prayer and retreat centers will enjoy a popular revival."[10] It is the image of Thomas Merton, not that of John Courtney Murray or John Paul II, that best symbolizes the open future where emphasis is placed on the spiritual life.

I leave you with three images for meditation.

First, an image about interreligious relationships. In October 1999 in Chicago, an interfaith coalition including the Catholic cardinal, the executive director of the Chicago Board of Rabbis, and a few Methodists and Presbyterians asked the Southern Baptists to call off a summer visit of thousands of evangelizing missionaries into Chicago neighborhoods. The Baptists said that they had "a message that we think will bring encouragement and hope to people." But the other religious leaders worried that the "campaign" might "contribute to a climate conducive to hate crimes." Seeking converts is one thing, a rabbi said, "but bringing in 100,000 outsiders changes everything."[11] It does and should. So what does deep commitment to one's faith mean for our relationship to one another?

Second, an image for meditation on the naked public square. In December 1999 at the World Parliament of Religions in South Africa, delegates affirmed the rich diversity of world religions and offered one another encouragement to remain faithful to their own traditions. There was not a hint of desire to convert. At the same time, the delegates worked hard (with only limited success, they admitted) to develop a global ethic that might unite the great religions in support of the human family in the face of extremely serious global problems. The majority was persuaded that a human future requires the kind of mass mobilization of talent and energy usually inspired by religious belief, not an ethical common denominator. How to reconcile serious religious beliefs, which truly are different, with the need for serious commitment to one another and our earth? Indeed, how?

Finally, an image that helps me with the other two: a summer afternoon thirty years ago with that quintessential American religious seeker, Thomas

Merton. He dwelled in the deepest recesses of the Catholic subculture, a Trappist monastery, and his departure from the world had been a major countercultural event. But on that day, there was a new enlightenment about solidarity:

> In Louisville, at the corner of Fourth and Walnut, in the center of the shopping district, I was suddenly overwhelmed with the realization that I loved all these people, that they were me and I was theirs, that we could not be alien to one another even though we were total strangers. It was like waking from a dream of separateness, of spurious self-isolation in a special world, the world of renunciation and supposed holiness. . . . To think that such a commonplace realization should suddenly seem like news that one holds the winning ticket in a cosmic sweepstake.[12]

Merton went on from there to shatter more than one "contour" of American religion, to rock more than a few boats, and to build an amazing range of wonderful relationships, all the while pointing a way. And he did not leave the monastery.

NOTES

1. Robert Wuthnow, *Christianity in the 21st Century* (New York: Oxford University Press, 1993).

2. See David J. O'Brien, *Isaac Hecker: An American Catholic* (Mahwah, N.J.: Paulist Press, 1992).

3. Timothy L. Smith, "Religion and Ethnicity in America," *American Historical Review* 83 (1978): 1155–85.

4. "Religious Diversity and Immigration: An Interview with R. Stephen Warner," *Ethics and Policy,* fall 1997, 3.

5. Nancy Ammerman, "Whose Story Is It? Who Says Churches Are in Trouble?" *Ethics and Policy,* fall 1997, 4–7.

6. "Statement of Bishop Joseph Fiorenza of the National Conference of Catholic Bishops," *Origins,* April 27, 2000, 6.

7. Jonathan Rosen, "Abraham's Drifting Children," *New York Review of Books,* March 30, 1997, A19.

8. Peter Steinfels, "Beliefs," *New York Times,* November 30, 1996, A15.

9. Thich Naht Hanh, *Living Buddha, Living Christ* (New York: Riverhead Books, 1995), 88.

10. David J. O'Brien, "Young and Catholic: Will Our Children Be Churched?" (paper available from the author).

11. "Group Seeks to Moderate Baptists' Drive for Converts," *New York Times,* November 29, 1999, A19.

12. Thomas Merton, *Conjecture of a Guilty Bystander* (New York: Doubleday, 1968), 156–57.

2

American Catholics: Neither out Far nor in Deep

CHESTER GILLIS

As is often the case, last year while delivering a paper at a conference, the most insightful exchange involved a member of the audience who commented on the thesis of my paper and its relationship to his own cultural and religious circumstance. The paper chronicled the development and deconstruction of a Catholic subculture in America, arguing that the immigrant Catholic population, outsiders to the mainstream economic, religious, social, and political culture, carved out a space for themselves that at the same time conferred an identity on them and confirmed their marginalized status. This Catholic "ghetto" peaked in the 1950s and has seen its gradual dissolution in the post–Vatican II (Second Vatican Council) period. Put briefly, Catholics have assimilated to the larger culture, resulting, on the one hand, in greater acceptance and influence in America, and on the other, a loss of many of the particular marks of identity that made them unique or different. The questioner criticized American Catholics for having assimilated into the larger culture, surrendering homogeneity, cohesion, and many traditions in the process. He offered details of his personal life that testified to his immigrant community's resistance to assimilation and its consequent loss of identity. He identified himself as a thirty-two-year-old Korean who, though engaged to be married, still lived with his parents, spoke Korean at home, and worshiped in a Korean-speaking Christian church. He proudly asserted that he and the members of his church had not unwittingly taken on the cultural habits of America but rather had maintained their traditions and preserved their ethnic identity. I told him that I admired his tenacity and respected the preservation of his cultural and religious heritage. However, I challenged his assertion that his community would never surrender to the patterns of the broader culture and be assimilated. I did so with two direct and simple questions. "Do you intend to have children?" "Yes," he responded. "Do you expect your children to live with you and speak only Korean at home until they are thirty-two years old?" He sat down.

During his life, the poet Robert Frost poignantly symbolized America in his person and his work. The Frost poem from which I take the title of this chapter seems most appropriate because American Catholics in their history found their relationship to American culture to be neither out far nor in deep. Since the beginning, they have been a part of America; never far from what made America the melting pot it is. However, until very recently, they have not been in deep representing the politically and economically elite in our culture.

HISTORY: 200-PLUS YEARS OF IMMIGRATION

American Catholics, like many other religious groups in the United States, represent a diverse collection of immigrants united by religious identity. Historically and today, Roman Catholics in America comprise multiple ethnic identities mirroring the patterns of immigration into the United States. At one time, they arrived from Poland, France, and Ireland, among other European countries; now they come from Vietnam, the Philippines, Mexico, and Latin America. However, a nation of immigrants did not bear a religion of immigrants. Their religious identification, Roman Catholicism, preceded their sojourn to America. They did not come to America seeking a new religious identity, for their religion securely anchored their identity, perhaps more surely than any other characteristic. In America's 200-plus years, Catholic immigrants trickled in during the colonial period, flooded the country's shores during the nineteenth century, and continue to arrive today in a moderated but steady supply. In the process, they have assimilated the ways of American society and culture and have been assimilated by their American experience.

This relationship between Catholic immigrants and American culture continues today for Latino/Latina and Asian immigrant Catholics. Laotian Hmongs find refuge in Catholic parishes in places as distant and different as Rhode Island and North Carolina. Mexican Americans in California and the

Southwest gather for mass in Spanish in parishes, some of which once served only Anglo populations. Salvadorians and Nicaraguans from Central America celebrate liturgy together midmorning on Sundays in the same churches that later host Mexican worshipers.[1] At St. Boniface Church in the Diocese of Orange in Southern California, masses are celebrated in Vietnamese, Spanish, and English, accommodating an ethnically mixed population of recent immigrants from Mexico, Latin America, and Vietnam as well as a rooted Anglo population. On any given Sunday, mass is celebrated in forty-seven different languages in the Archdiocese of Los Angeles. On the East Coast, a similar phenomenon occurs each Sunday in the Archdiocese of Washington, D.C., where mass is celebrated in Croatian, Chinese, and Korean, among a host of others.

As Ana María Díaz-Stevens indicates in chapter 4 of this volume, not all contemporary Catholic immigrants favor assimilation. Many in the growing Latino/Latina population prefer to preserve their cultural heritage and language, insisting that the Church attend to their spiritual needs in ways that demonstrate sensitivity to and respect for their heritage. They do not wish to be forced into a homogenized "American" Catholicism that is dominated by persons and patterns formed by the ancestors of those descended from a select group of European cultures. If this singles them out as the exception, they argue that it is about time that the Church in America recognizes their particular talents, growing numbers, and unique contributions without insisting that they emulate the linguistic, religious, and social patterns of the hegemonic majority. And not all immigrants have had the opportunity to assimilate. Many African American Catholics find themselves marginalized within their Church and the larger American culture. Because of abiding prejudice, the majority of them do not enjoy the same economic power and social mobility as white Catholics. Their opportunities for political, economic, and educational advancement remain limited and sometimes come at a high personal price. Thus, they do not easily fit under the rubric of assimilation being described here.[2]

Nevertheless, immigration and American Catholicism present an inseparable relationship and a history of marginalization, prejudice, hard work, loyalty (to both the Church and the country), self-identification, struggle, and assimilation. The road to assimilation has proved long and sometimes painful. The Protestant majority who founded most of the colonies (Maryland, founded by Catholics, being one exception) came to America in part to escape religious tyranny yet practiced a tyranny of their own by establishing some form of Protestantism as the religion of nine of the original thirteen colonies. Small in number and viewed with suspicion by the Protestant colonists, Catholics found it difficult to practice their faith in colonial America, often encountering restrictive legislation and personal prejudice. Their allegiance to a foreign power, Rome, created distrust and cast suspicion on their loyalty to their adopted homeland. Religious freedom in the colonies meant not freedom to practice any religion but rather freedom to practice Anglican or Protestant religion. Papists, as they were called, were relegated to the status of outsider or second-class citizen. Michael Zoller, in his book *Washington and Rome,* summarized Protestant treatment of American Catholics: "Anti-Catholicism became the major common point characterizing an otherwise unmistakably diverse Protestantism. Conversely, Catholics developed a sense of being a minority that had to overcome resistance to win a place in America."[3] This history of prejudice stretched into the twentieth century as testified to by Paul Blanchard's 1949 characterization of American Catholics in his book *American Freedom and Catholic Power:*

> Unfortunately the Catholic people of the United States are not citizens but subjects in their own religious commonwealth. The secular as well as the religious policies of their Church are made in Rome by an organization that is alien in spirit and control. . . . They are compelled by the very nature of their Church's authoritarian structure to accept nonreligious as well as religious policies that have been imposed upon them from abroad.[4]

Some would contend that this prejudice still manifests itself today. When presidential candidate George W. Bush spoke at Bob Jones University during the 2000 presidential campaign, for example, some interpreted it as an endorsement of the anti-Catholicism exhibited in the history of that institution. Such anti-Catholicism was also evident in the congressional leadership's initial preference for a chaplain from a Protestant denomination, which was later reversed with the appointment of the Chicago priest Father Daniel Coughlin to the post. Regardless of the degree to which anti-Catholic prejudice exists today, the prejudice that Catholics have encountered historically has both marginalized and galvanized them. It helped them form a more or less cohesive social unit, gave them a particular identity, and encouraged them to form organizations designed to serve their particular needs. For most of their history, this dialectic between marginalization and identity marked the Catholic community.

THE CREATION OF A CATHOLIC SUBCULTURE

When Catholic immigrants arrived in America, the influential and established Protestant population was not about to make room for them, except as blue-collar workers, renters, and social outsiders. This unwelcoming environment caused American Catholics to create a separate subculture that would provide them with an identity, mirror the larger culture, and offer them the opportunity to belong to organizations ranging from the explicitly religious to the quasi-secular. As Charles Morris chronicles in his insightful book *American Catholic*,[5] in the pre–Vatican II era of the 1930s to 1950s, the Catholic subculture flourished, giving birth to numerous organizations, including, among writers and publishers, the Catholic Press Association, the Catholic Writers' Guild, and the Catholic Book Publishers Association. Serving those in the professions were the Catholic Economic Association, the National Council of Catholic Nurses, the American Catholic Psychological Association, the Catholic Physicians' Guild, and the National Catholic Education Association. Catholic academics formed the American Catholic Philosophical Association, the Catholic Anthropological Association, the American Catholic Sociological Society, the American Catholic Historical Association, and the Catholic Poetry Society of America. For the working person, Catholics created the Association of Catholic Trade Unionists. Catholics in the media joined the Catholic Broadcasters Association.

Social organizations complemented these professional societies with the establishment of men's organizations, such as the Knights of Columbus, and women's organizations, such as the National Council of Catholic Women. Young people joined the Catholic Youth Organization because they were excluded from or refrained from joining the YWCA or YMCA. To fulfill their spiritual needs, Catholics formed and joined in large numbers the Holy Name Society and the Rosary and Altar Society. The Catholic Book Club recommended wholesome reading to Catholics and encouraged them to read books with explicit or implicit Catholic themes. The Catholic Hour on television, hosted by the skilled orator Bishop Fulton Sheen, brought Catholic doctrine into the living rooms of millions of Catholics and non-Catholics alike.

In the public culture, the Catholic Legion of Decency acted for Catholics as a moral watchdog over the film industry, rating films with categories from A1, acceptable for viewing by all, to "O," morally offensive (commonly referred to as condemned). Older and middle-age Catholics will remember well the influence of the Church in the entertainment sphere. Parents regularly consulted the weekly list of film ratings in the diocesan newspaper before they would allow their children to go to the movies. They themselves would not want to be seen coming out of a movie theater that was showing a movie that had been condemned by the Legion of Decency. Well-known films such as *The Blue Angel* (1930) with Marlena Dietrich, *Two-Faced Woman* (1941) with Greta Garbo, and *The Pawnbroker* (1965) with Rod Steiger were condemned or altered before distribution in order to receive a respectable rating. The Church wielded a sweeping influence over this element of American culture.

This review process continues today. Two recent popular films reviewed and classified as morally offensive by the National Conference of Catholic Bishops include *American Beauty* (a film that garnered several Academy Awards, including best picture) and *The Matrix*. According to the official reviews, the unfavorable rating of *American Beauty* is due to brief, gory violence; sexual situations, including adultery, masturbation, and nudity; and some profanity and recurring rough language. The unfavorable rating of *The Matrix* is due to excessive violence and recurring profanity. But the contemporary film industry exhibits less concern about Church censorship, and average Catholics are ignorant of or readily dismiss Church ratings of films.

Though suspect that they were beholden to a foreign power in Rome, Catholics demonstrated patriotism and loyalty as Americans. For example, during World War II, Catholics enlisted in the military in large numbers, even though there was less pressure to prove their patriotism as their numbers and influence grew. From 1940 to 1960, aided by the postwar baby boom, the Catholic population doubled. The 1950s saw the largest expansion of schools and churches since the Councils of Baltimore held in the mid-nineteenth century. Catholics established an educational system second only to the public school system. Catholic elementary schools operated by orders of religious women and secondary schools staffed by nuns, brothers, and priests educated a substantial portion of the Catholic population. As the population moved to the suburbs, bishops and pastors expanded their landholdings, physical plants, and programs, delving into the pockets of Catholics to pay for them. The GI Bill paved the way to higher education for a generation of veterans, in-

cluding those matriculating at Catholic colleges and universities in unprecedented numbers. Catholic women's and men's colleges dotted the American
landscape, catering to Catholic parents who were raising their sons and
daughters to be the first generation of Catholics to receive a college education.
Catholics continued to relish the mystery of the Latin Mass, revere the clergy
and sisters, fear punishment for sin, and act in a xenophobic manner toward
other Christians and non-Christians alike. Catholic culture reached its apex.

The answer to the question of whether a person could be a good Catholic and
a good American was a resounding yes. The 1956 nomination hearings for the
appointment of William J. Brennan Jr. to the Supreme Court provide an example of a prominent Catholic's unhesitating willingness to support the country.
When asked whether he might follow the pronouncements of the pope by
which he was bound as a Catholic over the requirements of his oath to uphold
the Constitution, Brennan responded, "What shall control me is the oath that I
took to support the Constitution and laws of the United States and so act upon
the cases that come before me for decision that it is that oath and that alone
which governs."[6] A few years later, while running for president, John F. Kennedy
would have to make a similar disclaimer during a speech to the Texas Baptist
Ministerial Association, reassuring his audience and all Americans that his
Catholicism would not interfere with his duties. Catholics carved out a space in
the public sphere, gained political recognition beyond precinct politics, and began to be trusted with responsibility for the welfare of the wider population.

At the same time that Catholic culture was so embedded, its foundations
were stirring. Catholics were assimilating into American society, becoming
wealthier, better educated, and geographically diversified. The majority was
no longer immigrant. Opportunities in business, government, entertainment,
education, and industry became available to Catholics in increasing numbers.
They did not yet hold sway over the top echelons of the professions, but doors
were opening that would change the economic, professional, and social status
of the rising generation. The gap between Protestants and Catholics was nar-
rowing as Catholics enrolled at Harvard, Princeton, and Yale, along with
Georgetown, Notre Dame, Boston College, and Holy Cross.

THE BREAKDOWN OF CATHOLIC SUBCULTURE

Catholics created a subculture in America that constituted a clearly identifiable social unit, providing security and identity for the immigrant community. Catholic subculture gave a space for Catholics to participate, a cohesive

content to their beliefs and practices, and a much-needed identity. However, this cohesive subculture has diminished in the past forty years as Catholics have been increasingly assimilated into the larger culture. American Catholics today make up 23 percent of the U.S. population. Their family size reflects the national average, their median income is higher than the national average, and they progress further in education than the average citizen. They occupy positions of power in all areas of the public and private sectors. They no longer are found only in certain regions of the country, though they remain concentrated in some areas (e.g., the Northeast) and are more sparsely distributed in others (e.g., the Carolinas). Looked at statistically, they resemble their Protestant counterparts. Many prominent figures in business, politics, education, and the arts are Catholic. Martin Sheen, star of the popular television show *The West Wing,* three members on the U.S. Supreme Court (Kennedy, Scalia, and Thomas), and political commentators Cokie Roberts and Tim Russert are Catholic. Today, Catholics may seem indistinguishable in American society, yet they have only recently emerged from their cohesive subculture to take their places in a pluralistic America.

Nevertheless, vestiges of Catholic subculture remain. Churches still have committees, social events, education programs, outreach, and support groups that involve many parishioners, and some churches continue to rely on bingo for income. However, even within the Catholic subculture, structures and organizations are changing, being redefined or replaced. Although a number of traditional Catholic organizations continue today—some still vibrant, others with dwindling membership and activity—they are joined by a new breed of Catholic organization not found in the pre–Vatican II Church. These new creations include the Catholic League for Religious and Civil Rights, Catholics for a Free Choice, the Conference for Catholic Lesbians, CORPUS (Corps of Reserved Priests United for Service), the Association of Hispanic Priests, the Brotherhood and Sisterhood of Catholic Laity, Women of the New Covenant, Catholics Against Capital Punishment, the North American Conference of Separated and Divorced Catholics, the Young Catholic Apologists, and Dignity.

Catholics are also welcome in the activities and organizations of the larger culture, a development that introduces competition for their time and energy. Opportunities afforded by Catholic traditional organizations compete with children's sports teams sponsored by the town, city, or county, not the Church.

Such opportunities bring with them professional demands for husbands and wives, public school activities, a social life that includes friends of other or no religious persuasion, and the temptations of the larger culture to get ahead, consume more, and be entertained. Catholicism not only represents a "culture within a culture" but also interacts with and influences American culture as a whole. Catholics interact with the larger culture while maintaining their particular Catholic beliefs and practices that sometimes set them apart from popular culture. Thus, they support public schools with their taxes but also sustain an extensive system of parochial schools with their private contributions and tuition payments. Many non-Catholic students attend these institutions, ranging from elementary to university education, and experience Catholic culture in this educational context. The Church runs nursing homes, hospitals, and orphanages that serve a religiously mixed population. Catholic dioceses publish newspapers informing their own constituents and the larger public of the positions and activities of the Church internationally, nationally, and locally. The American bishops speak out regularly on controversial moral issues that have political and social ramifications. Catholics follow cultural patterns as readily as others do in America, but they also attempt to influence and sometimes transform the larger culture (in this they meet with limited success but continue their efforts nevertheless).

Bishops publicly defend the sanctity of human life in all its phases. Many Catholics ask to be excused from work on Good Friday afternoon. Catholic newspapers and journals find their way onto coffee tables in many homes. Shreds of palm hang loosely behind crucifixes and holy pictures in bedrooms and kitchens. Children in every state wear uniforms identifying them as members of parochial schools. Catholic culture is not gone, but it may take a sensitive eye to see it in the twenty-first century.

The Church's presence in American culture is evident in areas as widely divergent as public policy (e.g., the official Church's opposition to same-sex partner benefits) and individual tax forms (e.g., tax-deductible charitable contributions). When Peter Jennings of ABC News hosted *The Search for Jesus* on prime-time television, many expert Catholic scholars were consulted. When the pope visits the United States (or any country for that matter), news media cover the event. When Cardinal O'Connor of New York died and was succeeded by Archbishop Egan, national coverage rivaled local reports. When Catholics participate in the annual Right-to-Life March in Washington, they do so because they believe that they can influence the Supreme Court to re-consider (and reverse) *Roe v. Wade.* Catholics, often equally influenced by the larger culture, adopt patterns, behaviors, and beliefs that originate with or manifest themselves in secular society and sometimes conflict with official Catholic teachings. Thus, they exhibit prejudice in similar ways to non-Catholic Americans, vote on the basis of self-interest over the public good, eat fast food, pollute the environment, and watch television as much as any other Americans. They attempt to influence the larger culture while simultaneously being held prisoner by it.

In recent years, a significant Catholic minority has voiced discontent with the assimilation process that began at Vatican II. They opine that American Catholics all too easily and unwittingly follow cultural trends that at their core represent values inconsistent with Catholic teaching and tradition. Assimilation, they claim, comes with a hefty price, namely, loss of identity. Catholics created a ghetto that may have trapped them to some degree, but the escape from that metaphorical and actual ghetto symbolized by separatism and prejudice has un-dermined identity. These conservatives warn Catholics that they may be too eas-ily trading their Catholic identity for an American one and that American iden-tity on many fronts conflicts with their religious commitments. In deconstructing the Catholic subculture created over the first half of the twenti-eth century, Catholics fail to replace it with anything that is either substantive or specifically Catholic. They accuse Catholics of simply aping the ways of the icons of popular culture, be they from the world of entertainment, business, politics, or other dimensions of the contemporary American scene. In becom-ing fully American, they have sacrificed being fully Catholic, they say.

One component of the decline of the Catholic subculture can be attributed to Catholics' changing attitude toward Church authority. Vincent of Lerins, a fifth-century monk and saint, defined orthodox faith in his *Commonitorium* as doctrines that have been believed "always, everywhere, and by all the faith-ful." Such a definition of orthodoxy would be difficult to support in the con-temporary American church because significant evidence exists that doctrines are not held equally by all the faithful everywhere. This pertains even more widely to practices of the Church. The Roman Catholic Church in America to-day manifests a diversity and pluralism unequaled in its history. At the begin-ning of the third millennium, American Catholics no longer pay, pray, and obey the way in which their forebears readily did. Unlike their grandparents who generally held Church authority as compulsory, today's Catholics more readily perceive compliance as voluntary. The Church remains important in the lives of many Catholics, but it must compete for their attention and allegiance with social, cultural, and economic forces that pull them in different directions. While not a new tension for Catholics in America, the price for disobedience to Church practices is less costly now than a generation or two ago, when Catholics who disobeyed Church teachings often were subject to ecclesiastical and social disapproval. The Church, most often in the person of the pastor or parish priest through the vehicles of the pulpit or confessional, made it clear that certain beliefs or practices were sinful, or not in line with Catholic teachings or practices. In addition, family and friends often reinforced the Church's reprimand with their own disapprobation. Contemporary Catholics do not fear the institutional Church to the degree that previous generations did. The days when the Church dictated all facets of a Catholic's life are gone. The Catholicism of the 1950s had cultural supports and an institutional regime that cannot be retrieved at the beginning of a new century (despite the nostalgia and efforts by some to do so).

The areas in which the Church carries significant authority in a believer's life are fewer than in the past, and the authority is of a different type. This is due, in part, to the fact that American Catholics are (by and large) no longer an immigrant community, that the educational level of American Catholics today is much higher overall than in the first half of the twentieth century, that the economic status is greater, and that the social stigmas for noncompliance with Church dictates have greatly diminished. As Catholics assimilate into the larger culture, along with many other groups, distinguishing characteristics fade. Catholics blend in with others. Larger cultural forces influence them as they do all Americans. Their need for a Catholic ghetto now past, many Catholics attempt to forget that one ever existed. Assimilation hastens their homogenization. A shrinking minority of Catholic children attends parochial schools. Catholics, outsiders for most of American history, now appear as insiders in many dimensions that affect the larger American culture. They hold key positions in publishing, the film industry, television, and technology, to name a few of the sectors that significantly influence the larger culture.

The Church represents, on the one hand, a cultural force and, on the other, an institution shaped by the force of culture. While the Church no longer exhibits the sway on culture that it did in the pre–Vatican II era, when it deeply and directly influenced the cultural lives of Catholics and, in an incidental way, many non-Catholics, it still constitutes a presence and an influence. A number of American cultural forces work against the Church's agenda, forcing Catholics consciously to resist or oppose elements of culture that society as a whole accepts. Of course, Catholics do not always do so. Like other Americans, religious and nonreligious, they regularly follow cultural patterns. A church embedded in a culture cannot avoid this dialectic.

THE ATTEMPT TO REVIVE THE CATHOLIC SUBCULTURE

Some fear that if Catholics appropriate the habits of American society via assimilation, the Church will suffer a fate similar to mainline Protestant churches that have been steadily losing members since the second half of the twentieth century. Declining birthrates, competition from fundamentalists, the changing ethnic composition of society, the inability to innovate, social indifference to religious commitment, and a lack of uniqueness that distinguishes these churches one from another have all contributed to their declining membership. Some signs of such a condition within Catholicism already are in evidence. For example, the percentage of Catholics attending church weekly has declined from the pre–Vatican II period, when about two-thirds of Catholics attended, to the current rate of one-third.[7] At the same time, however, the Catholic population continues to grow in absolute numbers so that even though the percentage attending mass declined, dioceses have experienced an increase in the number of Sunday attendees. This fact, coupled with the priest shortage, results in various methods to accommodate the growth, such as larger suburban churches that seat more people and importing priests from Africa, the Philippines, and other places.

To prevent the Catholic Church from experiencing declining numbers as mainline Protestantism suffers, a more or less cohesive body of traditionalists and conservatives is mounting a campaign to revive the Catholic subculture. This effort is identifiable in a variety of groups, individuals, and activities in the Church. Michael Cuneo, in his sociological analysis in *The Smoke of Satan*, describes this phenomenon as the "Catholic underground" that represents a backlash against Vatican II reforms. While many of the groups that Cuneo describes are extremists, Catholics United for Faith and Opus Dei represent two prominent groups that include members who are fiercely loyal to Church teachings and often do not engage in extremist behavior or rhetoric. They desire to direct

Catholics to a path of obedience even to unpopular Vatican positions, such as prohibition of birth control, condemnation of homosexuality, and maintenance of an all-male clergy. "In the view of the CUF leadership, the rising generation of younger Catholics, who did not experience the dissent of the 1960s and 1970s, could help regenerate Roman Catholicism in the United States."[8]

Public attempts to retrieve or reinvigorate the Catholic subculture come from many quarters. For example, in the spring of 1998, the late John Cardinal O'Connor, then the archbishop of New York, considered by some to be the doyen of this movement to revive Catholic subculture, publicly objected to scheduling major league baseball games on Good Friday. In particular, he protested the 1:05 P.M. start for the New York Yankees–Cleveland Indians game at Yankee Stadium in the Bronx on Good Friday in April 1998. As a form of personal protest against such (in his view) insensitivity to the Catholic community that considers the hours from noon to 3 P.M. on Good Friday sacred, he said that he would not attend any major league baseball games that season. In a September 27, 1998, homily at St. Patrick's Cathedral in New York, Cardinal O'Connor stated, "In my personal judgment the Catholic Church, its teachings, its efforts, its agencies, are under stronger attack today than in my entire, by no means brief, lifetime of more than 78 years. We cannot just sit and be silent."

One group intends to create a community in Pennsylvania that will revive Catholic culture and live in a world apart. The vision of the Society of St. John is as follows:

> Liturgy. Priesthood. Education. Community. These are the pursuits of The Society of St. John, an association of priests and other clerics working in close cooperation with committed laymen who seek to revive holiness of life and Catholic civilization. The principal means of accomplishing this will be the solemn use of traditional Roman liturgy, the renewal of priestly life, classical education, and the building of small cities with a true Catholic culture to share with all. You are invited to join us in this pursuit.[9]

In the promotional literature for this proposed community, the leaders express a form of perennial philosophy in their description when they write, "We do not desire a mere return to a model of the past but a recapturing of the perennial." This community will live and work in one place that abides in faith. With the canonical approval of the bishop of Scranton, they intend to revive the community sense prevalent in the Middle Ages. To the naive observer, it may appear that they will rival the Amish in their home territory.

In the clerical ranks, the followers of French Archbishop Marcel Lefebvre formed the Society of St. Pius X (SSPX), a conservative (some would label it reactionary) movement founded in 1970 in Econe, Switzerland. Lefebvre died in 1991 but not before he ordained priests and bishops to serve in his order. The order has a checkered history, particularly in its relationship to the Vatican. Despite this conflict, "the SSPX remains the largest and best-known traditionalist initiative."[10] These priests celebrate the traditional Latin Mass in America for a community of followers estimated to number about 20,000. The society caters to Catholics who do not accept many of the changes initiated by Vatican II and some that reject Vatican II outright. They do not believe that the Church should accommodate modernity or initiate changes that allow contemporary theories (secular and theological) to influence Church teaching or practice.

Conservative Catholics launched a media effort to disseminate their message with Catholic Family Radio, which began operations in seven locations across the United States in October 1998.[11] In February 1999, the company announced plans to open ten new stations by the end of 1999. A number of wealthy Catholics are behind this effort, including investment strategist Peter Lynch, Domino's Pizza founder Tom Monaghan, and former Miami Dolphins coach Don Shula. Father Joseph Fessio, editor of Ignatius Press, who provides the clerical leadership for the effort, said that the theological content for the program will come from the Catechism of the Catholic Church.

In the past few years, a group of conservative Catholics founded a Catholic law school in Ann Arbor, Michigan, named Ave Maria. The freestanding institution claims to represent true Catholic thought and to train lawyers who will be completely loyal to Church teachings. Its backers believe that the current cadre of law schools affiliated with Catholic universities do not fulfill the mission of the Church doctrinally or ethically, thus their expensive and potentially risky endeavor.

The hierarchical Church promotes any number of strategies to maintain the subculture among Catholics and to advocate its principles in the wider culture. For example, the Church's stringent ethics regarding sexual behavior are countercultural. The Church consistently opposes lifestyles for Catholics that undermine the sacramental nature of marriage. Further, the Church defends a traditional view of the institution of marriage against either legislation or public policies that would alter the exclusive bond between a man and a woman that marriage recognizes. Bishops Joseph Charon, chair of the U. S. Bishops' Committee on Marriage and Family, and William Skylstad, chair of the Committee on Domestic Policy, issued a statement opposing same-sex unions on July 24, 1996, that said in part, "We oppose attempts to grant the legal status of marriage to a relationship between persons of the same sex."[12] And Cardinal Anthony Bevilacqua of Philadelphia wrote to the mayor of Philadelphia on June 7, 1996, expressing his strong opposition to extending benefits to city workers' partners in same-sex relationships.[13]

Perhaps the area in which the attempted renaissance of Catholic subculture is most pronounced is within a separately identifiable subculture of the larger subculture, namely, the clerical culture. Many seminarians and recently ordained priests are attempting to re-create a clerical culture in which "father knows best." Rome, as well as a fair number of American bishops, is encouraging this trend, calculating that seminarians in their twenties have not been tainted by the anti-hierarchical influences of the social experience of the 1960s in America. Members of the Church hierarchy are reaching out to this generation, hoping to re-create a clerical body that is obedient, conservative, and loyal. An October 1998 *New York Times* article describing American seminarians studying in Rome[14] provides evidence supporting this shift. Saying that their heroes are John Paul II and Cardinal Joseph Ratzinger (head of the Vatican's Congregation for the Doctrine of Faith), they favor a strong centralized authority in the Church. They think that in the 1960s and 1970s, the Church stumbled and lost its direction. They dislike dissension in the Church, readily embrace celibacy, and are generally more conservative than the professors who teach them and the seminary staff priests who guide them in their pastoral and spiritual training. As early as 1987, John Deedy, in his book *American Catholicism*, indicated that "national profiles are showing that young men choosing the priesthood are decidedly more conservative than their counterparts of 15 years ago."[15]

American dioceses that have burgeoning seminaries cater to this clientele. For example, Bishop Fabian Bruskewitz of Lincoln, Nebraska, recruits conservative seminarians. Regarding the dearth of vocations in the 1980s and 1990s, Elden Curtiss, archbishop of Omaha, Nebraska, wrote,

I personally think that the vocation "crisis" in this country is more artificial and contrived than many people realize. . . . It seems to me that the vocation "crisis"

is precipitated and continued by people who want to change the church's
agenda, by people who do not support orthodox candidates loyal to the magis-
terial teaching of the Pope and bishops, and by people who actually discourage
viable candidates from seeking priesthood and vowed religious life as the
Church defines the ministries.[16]

The Church also influences culture via Catholic education. In *Being Right:
Conservative Catholics in America,* Mary Jo Weaver chronicles the rise of conservative Catholic education. She writes,

> Indeed, disgruntlement with Catholic education, from preschool through col-
> lege, has led to increased involvement of Catholics in home schooling, the
> founding of new high schools, the revitalization of old colleges, the establish-
> ment of conservative institutes within Catholic universities, support for gradu-
> ate institutes to promote the defense of papal prohibition on artificial birth con-
> trol as articulated in Humanae Vitae, and professional associations for
> conservative Catholic intellectuals.[17]

Some fear that Catholic colleges and universities that interpret the Vatican
document on Catholic higher education, *Ex corde Ecclesiae,* too liberally will
soon follow the path that many originally Protestant denominational universities have trod, that is, surrendering their religious (e.g., Methodist, Presbyterian, or Lutheran) character and being identified only historically with these
churches. Princeton, Harvard, and Yale all have Protestant roots that they long
ago abandoned, and Duke and Syracuse exhibit little institutional connection
to their Methodist roots, even though all these institutions maintain divinity
schools or religious studies departments. Advocates of closer episcopal
scrutiny or control over Catholic colleges and universities seek to propagate a
particular understanding of the intellectual dimension of Catholic subculture,
and many would brook no dissent.

Writing in *The New Republic,* Charlotte Allen reviews the controversy at
Georgetown University about the lack of crucifixes in some classrooms. In her
concluding paragraph, she writes, "What Georgetown can do—and has done
in resolving the crucifix controversy—is to foster Catholic identity through
bolstering Catholic culture."[18] She defines "Catholic culture" as art and religion as opposed to "reports, recommendations, manifestos, or theories." Of
course, Catholic culture represents more than "art and religion." It includes

cultural habits, political convictions, religious practices and beliefs, disposi-
tions toward Church authority, and a host of other factors. While I do not
think that the advocates of a more prominent Catholic subculture are going
to prevail in their attempt to convert all or even a majority of Catholics to
their view of Catholicism, it would be a false judgment to conclude that the
Catholic subculture will soon disappear completely.

In the past forty years, America has witnessed the erosion of Catholic culture that supported and defined Catholics. Contemporary suburban neighbors do not define themselves primarily by their religion as their immigrant
ancestors did. In some gentrified urban settings, condominium and town-
house dwellers do not even know their neighbors' names, much less their religious persuasions. Neighborhoods are more likely to group together similar
economic classes than they are Catholics, Protestants, Muslims, or Jews. In the
sprawling suburbs, most people do not notice whether their neighbor's garage
door goes up Sunday morning. And if it does, it may be to permit someone to
retrieve the Sunday paper or to drive to pick up Grandma for brunch instead
of church. This fact, which many Catholics regret, signifies the assimilation of
Catholics into the wider American culture, just as Protestants and Jews before
them and now Muslims, Hindus, and Buddhists after them.

Much of the tension over identity in the American church has to do with
American society and culture (to which Catholics contribute and by which
they are affected). Americans are democratic; Catholicism is not. Americans often follow or even set trends. Seldom has the Church been accused
of being trendy. Americans live in a pluralistic society that values tolerance
for many views and practices; the Church holds moral and dogmatic positions that do not abide tolerance in its beliefs or practices. Americans live
in an affluent, developed, and materialist country; the Church promulgates
the gospel mandate to identify with the poor. Americans prize their independence; the Church "takes care of" her children. Often Americans are
asked to compete and win at work; the Church asks them to form a community of forgiveness and compassion. Americans demand reasonable answers to difficult questions from their political leaders; the Church asks
them to accept some things on faith alone or on the sole basis of the authority vested in the Church. It is no wonder that American Catholics
sometimes find it difficult to be both. What their culture espouses their
Church sometimes contradicts.

Some of the problems that the Roman Catholic Church in America faces can be overcome with greater effort, more sensitivity, and clear vision. Others appear beyond its immediate control. This is due, in part, to its ties to Rome, which prevent it from embarking on national initiatives that conflict with the Vatican's agenda, and in part to American culture, which shapes Catholics in the same way that it shapes other citizens. The Church can, however, frame its response to culture, inform and form its constituency, offer alternatives where possible, and provide reasons to resist cultural pressures when necessary.

Contemporary Catholics in America differ from previous generations in that they are not subject to as much suspicion or exclusion because of their Catholicism (although some may be because of their race, ethnicity, or economic status). Some willingly adopt the patterns of the larger culture; others resist such a move. In either case, increasingly they represent a significant constituency in American society and popular culture that can no longer be ignored.

NOTES

1. See Wade Clark Roof and Cristel Manning, "Cultural Conflicts and Identity: Second-Generation Hispanic Catholics in the United States," *Social Compass* 41, no. 1 (1994): 171–84.

2. For an insightful historical study of African Americans' relationship to Catholicism, see John T. McGreevy, *Parish Boundaries: The Catholic Encounter with Race in the Twentieth-Century Urban North* (Chicago: University of Chicago Press, 1996).

3. Michael Zoller, *Washington and Rome: Catholicism and American Culture,* trans. Steven Rendall and Albert Wimmer (Notre Dame, Ind.: University of Notre Dame Press, 1999), 68.

4. Paul Blanchard, *American Freedom and Catholic Power,* 11th ed. (Boston: Beacon Press, 1950), as quoted in Mark S. Massa, *Catholics and American Culture: Fulton Sheen, Dorothy Day, and the Notre Dame Football Team* (New York: Crossroad, 1999), 1.

5. Charles Morris, *American Catholic: The Saints and Sinners Who Built America's Most Powerful Church* (New York: Times Books, 1997), 160–61.

6. Samuel A. Mills, "Parochiaid and the Abortion Decisions: Supreme Court Justice William J. Brennan, Jr. versus the U.S. Catholic Hierarchy," *Journal of Church and State* 34, no. 4 (1992): 753.

7. For recent statistics, see Bryan T. Froehle and Mary L. Gautier, "Catholic Behavior and Values," in *Catholicism USA: A Portrait of the Catholic Church in the United States* (Maryknoll, N.Y.: Orbis Books, 2000), chap. 2.

8. James A. Sullivan, "Catholics United for Faith: Dissent and the Laity," in *Being Right: Conservative Catholics in America*, ed. Mary Jo Weaver and R. Scott Appleby (Bloomington: Indiana University Press, 1995), 132.

9. www.ssjohn.org.

10. William D. Dinges, "'We Are What You Were': Roman Catholic Traditionalism in America," in Weaver and Appleby, eds., *Being Right*, 242.

11. "Catholic Radio Company Plans to Open Station in Area," *Washington Post*, February 13, 1999, B8.

12. "Bishops' Statement," in *1997 Catholic Almanac*, comp. and ed. Felician A. Foy, O. F. M., and Rose M. Avato (Huntington, Ind.: Our Sunday Visitor, 1996), 51.

13. "Domestic Partners," in *1997 Catholic Almanac*, 51–52.

14. Alessandra Stanley, "U.S. Catholic Seminarians Turning to Orthodoxy," *New York Times*, October 3, 1998, A3.

15. John Deedy, *American Catholicism: And Now Where?* (New York: Plenum Press, 1987).

16. Elden Curtiss, "Crisis in Vocations? What Crisis?" *Our Sunday Visitor* 84, no. 23 (October 8, 1995): 18.

17. Mary Jo Weaver, "Self-Consciously Countercultural: Alternative Catholic Colleges," in Weaver and Appleby, eds., *Being Right*, 301–2.

18. Charlotte Allen, "Crossroads," *The New Republic*, February 15, 1999, 21.

3

Crossing the Borders: Evangelicalism and Migration

RANDALL BALMER

Evangelicalism and migration are no strangers in American history. The first European immigrants to settle permanently in the eastern part of North America brought with them the rudiments of what we now know as Evangelicalism. The Puritans of New England, followers of Martin Luther and children of the Protestant Reformation, held to the Bible as their sole authority, and they approached that Bible in an egalitarian way: Everyone had both the opportunity and the obligation to read and interpret the Scriptures for themselves, a circumstance that gave rise to the remarkable fissiparousness that has come to characterize Protestantism in America.

The second immigrant stream to shape Evangelicalism in America came from the European continent, a movement known as Pietism. Formulated in reaction to the arid scholasticism that had come to characterize Protestant theology, Pietists emphasized the importance of spiritual ardor and warmhearted religious conversion. Pietist immigrants established a foothold in the middle colonies, and in one of the most remarkable combustions in American history, Pietism combined with the remnants of New England Puritanism to create the colonies-wide revival known to historians as the Great Awakening. The hallmarks of the revival were the twin emphases on religious conversion and biblical authority, which became the central defining characteristics of American Evangelicalism itself.

A subsequent revival, known as the Second Great Awakening, convulsed three theaters of the new nation at the turn of the nineteenth century: New

England, the Cumberland valley of Kentucky, and western New York. Evangelicalism, thereby rooted securely in American soil, went on to set the political agenda for most of the nineteenth century. Its continued vitality more than two centuries later (polling data suggest that Evangelicals make up anywhere from 25 to 46 percent of the U.S. population) makes Evangelicalism the most influential social and religious movement in American history.

Evangelical migrations in the nineteenth century came from northern Europe, especially Scandinavia and the Netherlands. Like the wave of Pietism a century earlier, these immigrants protested what they considered the empty formalism of traditional orthodoxy and state churches. They had organized in what the Pietists had called conventicles in the Old World, but in the New World they formed their own communities (such as the Janssonist colony in Bishop Hill, Illinois) and eventually their own denominations: the Christian Reformed Church, the Evangelical Covenant Church, and the Evangelical Free Church, among others.

Understanding the interrelationship between Evangelicalism and migration will require one more historical digression: the Azusa Street Revival in Los Angeles, which lasted from April 1906 approximately through 1909. On the first day of the new century, January 1, 1901, a Pentecostal revival had broken out in Topeka, Kansas, after a student at Bethel Bible College there, Agnes Ozman, began speaking in tongues under the influence of the Holy Spirit. The revival spread throughout the lower Midwest to Texas, where an African American waiter, William J. Seymour, took up the message and brought it to Los Angeles early in 1906. Shortly after his arrival, the revival shifted to 312 Azusa Street, where those in attendance reported divine healings, speaking in tongues, and all manner of spiritual blessings. The Azusa revival, moreover, was racially and gender inclusive. More important, those affected by the Azusa Street revival fanned out across North America, to Latin America, and throughout the rest of the world, thereby planting the seeds for the immigration of Pentecostals to the United States a century later.

Beginning late in the twentieth century, evangelical immigrants began arriving from around the world, but primarily from Latin America, Africa (especially Nigeria, Zimbabwe, and Liberia), India, and Southeast Asia (especially Korea and the Philippines). This influx of Evangelicals should prompt a note of caution into any discussion of America's changing religious complexion. Yes, as has been marvelously documented by Diana Eck and others, the

United States is a religiously pluralistic nation, arguably for the first time in history, with Muslim mosques; Hindu, Shinto, and Buddhist temples; and Sikh *gurdwaras* now dotting the landscape. Despite these important changes, however, as R. Stephen Warner points out, America is still an overwhelmingly Christian nation, and even the majority of immigrants themselves are Christian, most likely evangelical Christians.[1]

The most notable provenance for evangelical immigration is Latin America. The incursion of Evangelicalism into Latin America has been fraught with contention and controversy. Ever since the arrival of Spanish conquistadores at the turn of the sixteenth century, Latin America has been overwhelmingly Roman Catholic, but the steady growth of Evangelicalism in the twentieth century, especially in the years since World War II, has altered the religious landscape of Latin America. "Almost unnoticed, without permission or ceremony," Richard Gott wrote in 1995, "Latin America is moving seamlessly from the unquestioned rituals of the Roman Catholic faith into the uncharted waters of Protestantism."[2] Evangelicals are enjoying success in the very precincts where Catholic missionaries have long been active. "Never before since the Reformation," according to Chilean sociologist Claudio Veliz, "have so many Catholics converted to Protestantism in such a brief period of time."[3]

The initial evangelical invasion of Latin America was caricatured as American cultural imperialism, fueled by massive amounts of money and conveyed by "Anglo" missionaries, but Evangelicalism, especially Pentecostalism, in Latin America is now an indigenous movement, with its own leadership and resources—and enormous popular appeal. A Roman Catholic priest has compared the spread of Pentecostalism in Latin America to "a tidal wave that nothing can stop."[4]

Evangelicalism in the 1970s and 1980s did little to challenge the right-wing regimes that blanketed Latin America; indeed, it provided a measure of legitimation to the military governments of Chile's Augusto Pinochet and Rios Montt, president of Guatemala and an Evangelical. Contrary to popular stereotypes but consistent with the early years of the movement in North America, Pentecostalism has appealed primarily to the poor and to the marginalized in Latin America, offering the basis for civic renewal at the grassroots level as well as personal transformation.[5] Pentecostalism differs markedly from its evangelical sibling fundamentalism, with its nationalistic overtones; Pentecostals carry less baggage. Their steadfast suspicion of "worldliness," their ideas about the separation of church and state, and their emphasis on personal regeneration, moreover, make Pentecostals even less likely to mount large-scale political reforms. "Evangelical Christians are," in David Martin's words, "ambitious at most to constitute an effective pressure group, pressing corporate institutional interests and broad moral principles, and generally acquiring a voice in the public forum."[6] In the domestic arena, as several observers have noted, evangelical sensibilities have appealed especially to women because its egalitarianism attenuates some of the machismo characteristic of male-dominated Catholicism.[7] Some evidence even suggests that, among immigrants to the United States, Protestant men are more likely to attend church on a weekly basis than women.[8]

In part because of John Paul II's relentless attempts to suppress liberation theology and in part because of the abuses associated with Marxism in the region, Pentecostalism has replaced liberation theology as the "theology of the people" in Latin America. Put starkly, Leonardo Boff and Gustavo Gutíerrez have been supplanted by Luis Palau and Jimmy Swaggart. There are approximately 40 to 50 million Evangelicals in Latin America, about 10 percent of the population, as well as three million Mormons.[9] David Stoll had argued that Pentecostals are growing in Latin America at five or six times the rate of the general population.[10] Pentecostals have been especially successful in Brazil, Chile, and Guatemala, at times providing a language of popular dissent against authoritarianism, both political and ecclesiastical. Evangelicals make up about 15 percent of the population in Brazil, 20 percent in Chile (where some observers believe that, in terms of actual church adherence, Protestants now outnumber Catholics), and 30 percent in Guatemala.[11] Those numbers do not begin to account for enclaves of evangelical strength elsewhere in Ecuador and Central America.

What is the appeal of Evangelicalism in Latin America? Part of it is, most assuredly, a reaction to Roman Catholicism, which, despite the efforts of liberation theologians, has been associated with elite Latin culture. For many Latinos and Latinas, Roman Catholicism represents the old order and, to them, poverty; Evangelicalism, with its theological emphasis on egalitarianism and its offer of a kind of spiritual upward mobility, is enormously attractive. Evangelicalism in North America has always been peculiarly adept at popular communications and sensitive to market forces. Its history can be read as successive attempts to bring religion to the people—whether the open-air preaching of George Whitefield and itinerant preachers in the eighteenth century, the camp meetings and the colporteurs of the nineteenth, or the electronic preaching over the airwaves in the twentieth. These same techniques have been used to great advantage by Evangelicals in Latin America as well. The attractions of Evangelicalism for Latinos and Latinas seem only to increase as they immigrate to North America. While most Latin Catholics certainly remain in the Roman Catholic Church and Catholicism still claims the allegiance of more immigrants overall than any other religion,[12] many Hispanic immigrants gravitate toward parishes affiliated with the Catholic charismatic renewal movement, with its unmistakable overtones of Pentecostalism in the enthusiastic worship and the belief in miracles. The Roman Catholic hierarchy seems uncertain about its response to this phenomenon. On the one hand, it cannot deny the renewal force of charismatics, but spiritual phenomena are, by their very nature, unwieldy and unpredictable, not easily corralled by ecclesiastical conventions.

Other Latinas and Latinos bring their evangelical convictions and practices with them, while still others use the occasion of crossing the border to shift religious affiliations from Roman Catholicism to Evangelicalism. Some are quite conscious and articulate about that choice. They gravitate toward the increased freedom of choice they detect in Evangelicalism as opposed to Catholicism. They see greater opportunities for advancement and upward mobility, and they are eager to distance themselves from the faith that many associate with the grinding poverty that they have sought to escape by heading north.[13]

The Roman Catholic hierarchy has had to do battle with Protestants over the hearts and souls of Hispanics for half a century. As early as 1955, bands of Baptist ministers fanned out into the camps of migrant workers in eastern Texas, seeking conversions to Protestantism. The Catholic Church responded with priests and social workers "so that spiritual services may be given to them and they may be kept from Protestant proselytizers."[14] The Bishops' Committee for the Spanish-Speaking also provided a kit for distribution to the workers. It included a picture of Our Lady of Guadalupe for posting on the front door of migrants' quarters with the inscription (in Spanish), "This is a Catholic home and Protestant propaganda will not be admitted."[15]

Protestantism has retained an appeal for Latinas and Latinos crossing the border into the United States. Part of the appeal is that Evangelicalism, especially Pentecostalism, provides tangible help to new immigrants. Throughout American history, religious communities have offered various services to immigrants. The best example would be the settlement houses in places such as Brooklyn or Chicago, where newly arrived immigrants could live until they found jobs and suitable housing. Within ethnic Catholic enclaves, the Church provided a whole range of social services, ranging from language instruction and employment bureaus to professional guilds. Even the construction of a church building provided employment for workers and also announced to the larger community the availability of such skilled labor. More recently, the emergence of Islamic community centers among Muslims is an example of how religious groups provide a kind of cultural shelter for new immigrants.

The evangelical community, because of it decentralized character, functions in similar, albeit less formalized, ways. A Latino or Latina coming to, say, the Coachella Valley of Southern California, for example, will plug into kinship networks but also into the network of the Latin Pentecostal community. That community, in turn, helps in the search for housing and jobs and may provide day care in addition to the regular worship, social, and educational opportunities normally associated with churches.

In addition to help at the local or congregational level, Evangelicalism provides larger networks of affiliations—a vast and interlocking world of congregations, denominations, publishing houses, seminaries, mission and relief societies, Bible institutes, Bible camps, and the like. All this constitutes what I have called the evangelical subculture in America.[16] For Evangelicals generally, the evangelical subculture provided a refuge from the larger world, a zone of safety against the depredations of American society beginning in the 1920s. Evangelicals, who regarded themselves as an embattled minority, especially in the middle decades of the twentieth century, used the safety of the subculture not only as a defense but also as a kind of staging ground for their reentry into the broader American society late in the twentieth century.

Although Evangelicals, especially white Evangelicals, must still combat the evils of racism within their own ranks, there is some evidence that the evangelical subculture—or at least a part of the subculture—is available to those crossing the borders into the United States. Just as the Roman Catholic Church has historically provided an institutional network to ease Catholic immigrants into American society, so too Evangelicals are providing parallel institutions, although (given the general character of Evangelicalism in contrast to Catholicism) they tend to be less centralized, less hierarchical, and somewhat less interconnected.

The function of the evangelical subculture, however, is the same as that traditionally offered by the Roman Catholic Church. The evangelical subculture provides shelter and nurture—the safety of a like-minded community within an alien, sometimes hostile society.

Although I generally resist socioeconomic explanations as reductionistic (and they serve, at best, to only partially explain religious convictions or behavior), there is no denying that Evangelicalism, with its emphasis on thrift, sobriety, and domestic responsibility, has had a profound influence in the social and economic sphere. Max Weber's *The Protestant Ethic and the Spirit of Capitalism* has long served as an effective tool for explaining evangelical behavior in the marketplace. The role of revivals in constructing a middle class in America has been demonstrated by historians of American Methodism and by Paul E. Johnson's study of Rochester, New York, during the Second Great Awakening.[17]

In Latin America, these quintessentially Protestant values—thrift, sobriety, and domestic responsibility—have provided for the emergence of a middle class within a society that has never had a middle class in its history. Latinos and Latinas who cross the border find Evangelicalism a convenient and useful conduit for entering the middle class in the United States. Not all of them make it, of course, and for many the road is long and arduous; it requires a generous outlay of the personal and social virtues associated with Evangelicalism, not least of which is the temperance to resist the blandishments of American consumerism. But just as assuredly as Methodism has historically been coterminous with middle-class demographics and just as assuredly as Evangelicalism provided a kind of halfway house for members of the counterculture on their way to reclaiming middle-class status in the 1970s,[18] so too Evangelicalism offers Latinos and Latinas the safest, most direct, and most efficient passage into the middle class and, therefore, into the heart of American society.

NOTES

1. See Guillermina Jasso, Douglas S. Massey, Mark R. Rosenzweig, and James P. Smith, "Family, Schooling, Religiosity, and Mobility among New Legal Immigrants to the United States: Evidence from the New Immigrant Survey Pilot," in *Immigration Today: Pastoral and Research Challenges*, ed. Lydio F. Tomasi and Mary G. Powers (Staten Island, N.Y.: Center for Migration Studies, 2000), 52–81.

2. Richard Gott, "The Latin Conversion," *The Guardian Weekend*, June 10, 1995, 14.

3. Quoted in Gott, "The Latin Conversion," 14.

4. Quoted in Gott, "The Latin Conversion," 14.

5. See, for example, David Martin, *Tongues of Fire: The Explosion of Protestantism in Latin America* (London: Blackwell, 1990); David Stoll, *Is Latin America Turning Protestant?: The Politics of Evangelical Growth* (Stanford, Calif.: Stanford University Press, 1990); John Burdick, "Struggling against the Devil: Pentecostalism and Social Movements in Urban Brazil," in *Rethinking Protestantism in Latin America,* ed. Virginia Garrard-Burnett and David Stoll (Philadelphia: Temple University Press, 1993), 20–44; Christian Smith, "The Spirit and Democracy: Base Communities, Protestantism, and Democratization in Latin America," *Sociology of Religion* 99 (summer 1994): 119–43; and Harvey Cox, *Fire from Heaven: The Rise of Pentecostal Spirituality and the Reshaping of Religion in the Twenty-First Century* (New York: Addison-Wesley, 1996).

6. David Martin, "The People's Church: The Global Evangelical Upsurge and Its Political Consequences," *Books & Culture,* January/February 2000, 13.

7. Compare Martin, "The People's Church"; Cox, *Fire from Heaven.*

8. Jasso et al., "Family, Schooling, Religiosity, and Mobility," 52–81, esp. tables 12 and 13.

9. Martin, "People's Church," 12.

10. Cox, *Fire from Heaven,* 68.

11. Cox, *Fire from Heaven,* 14–15; Gott, "Latin Conversion," 16.

12. See Jasso et al., "Family, Schooling, Religiosity, and Mobility," 52–81, esp. table 7.

13. See, for example, the treatment of a Hispanic Pentecostal congregation in Indio, California, in *Mine Eyes Have Seen the Glory,* three-part PBS documentary, WTTW television, Chicago, 1993, part 3.

14. Quoted in Chester Gillis, *Roman Catholicism in America* (New York: Columbia University Press, 1999), 78.

15. Gillis, *Roman Catholicism in America,* 79.

16. Randall Balmer, *Mine Eyes Have Seen the Glory: A Journey into the Evangelical Subculture in America,* 3rd ed. (New York: Oxford University Press, 2000).

17. Paul E. Johnson, *A Shopkeeper's Millennium: Society and Revivals in Rochester, New York, 1815–1837* (New York: Hill & Wang, 1979).

18. See Steven M. Tipton, *Getting Saved from the Sixties: Moral Meaning in Conversion and Cultural Change* (Berkeley: University of California Press, 1982).

4

Colonization versus Immigration in the Integration and Identification of Hispanics in the United States

ANA MARÍA DÍAZ-STEVENS

Scholars of immigration remind us that it is useful to treat the immigration experience as a process with several phases or as a journey with several stops.[1] But rather than begin with the process of relocation, as some do, I believe we must first start with an analysis of the social, cultural, economic, and political conditions in the so-called sending society that push the people to seek a new environment. Then we can better analyze the experience of relocation, with its direct effects on material culture: food, clothing, living arrangements, and the like. A lag time, or anomie, in which most immigrants experience the inconsistencies between their expectations and the reality of their new circumstances usually follows relocation. It is during this lag time that new arrivals are generally most vulnerable to radical change such as through religious conversion[2] or, in a negative sense, through substance addiction, crime, or family disintegration. Eventually, there comes a period of adaptation or acculturation during which substitutes are found for the guiding traditions of the past or the traditions undergo adaptation or transformation. Strategies of integration and resistance are devised to incorporate what is found to be useful in the new circumstances and to resist those elements that tend to undermine group identity.

An additional factor to be taken into consideration in today's world is the rapid development of technology, which has changed the way we view and relate to our immediate surroundings and the world at large. For example, there was a time when geography was central to the notion of community. But the importance of geography in community formation has undergone a shift in modern times, particularly during the past fifty years. The elements that bind people together can easily transcend the geographic community in which they live. The fact is that people living in the same building or side by side in suburban settings may not know each other or even care to make acquaintances. On the other hand, community can be created and maintained among people nationally and internationally with the aid of new technologies in transportation and communication. Thus, it is relatively easy for im/migrants to keep close contact with their places and cultures of origin.[3]

EXAMINING THE QUESTION

Immigrants often choose a place of relocation for what it promises in terms of housing, employment, education, socioeconomic opportunities, and even what is perceived as its level of acceptance of newcomers. Sometimes choice is a luxury, however, and people end up in a particular location because they have no other place to go or because they are joining already established members of their families. And while immigrants hope that the new environment will be better than what they left behind, the need for some sense of continuity often leads them to look for places to live that physically or culturally resemble their old environment. Thus, immigrants are often found clustered in certain regions, cities, or even ghettos. Among other things, city ghettos have provided a place where Hispanics/Latinos[4] can be in contact with other oppressed groups. These groups teach and learn from each other in ways that provide a bond and an identity separate from the dominant ethnic and racial groups of the society. Therefore, when we speak of integration, we acknowledge not only the impact of the core society on the particular group under consideration but also how that group has influenced and been influenced by other marginal groups as well as the influence that they all have on the core society itself. Integration is a multilayered and multidirectional process.

These are all issues that must be addressed in studying the ways in which Hispanics adapt to American society. In addition, it must be recognized that the Latino/Hispanic community exhibits certain characteristics that distinguish it from other immigrant groups. Like many other minority populations in the United States, the Hispanic community has had a long history of poverty and educational neglect that has resulted in nearly unbearable socioeconomic conditions. But while many other immigrants have been able to escape such circumstances, Hispanics today are the poorest among the poor with little hope for improvement. (Native Americans share this general condition but are not classified as immigrants.) In the past few decades, while other racial and social groups have demonstrated increases in economic and educational levels, Hispanics in general and Mexican Americans and Puerto Ricans in particular evidence the opposite.[5] But the distinctiveness of the Hispanic community is based on commonalities other than the socioeconomic plight of its members. It is these common factors—shared conditions, experiences, and values—that this chapter addresses.

The Hispanic experience in the United States must be seen in the historical context of American contact with people of Hispanic origin, including encroachment on their lands and their subsequent colonization. Acknowledging these realities is absolutely necessary if we are to understand present-day Hispanic demographics and the role of religion, culture, and language in the process of Hispanic or Latino identification in the United States.

DEMOGRAPHICS

The undercount of Hispanics through the U.S. census in the past has been a source of conflict and contention among leaders of the Hispanic community, the U.S. Bureau of the Census, and other government agencies that apportion moneys and services on the basis of demographics. That there has been an undercount cannot be easily disputed. It is based on two factors: One is the inability or the unwillingness of the designer of the census to develop adequate mechanisms to gain a correct count, and the other is the ability of undocumented immigrants and other members of the community to elude the census takers. These realities notwithstanding, present demographic data give us a good indication of the growth and importance of the Hispanic community in the United States.

The Latino/Hispanic population of the United States nearly doubled between 1970 and 1990. In less than twenty years, the number of Hispanic churches, associations, and representative bodies in schools, business, and social life has grown accordingly. A 1996 report by the Bureau of the Census states that by 2010, Latinos or Hispanics will be more numerous in the United States than African Americans. The projection is that by 2020, Hispanics will constitute almost 15 percent of the total U.S. population (some 47 million) and that by 2050 that number will increase to 25 percent, or about 95 million.[6]

Because this population has a higher birthrate and a lower median age than the general population, the Hispanic population does not have to depend on immigration for its continuous growth. In a nutshell, Hispanic families are larger and younger and have more children than non-Hispanics. Even if immigration from Latin America and the Spanish-speaking Caribbean were to stop tomorrow, the natural increase in this population would outstrip that of both Euro-Americans and African Americans.

Immigration, of course, even further increases the population of Latinos/Hispanics in America. Instead of losing their identity to merge into the Euro-American stew, however, new immigrants assimilate into the Hispanic culture that dates back centuries, rose dramatically during the late 1960s, and continues to the present time. Despite discrimination and societal pressures to forsake Hispanic language and culture, Hispanics overwhelmingly have maintained both.[7] For the majority of Hispanics, culture, language, and religion continue to be the mainstays of Hispanic identity in America. This has been well recognized by scholars interested in the integration process of immigrants. All these factors, but most especially the issue of language, are taken into serious consideration by advocates of assimilationist policies such as the "English Only" movement. A fourth important factor, often ignored but of crucial importance to the sense of identity of Hispanics in America, is the history of American colonization.[8]

Gallup and Castelli, for example, reported in 1989 that although Hispanics reflect the national average of 28 percent unchurched (not affiliated with a particular church and not attending church regularly), only 5 percent of all Hispanics are nonreligious and even the unchurched reported religion as very important. Hispanics (29 percent) even outperform whites (22 percent) or blacks (20 percent) in Bible study or membership in a prayer group. Gallup and Castelli also reported that only 3 percent felt unwelcomed in church because of ethnicity. The fact that they are segregated by ethnicity and language, to begin with, may account for their feelings of warm reception and acceptability.[9]

The National Survey of Religious Identity reported that two out of three Latinos (65.8 percent) identify themselves as Catholics. This survey included 130,000 interviews in all and more than 5,000 for Latinos alone. Overall, it found that only 2 percent of the Latinos identified as Pentecostals. Roughly one out of four identified as Protestant. These findings can be compared with a similar identification item in the 1989–1990 Latino National Political Survey. Protestantism is highest among Puerto Ricans and lowest among Cubans, except for those in Texas.[10] In summary, Catholicism remains the religion of two out of three Latinos, and evangelical forms of Protestantism are preferred by half of the non-Catholic Latinos.

There are no reliable data for the number of Latinos who practice other types of non-Christian or syncretized religions. Santeria, once thought to be practiced predominantly among the lower Cuban classes, was brought to Puerto Rico by the Cuban exiles. In New York, it syncretized with Puerto Rican *espiritismo karde-ciano* to form what some have termed *santerismo*. It is widely practiced in the United States, where there is a sizable Cuban population, and it has spread to the Latino population in general. Beyond segments of the Catholic community, it has found its way into the practices of people of other traditions, such as Jewish and Protestant. Among Puerto Ricans, another religious phenomenon is the attempt to reconstruct a Taino (native Puerto Rican indigenous) spirituality borrowing from other Native Americans rituals and practices. In addition, there are among the Latinos those who practice *curanderismo* and are involved in New Age religions. The overwhelming majority of Latinos, however, as the previously discussed data show, identify themselves as Christian in their beliefs and practices.

A BRIEF HISTORICAL REVIEW

The two largest groups within the American Latino community are the Puerto Rican and the Mexican. I believe that the history of U.S. relations with these two countries provides clues as to why these immigrants, in particular Puerto Ricans, are not integrating into American society in ways predicted by sociologists and other scholars. It may also shed light on the reality of the Latino community in general. The first thing history reveals is that not all Hispanics/Latinos are immigrants. Including the Puerto Ricans born on the island, nearly 70 percent of all Hispanics have been born as U.S. citizens. Puerto Ricans and Mexicans constitute the majority of that 70 percent, although the importance of other Hispanic immigrants over the past fifty years cannot be denied. In New York City and Dade County, Florida, for example, groups such as the Dominicans and the Cubans, respectively, account for the largest Hispanic constituencies. American economic policies, coupled with political unrest in various regions,[11] has produced a steady flow of immigrants from the Spanish-speaking Caribbean and Central America that has kept the Latino community in a continuous process of reintegration and identification.

Unquestionably, a sense of identity as unique national groups and as members of a larger Latin American community has been present among people who share a language,[12] certain cultural traits, a history of Spanish colonization, and in most cases a religious tradition. The commonalities shared by the diverse Hispanic groups and their lived experience as they relate to one another in this society have been instrumental in strengthening their awareness of common historical ties and refashioning their consciousness as members of that large Latin American/Hispanic family that we have called "pan-Hispanicismo" or "pan-Latinismo."[13] The Puerto Ricans and the Mexicans, however, have an additional reality in common, namely, a history not only of U.S. political and economic domination but also of territorial invasion and colonization.

Because they are continually receiving new members from Latin America and the Caribbean, Hispanic communities are constantly being cast in the immigrant mold. This perception leads scholars, educators, religious leaders, and politicians in the core society to expect these groups to follow the old immigrant paradigm of fairly rapid assimilation. But when the assimilation of Hispanics fails to take place as swiftly as it did with European immigrants, there is cause for surprise and finger-pointing. Lack of integration is seen as a failure on the part of Hispanics themselves rather than on the part of the receiving society; Hispanics are thus held responsible for their economic and social marginalization. If they are not educated, it is because they are "uneducable"; if they are unemployed or underemployed, it is because they are "lazy" or "refuse to learn English like everybody else."[14] Most observers seem to forget that the quest to assimilate people of Hispanic origin transcends the Hispanic population within U.S. borders. The persistent view that the lands south of the Rio Grande and the Caribbean constitute a "backyard" for America reinforces the quasi-religious belief that the United States has not only the right but also the obligation to impose its values and mores, its language and culture, its ethos, and even its religious traditions on the entire American continent.

Manifest destiny impelled the United States to invade northeastern Mexico so that by the mid-nineteenth century it had annexed Azatlán, the vast territory and natural resources of present-day Texas, Arizona, New Mexico, California, and Colorado. But the history of the Mexican population of the present-day Southwest does not begin with American intervention in the area. It has its origin in a society and culture established a hundred years before the Pilgrims landed at Plymouth Rock and centuries before the United States invaded their lands. Further, the back-and-forth movement of people between the borders of the United States and present-day Mexico has been a constant occurrence. People do not always abide by official laws, in this case because identity is in part forged out of resistance to what is perceived as a foreign imposition. The political boundaries set after the U.S. takeover of Mexican territories have proven ineffective in curtailing the movement of Mexican-origin people within an area that they consider home.

Fifty years after the takeover of Azatlán, what was left of the Spanish Empire in the Caribbean and Asia was seized for its strategic position. The nomenclature of the Cuban–Spanish War (recast as the Spanish–American War) was not the only thing changed by the U.S. intervention in the Caribbean in 1898. This successful effort helped alleviate the American economic depression of the 1890s by adding captive foreign markets and opening up a window of opportunity for the spread of U.S. political,[15] cultural, and economic influence beyond the North American continent.[16] The Caribbean became an American "lake" as the United States set up military outposts throughout the islands in order to protect its national interests in the surrounding regions. Thus, Puerto Ricans, coming from a Caribbean island colonized by the Spaniards in 1508 and invaded by the United States in 1898, have become a recognizable presence on the North American continent. Citizens since 1917, their movement back and forth has continued unimpeded to the present day.[17]

It took little more than half a century for the United States to extend its borders from the Atlantic to the Pacific coast and then to the Caribbean, "from sea to shining sea" as the "Star- Spangled Banner" affirms. The United States grew at the expense of the native and *mestizo* peoples by taking 75 percent of their land. There is ample evidence found in official and unofficial documents that the events leading to the acquisition of northern Mexico and Puerto Rico were planned and executed with forethought and force, "acquired" for their mineral wealth as well as their political and strategic advantage.[18] But in order to annex these lands that served so well the economic, political, and military interests of its Euro-American population, the United States was forced to protect residents under its flag, albeit as citizens with second-class status.

The inferior socioeconomic position of Puerto Ricans and Mexican Americans[19] today supports the argument that on the whole, both groups were made strangers in their own lands and deprived of participation in social progress and economic prosperity.[20] This point must be asserted forcefully because there is a tendency to attribute lack of so-called assimilation to the fact that one has recently arrived as an immigrant or is not able to speak English. Sociological studies have shown, however, that recent immigrants from Latin America often succeed better in school and in the workplace than Puerto Ricans born in the United States. It has also been demonstrated that Hispanics who have retained language and other cultural traits, such as extended family relationships, are healthier than those who have not. In the general Hispanic community, the infant mortality rate among those who have clearly retained a Hispanic identity as well as cultural ties is lower than among those who have lost such cultural traits. And among Puerto Ricans, there is a higher infant mortality rate of children born to parents in the mainland than among children born to parents on the island.

Meanwhile, the culture, language, and religion of Hispanic people have been portrayed in pejorative terms and as inferior to those of the United States. In the past, it was a common assumption that Hispanics needed to be enlightened by the Anglo-Saxon civilization and liberated from the "superstitions and obscurantism" perpetrated on them for centuries by Spain and Rome. Josiah Strong, a Protestant preacher of the nineteenth century, forcefully proclaimed that the Anglo-Saxon race represented the "largest liberty, the purest Christianity, the highest civilization—having developed peculiarly aggressive traits calculated to impress its institutions upon mankind."[21] And one of the institutions that Americans thought should be perpetrated on people of Latino origin was its own brand of religion.

There are current studies that demonstrate a high rate of conversion of Latin Americans and Spanish-speaking Caribbean people to Pentecostalism, mainline Protestant churches, and other religious groups, such as the Church of Jesus Christ of Latter-Day Saints, Seventh-Day Adventists, and the Jehovah's Witnesses. Some point out that present-day immigration from Latin America and the Spanish-speaking Caribbean is self-selective in terms of religion—Protestantism being overrepresented among the immigrants. I would like to offer a word of caution. In speaking of the conversion experience in Latin America and the Caribbean, care has to be taken not to confuse nominal Catholicism with the practice of Catholicism. Being baptized a Catholic may give a person a legitimate claim to be counted as one, but it does not guarantee adherence to the doctrines and practices of the Catholic faith. When such a person "converts" to Protestantism, it is questionable whether it can be said that the Catholic Church has lost yet another member. Second, one must make a difference between "conversion" theologically speaking and mere "denominational switching." There is what I call in the Hispanic community a "revolving door Christianity," and sometimes people end up where they began. In other cases, after "switching" one or more times, the person simply gives up institutional religion altogether and reverts back to home religion, popular religiosity, or no religious practice at all. In terms of the numbers and rates of "conversion," we are in desperate need of a comprehensive study that includes "multiple switching," "dropout" rates, and return to original denomination. The factors that influence the "conversion" experience also need to be better documented, including family ties, economic and political circumstances, health, education, spirituality, personal fulfillment, and the like.

The researcher needs to be fully acquainted with religious and cultural practices in the Hispanic community. Syncretism is commonplace. Among Hispanics, it is not uncommon to find people simultaneously practicing in different denominations and sometimes even in different religions or combining religious elements that to the outsider may seem incompatible. A person may go to the *curandera* to ask for a remedy for his or her headache on Monday; when the pain persists on Tuesday, he or she may seek the help of a *santero;* on Wednesday, he or she may turn to home remedies and prayer before the home altar; on Thursday, the person may decide that perhaps going to hear the Pentecostal preacher at the storefront church will offer a diversion from the pain and that his blessing may even take it away; on Friday, there is a rosary and novena at the local Catholic church (perhaps prayers to the Virgin may help; if not, perhaps it is time to go to the doctor); on Saturday, after taking the medication the doctor has prescribed, the headache subsides, and in the afternoon the person decides "to repent" and go to confession to tell the priests what has taken place during the week; and finally, on Sunday, the person returns to the Catholic liturgy of the Mass and the Sacrament of the Eucharist. There may have been a time when such behavior was thought to be exclusive of those identifying themselves as Catholics, but more and more we find a similar behavior among adherents to Protestantism and other religions.

THE ROLE OF RELIGION

Religion offers a sense of identity that in turn is an important ingredient for group cohesiveness. It has been argued that religion offers the immigrant group a "place" of strength from which to voluntarily seek assimilation into the core society. When the religious belief system is the same as that of members of the core society, a sense of commonality and shared values between the subordinate and the core group is expected and with this a diminishing of tension and conflict. All too often, however, religion is also used to counteract the indigenous belief system on which the values, norms, and ethos of the conquered people rest. As such, the religion of the invaders is an effective tool in the conquest and colonization of acquired territories.

Clearly, the role of religion both as shared beliefs and as imposed values has been played out in the case of Puerto Ricans and Mexican Americans. The Catholic Church, for example, has clearly extended services to the Latinos because it considers this to be a pastoral imperative. Thus, it has provided a place of identity for these peoples. But the Catholic Church, like any other social institution, must keep the allegiance of its members in order to strengthen its own visibility and social clout.[22] A strong membership is seen to constitute a strong church, a factor in the relations of both Catholicism and Protestantism vis-à-vis the Hispanic community. While churches have used their spiritual, intellectual, and material capital to minister to Hispanics, too often they also display a sense of condescension—a kind of "religious imperialism" and "pious colonialism" at its best—in which Latino ways are clearly seen to be inferior to those of the core society.[23] The construction of a Protestant orphanage in Puerto Rico, for example, prompted these remarks: "It is no slight task laid upon our Government by Divine Providence to bring the people of Porto Rico[24] to the highest standard of American citizenship—and nothing short of that will satisfy God."[25]

In 1906, the annual report of the Board of Missions of the Presbyterian Church in the United States had the following to say about its work in Puerto Rico:

> Under the influence of our commerce and schools and religious philanthropic agencies the character of the people is being transformed. But if the great masses of these are to be lifted out of darkness into the light and prepared for the exercise of the prerogatives and privileges of American citizenship, then must the work of education and Christian evangelization not only be maintained, but also enlarged and persecuted with new vigor and earnestness.[26]

Thus, religion, educational, and business interests were linked together in a U.S. messianic quest that purported to bring civilization and progress to these conquered lands. In reality, it was setting the basis on which a new sphere of political and economic influence extended from south of the Rio Grande to include the Caribbean and eventually Central and South America. In the process, the excellence of Anglo-American Protestantism over Catholicism was often stressed, as was Anglo-Saxon language and culture over that of the Spanish and Latin American peoples.

The American Catholic Church, however, was also culpable.[27] Catholic clergy did not urge New Mexicans, Californians, and Puerto Ricans to resist the invaders and rally around the Catholic faith as had happened for Catholics in Poland and Ireland when those countries were invaded. Instead, the Church fostered the notion that Latinos still living in their homelands were "immigrants" to America. Although Hispanics were a conquered people, missionaries often urged them to be grateful for new opportunities rather than to nurture resentment against an invading U.S. imperialism.[28] While Protestant missionary activity often betrayed an imperious sense of morality and religious superiority, the Catholic missionaries were intent on salvaging those traditions within Latino Catholicism that were not an embarrassment to their church as an "American" institution. It is these missionary practices and their underlying philosophical underpinnings that we refer to as "pious colonialism."[29]

When there was openness toward incorporating Puerto Rican and Mexican cultural values in the ministry, it flowed from the premise that these were members of an ethnic group on the way to eventual assimilation. Such was the case with the Puerto Ricans living in the homeland. This view prevailed even among those who saw Latino and Puerto Rican Catholicism in a brighter light. The dedicated clergy, in effect, sought to lessen the evil effects of colonialism, but they scarcely challenged colonialism itself with its imposition of a different worldview, culture, and language.

Looked on as foreign immigrants rather than as internal migrants from colonized parts of their countries, Mexicans and Puerto Ricans have been expected to abandon the use of the Spanish language so as to be assimilated into American society. The low regard for things Hispanic on the one hand and exaggerated esteem for Anglo-Saxon culture on the other are still very much in evidence. Expressions of desire for Puerto Rican independence are often met with surprise that Puerto Ricans would not want to continue to be governed by the "most enlightened and progressive nation in the face of the earth." But Puerto Ricans cannot forget that it was this enlightened and progressive nation that took over some of their best agricultural lands to install their military bases and that such manipulations as the devaluation of the Puerto Rican peso allowed U.S. entrepreneurs to deprive Puerto Ricans of ownership of the sugar companies in less than two decades.

THE MIGRATION EXPERIENCE AND THE MAINTENANCE OF LANGUAGE AND CULTURE

American citizenship imposed in 1917 did not bring with it all the rights and benefits extended to the mainland population, but it did mean that Puerto Rican men could serve in World War I.[30] Prior to that time, Puerto Ricans thought of themselves as part of the larger community of immigrants of Spanish language and culture. But after 1917, the combination of being U.S. citizens and still sharing history, language, and culture with Hispanic groups placed the continental Puerto Ricans in an uneasy situation that endures to the present time.[31] During the first wave of Puerto Rican migration (1902–1945),[32] water travel took three days, making a return home extremely difficult. But some fifty years ago, when Operation Bootstrap was initiated in Puerto Rico with the backing of U.S. corporations and the approval of the U.S. government, air flight to the northeastern part of America took only seven to eight hours. This accelerated industrialization and urbanization of the island, in the process uprooting a large number of hinterland people.[33] Among them were many campesino Catholic families. They left the land they had occupied for generations to go first to the *barriadas* of Puerto Rican cities and ultimately to the city ghettos of northeastern United States.[34] From 1945 to 1964, approximately 30 percent of the island's population emigrated to the mainland, 40 percent if the children born to them in the United States are included. Not to be forgotten is the fact that Puerto Ricans migrated from a colony where English had been proclaimed the official language since 1911. The persistence of the Spanish language resulted not from the lack of exposure to English but from other causes. Therefore, perhaps the best explanation that even today Puerto Ricans who migrate to northern cities appear to be foreigners is their cultural resistance to colonialization.

Maintaining Spanish language and tradition has always been very important to religious expression than in other contexts. The piety of popular religiosity preserved an identity that was generally impervious to the seductions of Americanization. Thus, accommodation to the Spanish language, often intended as a means to introduce English, has become a major support to urban

COLONIZATION VERSUS IMMIGRATION

Latino identity. In areas such as New York, for example, where the Puerto Rican population has had few native clergy of its own, North American priests have tried to learn the language and culture of the people among whom they work. By this kind of reversal of the process of assimilation, with the Euro-American priests and sisters becoming somewhat Hispanicized, Hispanics have been able to maintain loyalty to the Church.[35] Clerics with a progressive vision also incorporated the traditional practices into the regular observances of the institutional religion and adjusted them to the urban reality.

In the 1960s, a well-established Puerto Rican and Mexican American community in the United States faced the challenge of new arrivals from the Caribbean and Central and South America. New issues of identity needed to be faced in terms of membership in particular groups and in the larger community. These arrivals served to remind Latinos of American intervention in Latin American and Caribbean affairs. Hispanics still come seeking political, educational, and economic freedom, and often the repression they feel here at the hands of officials of the Immigration and Naturalization Service and other government personnel resembles what they experienced in their own lands. Often, of course, political and military leaders back home are trained in the School of the Americas in the United States, meaning that refugees are fleeing from countries where the conditions they suffered bear the trademark of the country to which they are coming. In these circumstances, it is not uncommon to find mixed feelings of love and hate, admiration and disdain, hope and suspicion, and expectation and uncertainty.[36]

Although the process of integration into a pan-Hispanic or pan-Latino identity in the United States has had its ups and downs,[37] more often than not it has offered a sense of belonging and solidarity. Time and proximity, as well as political, educational, and other needs, have been the basis on which Hispanic or Latino solidarity has been built.[38] Marriage within the community, language, culture, and certain commonalities in the history of Latin America and the Hispanic Caribbean have made it possible for this pan-identity to be stronger for Hispanic/Latinos than for most other immigrant groups.[39] Religion has aided in the maintenance of Latino ethnic identity in ways that culture itself cannot because religion has a normative dimension; it holds individuals to a standard that integrates public behavior and personal morality in ways that culture cannot.

Among the things that preceded Puerto Rican immigrants to the United States were the suppression of religious devotions on the island, such as *la misa del gallo;* the destruction of religious artifacts, such as the famous *santos de palos;* and the imposition of the English language as the medium of instruction in Puerto Rican schools. Overt and covert pressure pushed Catholicism in Puerto Rico to exchange the simplicity of the agricultural world with more complex psychological and social meanings. But neither pressure nor official condemnation necessarily translated into public acquiescence. Centuries-old rituals cannot be eliminated with the stroke of a pen or official pronouncements. Whether on the island or in New York, the new adaptations made can be viewed not as capitulation but as recycling, as reinventing, and ultimately as a source of resistance. This has not been too hard for the Puerto Ricans in the United States; by the time the immigrants arrived in New York, they had had years of experience in resisting U.S. culture in the homeland. It must be remembered that Puerto Rican Catholicism emerged during Spanish colonization but evolved for four centuries before it met with U.S. Protestantism and political structures.

Through religion, groups keep in touch with the past, acknowledge the present, and even project the future. Religion and its traditions give believers a sense of purpose, of belonging, and of being one with each other—with previous generations and with those to come.[40] The maintenance of religious traditions always depends on a strong sense of community. This is certainly the case in terms of the Hispanic community. Remembering, transforming, and passing on cultural and religious traditions in new social circumstances to subsequent generations are part of the adaptation process and also guarantee in great measure the preservation of the group's unique identity. By necessity, this process involves religious imagination. Many of the traditions of the country of origin fall by the wayside, but others take root and are strengthened in the new location. Transformed or reinvented, they may even find their way "back home" to the country of origin, such as *las posadas* (celebrated around Christmas) *la pastorela* (celebrated at Epiphany), and *día de los muertos* (day of the dead) among Mexican Americans. The reenactment in the barrio streets of Jesus' passion on Holy Thursday is a sacramental act that has been resurrected and is now commonplace among the diverse Hispanic groups of this nation. Patron feast days—such as fiestas of *San Juan Bautista* or *Santiago Apóstol* for Puerto Ricans, *Caridad del Cobre* for Cubans, and *Nuestra Senora de Altagracia* for Dominicans—are other examples of religious traditions that have been adapted to the urban U.S. reality.[41] In ways that seem unique to

Latinos, religion in the barrios nurtures the revitalization of old traditions and the creation of new ones. This dynamic aspect of religion in the United States needs to be included in any comprehensive assessment of the future both of the Hispanic community in the United States and of American religion.

Puerto Ricans, like Mexicans, did not have to wait to migrate in order to encounter the United States and its value system. Before these people moved to the United States, the United States had moved into their homelands. Even so, the encounter of Puerto Ricans with U.S. personnel and political structure on their island did not fully prepare them for the reality of the migration experience. But it did help identify religious, cultural, and social traits in America deemed undesirable or detrimental to Puerto Rican identity. Furthermore, the Puerto Rican experience of contact with North Americans, first in their own island and then in the northeastern United States, no doubt helped pave the way for Spanish-speaking immigrants from the Caribbean and Central and South America. People from these regions, of course, are not totally unaware or untouched by U.S. political and economic influences in their own homelands. The contact between these groups reinforces historical allegiance to a pan–Latino-Americanismo dating back to the time of Bolívar and gives rise to a new consciousness of U.S. pan-Latinismo. Mutual contact acculturates Latin Americans to Hispanic norms, making the new arrivals more like the Hispanics/Latinos who have been born in the United States. But the process also works in the opposite direction: Hispanics acculturate to some aspects of a Latin American identity. The juxtaposition of the diverse Hispanic groups stimulates a complex process of asserting differences and searching for similarities, of cooperation and competition, and of re-creating the setting of the home country and adapting to the new urban circumstances.[42] In these dynamics, new configurations are created among the groups, and cultural identity is sharpened. As noted previously, tradition becomes a vehicle not only for preserving the past but also for facilitating constant adaptation to new circumstances, stimulating the religious imagination. In my opinion, this dynamic aspect of religion in the United States needs to be included in any comprehensive assessment of the future of both the Hispanic community and religion in the United States.

Last, in analyzing the assimilation process, we must consider the role of the Spanish language and bilingualism in relation to both education and religion. Within Catholicism, the democratizing effects of the Second Vatican

Council through new pastoral initiatives gave the U.S. lay leadership a more prominent role at the parish level. The first reforms of the Second Vatican Council, for example, affected the language of worship. The conciliar instructions indicated that the liturgy should be offered "in the language of the people." Because of the long-standing practice of offering services in Spanish that were different from those offered in English, this meant that Catholicism became bilingual. The Mass was to be said in Spanish for the Spanish-speaking people in the United States and in English for the English-speaking people. Thus, the decision of the U.S. bishops to consider Spanish as a "language of the people" effectively made the U.S. church a bilingual church.[43]

Bilingualism had an important effect on Latinos because it reversed the pattern of linguistic imperialism. Further, the Council's sympathetic view of popular religiosity also served to aid Hispanics in their new identification process, as this was an area of many commonalities calling for ritualization on the one hand and transformation through adaptation and reformulation on the other. Spanish-language services required music, hymns, and styles of expression that emphasized these differences. Instead of becoming more assimilated into the United States like European immigrants, Latinos have been distinguished from the English-speaking population through the use of Spanish. It is not only the Catholic Church, however, that has attempted bilingualism. Similar patterns have also been repeated in most Protestant and evangelical churches. The Board of Global Ministries of the United Methodist Church, through at least three of its divisions,[44] implemented national programs to meet the needs of its Hispanic constituency. In the 1970s, it began a program in Spanish for the ongoing Christian formation of Hispanic Methodist Women in the United States and Puerto Rico. An ecumenical endeavor, *Teología de las Américas*, sought to create a space for Hispanic religious leaders and theologians to formulate a theology consonant with the needs of Hispanics in the United States.

As a result of the 1965 reform of immigration laws, immigration from Latin America intensified, and new numbers were added to the enclaves of U.S.-born Latinos. The encounter between these two groups helps maintain and strengthen the traditions, culture, use of Spanish, and historical memory of the Hispanics. In the process, a new transnational identity as Hispanics or Latinos/as has been forged that often has been instrumental in paralyzing any movement toward assimilation. This has meant that the immigrant paradigm

of Americanization, loss of national language and identity, and assimilation
are no longer imperative.

In the late 1960s, a social movement that has been called "the Latino Religious Resurgence"[45] emerged within the churches, giving ample evidence of the strength and pervasiveness of this new identity. Hispanic culture was idealized in order to differentiate Hispanics from Euro-American believers, motivate members of the Hispanic community for collective identity, and justify a plan of action. Maintaining their identity as Mexican, Puerto Rican, Cuban, or other, Hispanics nonetheless began to stress similarities in terms of cultural traits. Through pastoral centers, theological books, and ministry among the people at the local level, as well as the Hispanic National Encounters of the 1970s and 1980s, Hispanics gave evidence that the different Latino nationalities had more in common with one another than with Euro-Americans. This journey toward a pan-Latino identity, which bore recognizable fruits in the 1980s (the "Decade of the Hispanics") is an ongoing process. What is taking place among Hispanics today calls into question the notion that the racial and cultural diversity of the United States produces a simple amalgamation into a homogeneous mixture where all differences are tolerated and enjoyed under the common set of values established by a Puritan ethic.

For all these reasons, as I have argued elsewhere, blindly adhering to traditional paradigms of assimilation to explain today's reality is like "pouring new wine into old skins." Clearly, paradigms cannot be treated as "one size fits all." A more enlightened approach takes into serious account both old and new factors that affect this process, including the history of previous contact between the host and sending societies, the length of time a group has lived in the host society, ongoing contact of im/migrants with the country of origin, and political, cultural, economic, and religious forces in the sending and receiving societies. Even the impact of transportation and communication must be addressed, as advancement in the technology of these fields and other related sectors of modern life has affected the maintenance of culture, language, and even sense of community. For example, at one time "community" was equated with the relationships established among people living within a specific geographic boundary, but this is no longer today's reality. One may occasionally have an opportunity to hastily greet the people next door without even knowing their last name. On the other hand, a person can maintain close contact with relatives and friends thousands of miles away. In my own case, I most certainly will be present at family reunions, weddings, and other rites of passages and feasts that bind us together even though this means traveling by car, train, or air to get to the place of celebration. What constitutes a community, then, is not only the geographic proximity of people who share language and culture with one another but also the accessibility of that language and culture through personal contact, radio, television, newspaper, telephone, regular and electronic mail, and frequent visits to and from the country of origin.

Hispanics' sense of identity, an increasing political visibility, the maintenance of the Spanish language and Hispanic culture, and the strength and creativity of their religious traditions seem to be causes of great pride to Hispanics at the same that they are of concern to others. If the persistence of these values, together with population growth, provides a valid indicator of the strength of Latinismo or Hispanicismo, then those advocating for such things as "English only" and a quick assimilation process indeed have a valid cause for concern. It can be argued that the growing numbers of Hispanics make them the crucial segment of the population who will determine the future of America. The spiritual quest of Hispanics today is an integral part of the spiritual quest of all religious believers in the United States. The experience of Hispanics, particularly that of Puerto Ricans and Mexican Americans in the American context, challenges the assumption that the role of colonization in the formation of these people is central to any analysis of their social, economic, or religious situation. It also poses serious questions, as has been demonstrated in this chapter, about the applicability of established paradigms for immigrant assimilation in general.

NOTES

1. See Alejandro Portes and Robert L. Bach, *Latino Journey: Cuban and Mexican Immigrants in the United States* (Berkeley: University of California Press, 1985).

2. Renato Poblete and Thomas O'Dea, "Anomie and the 'Quest for Community': The Formation of Sects among the Puerto Ricans," *American Catholic Sociological Review* 21 (spring 1960): 18–36.

3. Patricia Guadalupe wrote in her column "Political Poop" for a news service on the Hispanic community out of Washington, *Hispanic Link Weekly Report* (May 22, 2000), that "more than 10,000 Dominican residents of New York City traveled to their homeland to vote in the May 16 presidential elections, with many of them using

discounted air fares negotiated by three main political parties. Dominicans represent the fastest-growing Hispanic group in eastern United States. All three candidates campaigned heavily in New York, home to more than 600,000 *quisqueyanos* [Dominicans]. President Leonel Fernandez, who grew up in the Big Apple and is the only Latin American leader with a 'green card,' recently inaugurated a new cultural center in Manhattan with a $100,000 donation from the Dominican government" (2).

4. Henceforth, "Latino" and "Hispanic" will be used interchangeably. I find "Hispanics" a more inclusive term because it also includes people from Spain or of Spanish heritage.

5. For a more complete comparative economic and educational analysis of Latinos and other racial groups in the United States, see Ana María Díaz-Stevens and Anthony M. Stevens-Arroyo, *Recognizing the Latino Resurgence in U.S. Religion: The Emmaus Paradigm* (Boulder, Colo.: Westview Press, 1998).

6. U.S. Bureau of the Census, 1996.

7. There has been more coverage, both locally and nationally, of the Hispanic presence in the United States. On June 4 and 5, 2000, for example, the *Central New Jersey Home News Tribune* (dating back to 1879) carried a first-page article "Hispanic Influx Reshaping U.S." and "Hispanics Meet Mixed Reactions," where the impact of Hispanic demographics for the nation and for New Jersey are evaluated. It is of interest that three of the four photographs accompanying the two-part article are of cultural and religious significance.

8. There is a history of U.S. political and economic intervention in the Caribbean and Central America. In Guatemala and Costa Rica, for example, the exploits of the Banana Fruit Company have been amply documented. The same can be said of political intervention, such as the various military occupations of the Dominican Republic in the twentieth century. These events have found their way even into Latin American fiction. See the works of Gabriel García Márquez, especially *One Hundred Years of Solitude* (New York: HarperPerennial, 1991) and *The Autumn of the Patriarch* (New York: Harper & Row, 1976).

9. George Gallup and Jim Castelli, *The People's Religion: American Faith in the 90s* (Princeton, N.J.: Princeton Religion Research Center, 1989), 133–42.

10. Barry A. Kosmin, *The National Survey of Religious Identification 1989–1990* (New York: City University of New York, 1991); Barry A. Kosmin and Seymour P. Lachman, *One Nation under God: Religion in Contemporary American Society* (New York: Harmony Books, 1993).

11. There are those who believe that this will be ultimately detrimental to the United States. I believe it was Nobel Prize winner García Márquez who remarked that these policies and their subsequent consequences will cause a U.S. culture and society to be gutted out from within by an ever-growing Hispanic population within its borders.

12. I am very much aware of the fact that not all people coming from Latin America speak Spanish. In fact, there are those who do not know Spanish but who, once in the United States, find it necessary to learn it as a means to form part of the Hispanic community to which they first integrate before integrating into the larger society.

13. There are differences not only between the different nationality groups such as Cubans, Dominicans, and Guatemalans but also within segments of these groups themselves. The Mexican-origin group constitutes a very diverse population. Among themselves, the so-called Mexican Americans make differences between *nuevos mejicanos, mejicanos,* or newly arrived immigrants directly from Mexico, Chicanos, Californios, and so on. As the Mexican American population disperses throughout the United States and as new immigrants arrive from Mexico, new identifiers will probably arise.

14. This is not exclusive to Latinos. Victims are usually blamed for their situation in life. See, for example, Frances Fox Piven and Richard A. Cloward, *Poor People's Movement* (New York: Vintage Books, 1979).

15. For example, through the influence of the United States, an amendment was added to the Cuban constitution calling for U.S. intervention when the United States deemed it necessary to protect its interest in the Caribbean. This amendment was kept in the Cuban constitution until 1936. It is argued that by that time, the Cuban people had been so influenced by the United States as to make the amendment superfluous.

16. The U.S. political and economic domination has transcended the Hispanic reality on the island of Puerto Rico and the southwestern states and has extended throughout the Caribbean and Latin America as the United States spreads its "democratic principles and sphere of influence."

17. Bernardo Vega, a migrant during the first decades of the 1900s, documents his own experiences as a Puerto Rican migrant and that of the larger Colonia Hispana in his *Memorias de Bernardo Vega* (Río Piedras: Editorial Coquí, 1977), later edited by Cesar Andreu Iglesias. Though not large in number, it was a vibrant community composed mostly of Puerto Ricans, Cubans, and Spaniards.

18. In 1848, through the Treaty of Guadalupe Hidalgo and subsequently through the Gadsden Purchase and other such agreements, the United States gained control of northern Mexico. It did not take long, through both legal and illegal means, for the

"newcomers" (in this case the Euro-Americans entering the region) to lay claim to
the land, declaring previous ownership that went back hundreds of years and the
laws and practices on which that ownership was based no longer pertinent. With the
invention of barbed wire, the "newcomers" partitioned and segregated lands that had
been held and used in common for cattle grazing. Water sources were diverted from
their natural course, as depicted, for example, in the movie *The Milagro Bean War*. In
some areas, such as Nuevo Mexico, the elite classes of both groups formed
partnerships through intermarriages and other "legal" means while the masses were
left to fend for themselves as hired hands.

19. In the last four decades of the twentieth century, a large number of Mexican
Americans were dispersed throughout the United States. Like the Puerto Ricans,
mostly a rural population, the Mexican Americans now found themselves in the
great urban centers of this nation competing with other social minorities and ethnic
groups for employment, housing, education, and health care.

20. For example, the island of Vieques, a Puerto Rican municipality that has in vain
tried to rid itself of the Navy and its target practice amidst a civilian population
deprived of serenity and political voice.

21. Josiah Strong, *Our Country* (1885), cited in Ronald H. Chilcote and Joel C.
Edelstein, *Latin America: The Struggle with Dependency and Beyond* (New York: John
Wiley & Sons, 1974). Strong wrote thirteen years before the United States took over
Las Filipinas and Puerto Rico. It was of no consequence to Strong and others like
him that in large measure the wealth came from, or at the expense of, the same
people the Anglo-Saxon race deemed inferior.

22. See Ana María Díaz-Stevens, *Oxcart Catholicism on Fifth Avenue: The Impact of
the Puerto Rican Migration upon the Archdiocese of New York* (Notre Dame, Ind.:
University of Notre Dame Press, 1993).

23. By portraying Hispanics as scarcely above paganism, North Americans can
assume the role of righteous followers of Christ divinely chosen to save the
Hispanics from themselves.

24. The United States changed the name of Puerto Rico to Porto Rico, just as the
Spaniards had changed the indigenous name of Borik Island to Isla de San Juan
Bautista de Puerto Rico. The old name of Borik was kept in common parlance as
Borinquen.

25. David W. Creane at the dedication of the George O. Robinson Orphanage in San
Juan, quoted in Emilio Pantojas Garcia, *La iglesia Protestante y la americanization de
Puerto Rico* (San Juan: Prisa, n.d.), 23.

26. Pantojas Garcia, 23.

27. Another Puerto Rican author, Felix Padilla, examining the pre–Vatican II experience, states, "In the final analysis, Puerto Ricans became just another 'immigrant group' for the Catholic Church to accommodate, and this ambivalence disillusioned many Puerto Ricans. The church hierarchy saw the discrimination against Puerto Ricans, but it did not condemn it as part of American society. Instead, it sought to do charity by trying to alleviate suffering by serving as a buffer without attacking institutionalized racism. The church could not, due to its own relationship with American society, help Puerto Ricans resist the violation of their culture and personal identity." Felix Padilla, *Puerto Rican Chicago* (Notre Dame, Ind.: University of Notre Dame Press, 1987), 136–37.

28. Díaz-Stevens and Stevens-Arroyo, *Recognizing the Latino Resurgence in U.S. Religion*, 106.

29. Díaz-Stevens and Stevens-Arroyo, *Recognizing the Latino Resurgence in U.S. Religion*, 106.

30. Notably absent has been the right of islanders to vote for the president and other U.S. government officials. The island has no voting representation in either the House of Representatives or Congress, and the Puerto Rican resident commissioner has only voice but no vote. Puerto Rico cannot sign commercial treaties with any other nation. American vessels must be used for commercial transportation, and the postal service and customs are likewise controlled by the United States. Yet Puerto Ricans are inducted into military service. In armed conflicts, the rate of Puerto Rican fatalities has been higher than for Euro-Americans.

31. This, along with other social factors and characteristics of the Puerto Rican people, would affect the nature of their relationship with other Hispanics as well as their integration into U.S. society. The early Puerto Rican migration, from 1898 to roughly 1945, has been called the "Pioneer Migration." A second period registering a massive number of Puerto Rican migrants took place after World War II, from 1945 to 1965; this period has been called the "Puerto Rican Great Migration." At the end of this period, approximately 40 percent of the entire Puerto Rican population was constituted of migrants and the children born to migrants in the United States. Because of technological advancements in travel and communication, the period from 1965 to the present has been given the name the "Revolving Door Migration." Today there are approximately 3 million people classified as Puerto Ricans in the continental United States and another 3.8 million on the island.

32. The first wave, or Pioneer Migration, brought men to work mainly in the tobacco industry and factories of New York and New Jersey and in the Brooklyn navy yard.

33. The second wave, or Puerto Rican Great Migration from the end of World War II to the mid-1960s, coincides with a host of changes in Puerto Rico and the United States, including the demise of Luis Munoz Marín, the insertion of Puerto Ricans in New York City politics, the war on poverty, the Voting Rights Act, and the civil rights movement. This migration wave was characterized by low levels of education and a greater number of women and more family groups than in previous decades. While men were employed in farming and in menial work in hotels and factories, women were clustered mostly in the garment industry, which was undergoing a process of rapid displacement to Third World nations.

34. This is the phenomenon so vividly portrayed by Puerto Rican playwright Ren Marquis in *La carreta*, from which I derived the concept of "Oxcart Catholicism" for my book *Oxcart Catholicism on Fifth Avenue*.

35. Díaz-Stevens, *Oxcart Catholicism on Fifth Avenue*.

36. The case of the U.S. Navy on the Puerto Rican island of Vieques and the use of the FBI to remove peaceful demonstrators provides yet another opportunity for Hispanics to gauge the desirability of "assimilation" to U.S. society.

37. This is particularly so for the Puerto Ricans, in great part because of Puerto Rico's particular relationship with the United States and the sense of suspicion (sometimes even hostility) that it engenders. On the other hand, the fact that Puerto Ricans are citizens means that when newcomers arrive from the Caribbean and Central and South America, Puerto Ricans can and often do act as their spokespersons. Thus, citizenship for this group affects both their integration process in the Latino community and the Latino community's integration process into North American society.

38. See Felix Padilla, *Latino Ethnic Consciousness: The Case of Mexican Americans and Puerto Ricans in Chicago* (Notre Dame, Ind.: University of Notre Dame Press, 1985).

39. On the other hand, those who do not understand that integration into a society is a two-way process (which calls both for the readiness of the ethnic or immigrant group and for their acceptance by the core society) often believe that it is precisely this Hispanic sense of "peoplehood," with its attendant language and culture retention, that has kept the Latinos from readily assimilating into mainline U.S. society.

40. As the writer Edward Shils says, tradition creates a "sense of filiation, i.e. connectedness to other generations." Edward Shils, *Tradition* (Chicago: University of Chicago Press, 1981), 14.

41. It should be noted that in some public religious rituals, such as the reenactment of Jesus' Passion, members of diverse Christian churches—both Catholic and Protestant—participate. Rites of passage such as *La Quinceanera*, marking the passage of a young woman to adulthood, are now celebrated in Protestant churches using a manual prepared by the Instituto de Liturgia Hispana of the U.S. Catholic Conference.

42. With Dominicans among Puerto Ricans, however, the process has its own particularities because of the a pan–Spanish-Caribbean culture and the fact that a similar process of integration into Puerto Rican society is taking place with Dominicans in Puerto Rico.

43. Ultimately, the Catholic Church became not only bilingual but also multilingual as it sought to meet the needs of the diverse groups of immigrants within its midst.

44. The Women's Division, the Education and Cultivation Division, and the National Division.

45. Díaz-Stevens and Stevens-Arroyo, *Recognizing the Latino Resurgence in U.S. Religion.*

5

Some Praise Jesus, and Some Don't: Thoughts on the Complex Nature of African American Religious Identity and Those Who Interpret It

ANTHONY B. PINN

As recounted in spirituals and the blues, Africans in North America developed a worldview and sense of meaning premised on their "relocation" and its ontological, existential, and epistemological ramifications. The spirituals speak to this when Africans in the Americas sang,

> Don't be wary, traveller
> Come along home, come home.
> Don't be wary, traveller,
> Come along home, come home.[1]

Or, with the blues,

> Now I tell you mama now
> I'm sure gonna leave this town
> Now I tell you mam now
> I'm sure gonna leave this town
> 'Cause I been in trouble ever since I
> sat my suitcase down.[2]

Beyond examples in African American popular culture, the consequences of movement are notable in the general style of African American expression and in the fine points of African American life, including religiosity. From the early relocation of African gods to the Americas, even North America, to the African American appropriation of Christianity for subversive purposes, movement has entailed both trouble, as evidenced by the slave trade, and promise, as was the case with escape to the North and "freedom" associated with migration.

In the following pages, I explore the religious ramifications of movement as they relate to the development of a very complex sense of African American religious identity. In so doing, I give attention to the challenge of multiple religious identities in African American communities in four ways: 1) by briefly discussing religious diversity in African American communities resulting from three forms of movement—the slave trade, the Great Migration, and late twentieth-century immigration from the Caribbean; 2) by recounting the narrow focus of black religious studies and the challenge to this approach found in movement-generated religious diversity; 3) by presenting an alternate approach to religious identity through a rethinking of the nature of African American religious experience; and 4) by reformulating religious identity through attention to the body as the major site and symbol of religious experience, in opposition to the current preoccupation with doctrine as the defining characteristic of African American religious identity.

THE ATLANTIC SLAVE TRADE

Contact between Africans and Europeans during the fifteenth century was first centered on gold available on the western coast of Africa. Because of the potential wealth in mining, Europeans made an initial effort to restrict their exportation of human flesh to areas away from the Gold Coast to avoid conflicts that might hamper mining and trading. However, European expansion into the Americas provided a seemingly limitless supply of other resources, but securing this wealth required a substantial labor force. Early attempts to find labor involved indentured workers from Europe who often were secured through misleading information concerning profit-sharing opportunities. However, interested parties would not receive pay, and the benefits of their labor could not be secured until after the seven years of service were finished.[3] The benefits of indentured labor were limited, and the ability to secure indigenous labor—as either indentured or enslaved workers—was problematic at best. With time, this labor force proved impractical, and attention was given to the slave labor market already in operation in the Caribbean and Brazil.[4]

Having had their heads shaved and their bodies branded, Africans emerged from slave castles and holding pens, ate their "last meal," and were stripped, chained, and packed onto vessels (many with biblical names).[5] This started the long voyage into the unknown, marking the disruption of worldviews, cultural categories, language, and social structures. Although most of their time was spent in the crowded and dark holds, they were periodically brought to the deck, where they were examined for sores and other signs of illness. Time on the deck also included "exercise" and forced amusement, such as singing and drumming.[6] Those who did not die as a result of the poor diet, abuse (including rape), and disease-ridden conditions arrived in the "New World" to serve the labor needs of expansion-minded Europeans.

The first enslaved Africans in the North American colonies were brought to Virginia in 1619.[7] The first groups of enslaved Africans were small in number because of cost and other factors. But the importance of the African presence would increase. For example, one trade company, over the course of eight years (1680–1688), used 249 ships on journeys to Africa and, after losses due to death, brought more than 46,000 Africans back to America. Until 1707, roughly 25,000 enslaved Africans arrived in the North American colonies.[8] Although one might speculate that trading in slaves was a practice more likely associated with southern colonies, Puritans in New England began trips to Africa to gain slaves as early as the 1640s. There were enslaved Africans in New England, representing roughly 10 percent of the population by 1775, but the bulk of this forced labor was on the tobacco and rice plantations of southern colonies, where slaves represented a much larger percentage of the overall population. The rationale for the development of the slave trade in New England and the other British North American colonies is clear: Other forms of labor were problematic and costly. Enslaved Africans were easily identifiable, and this made escape more difficult than would be the case with Indians and Europeans. The physical difference between Europeans and Africans had broad implications.

Differentiated from the English, Africans became the "Other." Africans, who were distinguished in name (Negar or Negro) and by physical appearance, were often used as a measuring stick by which the English assessed themselves and their society in both religious and mundane terms. At its worst, differences in appearance, social habits, and cultural production were interpreted by the English in ways that painted Africans as barbaric and of less value.[9] Tied to this difference and degradation was a sense of Africans as religiously heathenistic, while the Puritans and other colonists possessed the truth to the extent that they were Christian (and English).

Many saw slavery as an opportunity to bring Africans into a proper understanding of God's word; in this way, they added to the Kingdom of God by converting the lost. Africans, the argument went, were capable of understanding the gospel if it was presented to them. For many influential colonists, such as Cotton Mather of Massachusetts, God placed Africans under the control of Puritans as part of a providential plan, and this fosters a responsibility that Puritans must accept with all sincerity and seriousness. Because God ultimately controlled the destiny of each human, Christians could not afford to neglect any soul. Nonetheless, Puritans and other Christian slaveholders faced a dilemma that pitted economic and social sensibilities against religion. Christianizing enslaved Africans could result in economic loss and social disorder. But failure to spread the gospel contradicted Jesus' calling of the redeemed to service: "Go therefore and make disciples of all nations, baptizing them in the name of the Father and of the Son and of the Holy Spirit, teaching them to observe all that I have commanded you; and lo, I am with you always, to the close of the age."[10] The relatively low number of Africans with recorded membership in Puritan churches bespeaks a continuing fear over the ramifications of Christianizing slaves.

In southern areas, Puritan preachers were supplanted by workers from the Society for the Propagation of the Gospel in Foreign Parts, which gave notable attention to converting slaves after 1702. The approach taken by the society met with some opposition because it entailed teaching Africans to read and write (in order to understand the catechism). In response to this opposition, the society advocated the benefits of conversion, and, when and where possible, it continued its work despite a short supply of ministers.

The Great Awakenings (beginning in the 1730s and then again in the early 1800s) marked a more energetic and less doctrinally focused attempt to "save" the slaves. However, the success of fiery services associated with these awakenings must not be overestimated. For example, the effects of the Great Awakenings among the Gullah of South Carolina were minimal. As a result, the challenge of converting slaves was amplified in areas such as coastal South Carolina, where mission efforts had little steam until the 1830s and faced the challenge of a large and somewhat insular black population.[11] Even when mission work was marked by what some considered success, early efforts to Christianize enslaved Africans were less than productive because the oppression of their flesh made status quo depictions of the gospel difficult for slaves to embrace. Many rejected Christianity.

Charles Long's work on New World religious formulations is important here. In *Significations,* Long argues that the oppressed must deal with two essential moments. The first is a recognition of their "second creation" as captive beings reduced in status by slavery. The second is recognition of their "first creation," a remembering of an early consciousness that is not limited to their objectification; it is a movement back to the fundamental humanity and worth of African Americans. In this way, religion within the context of early African American communities entails an effort to create an alternative consciousness, an alternate mode and expression of humanness, in history.[12] What is of particular importance for us is Long's refusal to confine this to the creation of African American Christianity. The opaque period, to continue in Long's framework, of African American religious development is complex and thick. And such a thick period of development in such an absurd space cannot be reduced to Christianity regardless of how unique its expression. Zora Neale Hurston argues that no one knows how many hearts are warmed by the fires of voodoo, and Long makes a similar appeal to a complex notion of religious identity. He writes,

> The church was not the only context for the meaning of religion. . . . The Christian faith provided a language for the meaning of religion, but not all the religious meanings of the black communities were encompassed by the Christian forms of religion . . . some of these extrachurch orientations have had great critical and creative power.[13]

Long's point is compelling, but what is the evidence? I think that Sterling Stuckey's *Been in the Storm So Long* points researchers in the correct direction. Drawing on Stuckey's work, it is inconceivable that the brutality of the slave institution completely wiped out African creative impulses and their articulation along the lines of some significant elements of African cultural sensibilities in general, and religious ones in particular. That is, Africans, even during the early years of their American presence, maintained artistic integrity and presented this in ways that speak to a diverse sense of religiosity, among other things.[14] The testimonies of slaves and former slaves speak to alternate forms of religious expression as alive on plantations. Charles Ball, for example, recalled that "at the time I first went to Carolina, there were a great many African slaves in the country. . . . Many of them believed there were several gods; some of whom were good, and others evil."[15]

Such information does not provide a systematic understanding of religious complexity, but it does raise important questions concerning the historical feasibility of black religious studies' preoccupation with black churches as *the* expression of black religiosity. There are certain religious beliefs and sensibilities that can be inferred from these findings that point to complex religious practices and identity. In other words, many enslaved Africans maintained rich ties to African religious thought and rituals, and when these could not be explored openly, they were celebrated and remembered in more subtle ways, one of which was the decorative arts. An example of this is found in the quilting tradition developed by enslaved Africans.[16] The argument is not that these quilts represent a pure link to African textiles and religious systems of meaning; rather, these quilts entail the introduction of certain African thoughts and principles into a new context, and what results is a variety of religious possibilities extending beyond the traditional church. In addition to these quilts, the collages that often marked the dwellings of enslaved Africans also held religious connotations. The collage style of wall covering was not merely a result of limited resources and utility. To the contrary, it was often understood that wall collages prevented harmful spirits from affecting those dwelling in the room in that these spirits would become preoccupied with reading the words and viewing the images present in the pieces of newspaper and so on and would then fail to do harm.

THE GREAT MIGRATION

Expressions of diverse religiosity in African American communities continued throughout the twentieth century. And the "voluntary" movement of African Americans called the Great Migration (the years following the Civil War through the first three decades of the twentieth century) is a lively marker of this progression. What is significant about this mass movement is not found in the literal number of African Americans who packed their belongings and headed elsewhere.[17] Rather, what is significant involves the socioeconomic, political, and cultural ramifications of this movement, the manner in which it would come to mark another major reformulation on the religious front.

The Emancipation Proclamation did little more than remove slavery's physical shackles. Economic, political, and social hardships persisted as African Americans were faced with limited gains through the period of Reconstruction and the reconstitution of discrimination through mob violence (e.g., the Ku Klux Klan) and legal as well as extralegal regulations referred to as Jim Crow regulations. Before 1919, more than 400,000 African Americans moved in response to economic opportunities in the North that, prior to World War I, would have been reserved for white Americans. These opportunities, combined with an assumed greater tolerance and sense of freedom in the North, made migration a more than pleasant prospect.

Migrants, however, would encounter a harsh reality. Reverdy C. Ransom, of the African Methodist Episcopal Church and one of its early Social Gospellers, spoke on the conditions faced by new arrivals in cities such as Chicago (1900). Ransom notes that African Americans faced strong discrimination in the North that resulted in their living in substandard housing at very high rents, having little green space and opportunities for constructive leisure, being intellectually stifled by inadequate schooling opportunities, and encountering health dilemmas because of crowded living conditions. What troubled Ransom as much as these conditions was the limited attention that churches gave to the plight of African American migrants, particularly those coming late in the migration pattern. He comments on the individualistic and elitist attitudes of churches and church leaders who argued that they were 1) financially incapable of addressing the needs of southern transplants, 2) unwilling to tolerate the "down-home" religious sensibilities of new arrivals whose practices ran contrary to the mainline/mainstream religious ethos embraced by many black churches, and 3) unwilling to surrender leadership positions to "unrefined" migrants. In response, and in keeping with his version of the Social Gospel, Ransom developed the Institutional Church and Social Settlement House as a way of addressing the needs other churches ignored.[18]

As Gayraud Wilmore's *Black Religion and Black Radicalism* suggests, Ransom's commitment to the needs and religious interests of migrants was not the norm within black church circles, as most churches rejected aggressive public positions and settled for a more docile and "acceptable" (accommodationist) perspective on urban crises. Although many churches attempted to provide some form of social outreach, the mass migration of African Americans is marked by a deradicalization of the mainline black church. Large numbers of new arrivals, complete with their "less refined" religious ways and economic difficulties, caused a strain on established churches that was responded to through a turn inward, individual salvation.[19]

Some migrants were able to assimilate into existing black denominations, while some others became members of black churches within predominantly white denominations. Still others joined Pentecostal and Holiness congregations. Another angle on religious identity played out during this period is of concern here, namely, "extrachurch" religious organizations. For example, the Moorish Science Temple (1913), founded by Timothy Drew or Noble Drew Ali, took Christian principles and added an understanding of African Americans as Asiatic or Moors and encouraged a familiarity with non-Western thought. It was argued by members of this group that their teachings included the thought of Muhammad, Confucius, Buddha, and Jesus. Other traditions, such as the Nation of Islam, emerged and embraced a similar form of nationalism. Of the two (the Moorish Science Temple and the Nation of Islam), the latter has held a more consistent place in African American communities. From 1930, with the first appearance of Master Fard Muhammad, through the ministries of the Honorable Elijah Muhammad and Malcolm X (before leaving the Nation of Islam in 1964) to the current work by Minister Louis Farrakhan, the Nation of Islam has remained a major religious force. Although the purpose and length of this chapter do not allow me to discuss it, one could easily add to the ranks of religiously oriented black nationalist organization Marcus Garvey's Universal Negro Improvement Association (and its African Orthodox Church). Garvey's movement represents the most significant African American mass movement in the history of the United States. Also of importance is the work of figures such as Father Hurley and Prophet Jones within the Black Spiritual Movement as well as Father Divine (Peace Mission Movement) and Sweet Daddy Grace (Universal House of Prayer for All Peoples).[20]

This hunger for alternative religious meaning and symbol systems continued during the period of the civil rights movement, in part sparked by the dissatisfaction of black-power advocates with the tone and programmatic of the Christian-dominated movement. This push away from the Christian church as a symbol of black enslavement often entailed a movement into African-based forms of religious practice.

IMMIGRATION FROM THE CARIBBEAN

In the Caribbean, in locations such as Haiti (Hispaniola), enslaved Africans had greater opportunity to maintain the basic dimensions of religious traditions coming from West Africa. Hence, it is reasonable to believe that "seasoned" slaves brought from the Caribbean into North American colonies carried African-derived religious practices to their new context.[21] Beyond this, the successful revolution in Haiti in the early 1800s resulted in the movement to North America (i.e., New Orleans) of some 10,000 enslaved Africans. Historical records complete with references to "snake worship" point to a Christocentric fear of voodoo-related practices abounding in New Orleans. Damballah (the voodoo god symbolized by the snake) is just one of the *lwa* (gods) whose presence was felt during Congo Square dances and more private gatherings controlled by Marie Laveau and other powerful religious leaders. Even when practitioners faced physical harm if their devotion was discovered by city authorities, the tradition continued to live and spread. Additional contact with voodoo is evidenced elsewhere in the United States, and its impact on the religious identity of African America is further enhanced by the immigration of Haitians. Karen McCarthy Brown's *Mama Lola* is just one example of voodoo as a religious component of life in the United States.[22]

In addition to the religious influence of Haitian voodoo on the United States, there is also strong evidence to suggest the impact of Cuban Santeria (Orisha worship). Early conversations concerning doctrine of God, for example, point to spiritual forces reminiscent of African deities associated with Santeria. The understanding that the saints (or gods) work in exchange for service or promises is maintained in American practices. In addition, it is not uncommon for it to be understood that these saints have particular days on which they should receive offerings and on which it is most profitable to ask for blessings and benefits. Candles, in most accounts, are a vital component of any altar because of the ways in which they "give life to the saints." At times, these saints are also given strong drink as a requirement. One informant, referring to St. Raymond but meaning (inferred from the conversation) St. Peter, indicates that the picture of St. Raymond must be given whiskey, beer, or wine before a request is made:[23]

An' Yo' put 'im [St. Peter] ovah de do'
If Yo' ain't got but a nickel
Try tuh git a nickel's wuth of beer
an' when Yo' gittin' up in de mawnin'
an' Yo' want a good time in yore house
an' some fellahs come in an' give yo' money

Yo' jes' throw beer on 'im [St. Peter]
jes' throw plenty beer on 'im an' light a white light
an' ah bet chew St. Peter gon'a open dat do'
Yo' git St. Anthony, yeah, a brown candle . . .
Yo' git a cigar . . .
Yo' git 'bout a little whiskey glass of whiskey see
'cause St. Anthony he's a Saint he laks cigahs
an' he wus a good-time man . . .
an' yo' wake up de nex' mawnin' an' Yo' see
de glass dry an' de cigah half smoked.[24]

Similarities between these practices found in the United States and the basic
principles of Santeria are further strengthened by the immigration of Cubans
during the late twentieth century.

According to most accounts, Cubans made their way to the United States
in notable numbers as a result of the Cuban Revolution. Although initially establishing themselves in Florida, with more than 400,000 in Dade County
alone by 1979, substantial Cuban communities began to develop further
north in cities such as New York and Washington, D.C.[25] Not all immigrants
from Cuba were practitioners of Santeria. However, those who were often
found themselves sought out for guidance and direction. (Major ceremonies
were not held in the United States until the 1960s.) Most of those who sought
guidance and embraced this religion were Latino/a. However, as Mary Curry
notes in her dissertation on Yoruba religion in New York, many African Americans found Santeria culturally and spiritually appealing. It is typically argued
that the first African American initiated into Santeria was Walter King (1959),
who was followed by several others in the early 1960s. As of the early 1990s, it
was estimated that roughly 5,000 to 10,000 African Americans practiced Santeria in New York alone.[26]

MOVEMENT AS A CHALLENGE TO BLACK RELIGIOUS STUDIES

The previous examples, I argue, fit into a more general ethos of critical ab-
sorbency marking African American communities for almost four centuries.
And once recognized, this requires an alternative understanding of what it
means to be African American and religious. Yet despite available resources
suggesting a plethora of religious forms within African American communities, much of what has passed as the study of African American religion, par-

ticularly by theologians, has been hopelessly biased toward the black Christian church. Joseph Washington's proclamation made several decades ago still
echoes in many contemporary discussions:

> In the beginning was the black church, and the black church was with the black
> community, and the black church was the black community. The black church was
> in the beginning with the black people; all things were made through the black
> church, and without the black church was not anything made that was made. In
> the black church was life, and the life was the light of the black people. The black
> church still shines in the darkness, and the darkness has not overcome it.[27]

Based on this assumption, much of the work done under the banner of
black religious studies has been apologetic, framed by a commitment to the
Christian faith as the ground of African American religious being. At times,
black religious studies makes concessions to non-Christian realities, yet its
conversation effectively excludes these realities as anything more than elements external to the true center of black religious experience: the Christian
faith. Even efforts to move beyond this dilemma, such as Will Coleman's
*Tribal Talk: Black Theology, Hermeneutics, and African/American Ways of
"Telling the Story,"* fail. Exploring slave narratives (Christian) and Da-
homean myths, Coleman seeks to develop a form of theology, "tribal talk,"
akin to black theology but with a much stronger concern for the hermeneu-
tical significance of previously overlooked sources. Yet his approach begs the
question: Are the Christian language and grammar guiding his comparative
project sufficient for the task?

Donald Matthews also believes that black theology is facing a crisis of
method based on a crisis of identity. However, his concern is more in keeping
with the critique offered by Cecil Cone years ago. It is a concern with the nature of African American resources (and the connection to Africa) used in the
construction of a unique Christian presence. I agree with Matthews that the
nondialectical discourse of traditional Christian theology (written-text
biased) embraced by black theologians is limited and problematic. Yet
Matthews maintains a certainty with respect to the reliability of cultural
memory that I find difficult to accept. It is my concern that this uncritical
acceptance of memory forces the same truncated (Christianity-biased) collection of theological resources and method Matthews finds objectionable.

Early in his text, Matthews writes,

> African peoples have carried on their cultural traditions and practices by vener-
> ating their ancestors. By honoring their ancestors, African people both remem-
> ber and re-create their cultural space. Until African Americans can remember
> without shame the pains and joys, the traditions and the practices of their an-
> cestors, they never will be truly free.[28]

This statement points to the assumption held by many in black theology that
our ancestor's sense of identity and positionality was intact and without question and that somehow we have lost this and must recover it. This is dangerous.
As Toni Morrison notes,

> Moving that veil aside requires, therefore, certain things. First of all, I must trust
> my own recollections. I must also depend on the recollections of others. Thus
> memory weighed heavily in what I write, in how I begin and in what I find to be
> significant. Zora Neale Hurston said, "Like the dead-seeming cold rocks, I have
> memories within that came out of the material that went to make me." These
> "memories within" are the subsoil of my work. But memories and recollections
> won't give me total access to the unwritten interior life of these people.[29]

Even Matthews talks about the secretive nature of slave gatherings and
memories yet assumes that African ritual practices could not survive in these
hidden spaces. This is because the slave narratives and spirituals are privileged
as resources for the doing of theology in ways that warp our understanding of
African American religious experience and identity.

His assertion that the spirituals are the foundational source of African
American religion ties him into this sense of Christian identity I believe he
seeks to challenge. This is the case because the spirituals are tied only to either
an embracing of or a challenge to Western Christian notions, and in this way
they do not necessarily point to the religious richness (extrachurch orientations) Matthews hopes to uncover. He, in my opinion, has not gone far
enough. Even Matthews's presentation lends itself to the assumption that the
best of African American religious identity is found in the Africanization of
Christianity.

Recent work by archaeologists that affirms the religious diversity promoted
by the triadic movement scheme concerning the evidence of religious diver-

sity within African American communities hidden in the ground should make it difficult to maintain this position with any integrity. In short, what we are learning about the religious life of enslaved Africans, combined with contemporary and overt appreciation for "non-Christian" forms of religious experience, serves as a challenge to narrow depictions of African American religious identity.

RETHINKING THE NATURE OF RELIGIOUS EXPERIENCE

Although the previous discussion of religious diversity is incomplete, I believe it does point to the reasonableness of thinking of African American religious identity as extending, in significant ways, beyond Christian denominationalism. This, again, certainly helps researchers better understand what it means to be black and religious in the United States, but at the same time it poses a challenge in that this recognition of religious diversity urges a rethinking of the nature of religious experience: How do we speak to religious and cultural complexity that we cannot fully describe or know? What language and grammar define our theological exploration of African American religious identity when this identity is so diverse and complex?

A revised understanding of the various layers of religious identity found in African American communities should push black religious studies into a comparative mode or stance. It is obvious, I believe, that religious experience and the religious identity it fosters cannot be adequately described through attention to doctrine and other elements that are bound to a particular tradition. Rather, I suggest that attention be given to two elements: 1) complex subjectivity and 2) the body as central concern of both religious identity and experience.[30]

I argue that religious experience entails the African American's recognition of and struggle for complex subjectivity; it is the struggle against essentialism, or the "first creation" discussed by Charles Long. Religious experience entails a human response to a crisis of identity (i.e., objectification), and it is the crisis of identity or "being" that constitutes the dilemma of ultimacy and meaning. The religious is a certain ordering or style of experience as opposed to a unique form of experience; it is a paradigm shift or perspective. So conceived, religious experience is historically situated and culturally bound—dealing with "the material world of outer nature" and "the human world of social life."[31] It is an assertion of being in the face of oppressive essentializing and dehumanizing forces. I am not suggesting a crude antiessentialism that denies the impact of race on African Americans. It is, to the contrary, recognition of race, but as only one of the factors affecting subjectivity in the context of the United States. Nor would I argue that religious experience is best understood on the level of the individual. To the contrary, it entails the development of individual subjectivity in the context of community.

This is a measured sense of autonomy; it is an autonomous existence in that it is associated with freedom from essentialism (as expressed through sexism, racism, classism, homophobia, environmental destruction, and so on), yet it does not entail a freedom from relationship and the obligations entailed by relationship. The key is individual subjectivity in creative tension with the demand for quality of relationships (community). In contrast, essentialism here is the reduction of a group or class of people to a single category or cluster of categories that promotes through law, social arrangements, and so on their subordination and the subordination of their power to define themselves in more wholistic terms.[32] This is most often cast in anti-black terms, yet essentialism can manifest as a pro-black stance, as in the case of the Nation of Islam, based on a racial or cultural essence. The latter is also harmful in that, as philosopher Robert Birt notes, "it tends to preserve (however clandestinely or in black face) all the conservative values of the white cultural hierarchy, and sometimes harbor[s] a secret contempt for black people concealed behind a rhetoric of glorification."[33]

Religion, in light of these comments, amounts to the collected stories of struggle for complex subjectivity, and theology is the articulation of these stories.[34] Finally, this struggle for complex subjectivity is played out in and on the human body.

AFRICAN AMERICAN RELIGIOUS DIVERSITY AND THE BLACK BODY

I am suggesting an understanding of the body both as constructed (as metaphor or symbol) and as a lived, as being a physiological and biochemical reality set in historical experiences. For some, this physiological body is problematic because it changes over time, hence changing the way it is experienced; yet for African Americans, some things do not change.[35] Therefore, the signs of age do not lessen many of the ways in which society seeks to essentialize the black body. In addition, some might argue that the body is not a unique mode of expression in African American communities. All humans share this physiology. Yet this shared human physiology is not enough to negate the value of the movement of black bodies for an understanding of the African American religious experience because, as Mary Douglas notes, this shared physical form does not produce universal symbols.[36]

Furthermore, the social system in which black bodies dwell determines patterns for the presentation and function of black bodies represented in religious experience as opposition and struggle. In short, the social system seeks to determine the ways in which the physical body is perceived and used.[37] Douglas notes that the social body and individual, physical body act on each other, the former attempting to define the possibilities of meaning and movement for the latter. They exchange meanings through a dialectic process of pressures and restrictions.[38] Yet whereas Douglas notes a type of concordance between the social and bodily expression of control, I argue for dissonance—bad faith—between the social body and black bodies that sparks and fuels the religious quest. With this in mind and because of the norm suggested earlier, black religious experience entails an effort to move beyond this exchange, beyond the pressures and restrictions—the essentializing tendencies—of the social system.

The connections between these two bodies—social and physical—also mean that liberation for black bodies must entail the restructuring of the social system. I am not suggesting that the two (the social system and black bodies) come apart. Rather, I am suggesting that the goal of religious experience is a transformation of both through the increased subjectivity of the latter. This is because the black body is not an image of society in the strict sense; rather, the essentialization of the black body promoted by the social system is meant to maintain the system by reflecting both the wishes and the fears of the social system. For example, the Christian concern with the body (vs. spirit) as threatening and dangerous if not controlled is played out on the African American physical form.[39] And African American churches, grounded in European Christian doctrine, also played into this process. Thus, early black churches sought to gain substantial rights in the larger society through the control or disciplining of the flesh. In the twentieth century, black Pentecostal churches in particular exemplify this thrust. The call to be in the world but not of it has often been played out as a need to bring the body under control. Think in terms of restrictions on sexual expression and dance, clothing and appearance, or pleasure in general.

Others have expressed a rejection of this social ordering through an embrace of the bodily movements rejected by many black churches. In other words, using the period of slavery as an example,

> by aestheticizing the black body, by putting its vitality, suppleness and sensuality defiantly and joyously on display, the black dancer [for example] repudiated slavery's evaluation of the slave body as brute physical labor, and constructed, for a time, a world of difference, sharply at variance with that which blacks were normally compelled to inhabit.[40]

Clearly, the relationship of control between the social system and the physical body is antagonistic for African Americans; it is a fight by individual persons for a reconfiguration of the former. The former seeks to disembody, to use Douglas's term, interactions in ways that for African Americans revolve around invisibility. For African Americans, social control and subjectivity (i.e., bodily control) are oppositional and adversely related. That is, the loss of control over black bodies (on a variety of levels) was a necessary component of the social system.

Religious experience, when viewed in light of the black body and its struggle against the social system, entails a stylized movement against warped depictions of African American identity and requires a movement beyond myopic discussion limited to Christian forms of expression. Religious experience understood in relationship to the development of identity or subjectivity and expressed in and through the body (as opposed to doctrine or institutions) gives a better sense of the multiple responses to the question of what it means to be black and religious. In short, this rethinking of religious experience and identity through the fight over and against the body is premised on this one idea: Some praise Jesus, and some don't.

NOTES

1. James H. Cone, *The Spirituals and the Blues* (Maryknoll, N.Y.: Orbis Books, 1991), 29.

2. Eric Sackheim, comp., *The Blues Line: A Collection of Blues Lyrics* (Hopewell, N.J.: Ecco Press, 1993), 161.

3. Abbot Emerson Smith, *Colonists in Bondage: White Servitude and Convict Labor in America, 1607–1776* (Chapel Hill: University of North Carolina Press, 1947), 9–10.

4. The slave trade, however, predates this period. In fact, by the ninth century a significant number of Africans were being exported to Muslim areas. And this practice would later involve Spanish and Portuguese export of Africans to Spain and Portugal. See J. E. Inikori, ed., *Forced Migration: The Impact of the Export Slave Trade on African Societies* (New York: Africana Publishing, 1982), 13–14.

5. Brantz Mayer's *Captain Canot, an African Slaver* (New York: Arno Press and the New York Times, 1968) provides the reflections of a slave trader on the nature of the Atlantic slave trade.

6. Edward Reynolds, *Stand the Storm: A History of the Atlantic Slave Trade* (New York: Allison & Busby, 1985), 47–50.

7. Historians are not certain what status Africans initially held in the North American colonies. It is possible that they were servants, as were many Europeans, and it is beyond question that some held status as free persons; yet by the middle of the seventeenth century, enslavement of Africans became institutionalized and addressed through legal codes in several colonies. As has been noted, indentured white servants played a role in agricultural development in New England and in southern colonies such as Virginia and Maryland. Before the 1600s, Africans in North American colonies worked under similar arrangements as European servants. It was not until England officially entered the slave trade that Africans undergoing the Middle Passage made their way to the North American colonies.

8. W. E. B. Du Bois, *The Suppression of the African Slave-Trade to the United States of America, 1638–1870* (New York: Longmans, Green, 1896), 5. For details on the slave trade and Middle Passage, see, for example, Edward Reynolds, *Stand the Storm*; Elizabeth Donnan, *Documents Illustrative of the History of the Slave Trade to America, Volumes I–II* (New York: Octagon Books, 1969); J. E. Inikori, *Forced Migration*; Frederick Bancroft, *Slave-Trading in the Old South* (Baltimore: J. H. Furst, 1931); and Winthrop D. Jordan, *White over Black: American Attitudes toward the Negro, 1550–1812* (Durham: University of North Carolina Press, 1968).

9. Winthrop D. Jordan, *The White Man's Burden: Historical Origins of Racism in the United States* (New York: Oxford University Press, 1974), 22–25. For information on this, see Cornel West, *Prophesy Deliverance! An Afro-American Revolutionary Christianity* (Philadelphia: Westminster Press, 1982), chap. 2.

10. RSV Matthew 28:19–20.

11. Margaret Washington Creel, *A Peculiar People: Slave Religion and Community-Culture among the Gullah* (New York: New York University Press, 1988), 2–4, 96.

12. Charles Long, "The Oppressive Elements in Religion and the Religions of the Oppressed," in *Significations* (Philadelphia: Fortress Press, 1986), 165–71.

13. Long, *Significations*, 7.

14. Sterling Stuckey, *Going through the Storm: The Influence of African American Art in History* (New York: Oxford University Press, 1994), 3, 4, 16–17.

15. Charles Joyner, "'Believer I Know': The Emergence of African-American Christianity," in *Religion and American Culture: A Reader*, ed. David G. Hackett (New York: Routledge, 1995), 188.

16. See Jacqueline L. Tobin and Raymond G. Dobard, *Hidden in Plain View: A Secret Story of Quilts and the Underground Railroad* (New York: Anchor Books, 2000), and Gladys-Marie Fry, *Stitched from the Soul: Slave Quilts from the Ante-Bellum South* (New York: Dutton Studio Books/Museum of American Folk Art, 1990).

17. Milton C. Sernett, *Bound for the Promised Land: African American Religion and the Great Migration* (Durham, N.C.: Duke University Press, 1997), 3.

18. See Anthony B. Pinn, ed., *Making the Gospel Plain: The Writings of Bishop Reverdy C. Ransom* (Harrisburg, Pa.: Trinity Press International, 1999), and Reverdy C. Ransom, *The Pilgrimage of Harriet Ransom's Son* (Nashville: A.M.E. Sunday School Union, 1949). Major black denominations also faced a membership and organizational crisis in the South because of the movement of African Americans resulting in diminished roles in southern churches.

19. See Gayraud Wilmore, *Black Religion and Black Radicalism: An Interpretation of the Religious History of Afro-American People* (Maryknoll, N.Y.: Orbis Books, 1983), chap. 6.

20. A full presentation of the historical development and ritual structures of these various traditions is beyond the scope of this chapter. My goal is to simply problematize narrow depictions of African American religious experience by pointing to the viability of various religious practices as shapers of African American religious identity. For more detailed information, see, for example, C. Eric Lincoln, *The Black Muslims in America* (Boston: Beacon Press, 1961); E. U. Essien-Udom, *Black Nationalism: A Search for an Identity in America* (Chicago: University of Chicago Press, 1962); Claude Andrew Clegg III, *An Original Man: The Life and Times of Elijah Muhammad* (New York: St. Martin's Press, 1997); Hans Baer, *The Black Spiritual Movement: A Religious Response to Racism* (Knoxville: University of Tennessee Press, 1984); Claude F. Jacobs and Andrew J. Kaslow, *The Spirituals Churches of New Orleans: Origins, Beliefs, and Rituals of an*

African-American Religion (Knoxville: University of Tennessee Press, 1991); Mother
Divine, *The Peace Mission Movement* (Philadelphia: Imperial Press/Palace Mission, Inc.,
1982); Kenneth Burnham, *God Comes to America* (Boston: Lambeth Press, 1979);
Robert Weisbrot, *Father Divine and the Struggle for Racial Equality* (Urbana: University
of Illinois Press, 1983); and Arthur Huff Fauset, *Black Gods of the Metropolis: Negro
Religious Cults of the Urban North* (New York: Octagon Books, 1970).

21. See Wilmore, *Black Religion and Black Radicalism,* 19–30.

22. Anthony Pinn, *Varieties of African American Religious Experience* (Minneapolis:
Fortress Press, 1998), 43. See also Leslie G. Desmangles, *The Faces of the Gods: Vodou
and Roman Catholicism in Haiti* (Chapel Hill: University of North Carolina Press,
1992); *Mama Lola: A Vodou Priestess in Brooklyn* (Berkeley: University of California
Press, 1991); Maya Deren, *Divine Horsemen: The Living Gods of Haiti* (New York:
McPherson and Company, 1953); and Jessie Gaston Mulira, "The Case of Voodoo in
New Orleans," in *Africanisms in American Culture,* ed. Joseph E. Holloway
(Bloomington: Indiana University Press, 1990).

23. Harry Middleton Hyatt, *Hoodoo-Conjuration-Witchcraft-Rootwork: Beliefs
Accepted by Many Negroes and White Persons These Being Orally Recorded among
Blacks and Whites,* vol. 1 (Hannibal, Mo.: Western Publishing, 1970; distributed by
American University Bookstore, Washington, D.C.), 869, 881–82.

24. Hyatt, *Hoodoo-Conjuration-Witchcraft-Rootwork,* vol. 2, 1220–21. I also make use of
this information in *Varieties of African American Religious Experience,* chaps. 1 and 2.

25. George Brandon, *Santeria from Africa to the New World: The Dead Sell Memories*
(Bloomington: Indiana University Press, 1993), 104.

26. Mary Elaine Curray, "Making the Gods in New York: The Yoruba Religion in the
Black Community" (Ph.D. diss., City University of New York, 1991), 12.

27. Joseph Washington, "How Black Is Black Religion?" In *Quest for a Black
Theology,* Eric Lincoln Series on Black Religion, ed. James J. Gardiner and J. Deotis
Roberts (Philadelphia: Pilgrim Press, 1971), 28.

28. Will Coleman, *Tribal Talk: Black Theology, Hermeneutics, and African/American
Ways of "Telling the Story"* (University Park: Pennsylvania State University Press, 2000);
Donald H. Matthews, *Honoring the Ancestors: An African Cultural Interpretation of
Black Religion and Literature* (New York: Oxford University Press, 1999).

29. Toni Morrison, "The Site of Memory," in *Out There: Marginalization and
Contemporary Cultures,* ed. Russell Ferguson, Martha Gever, Trinh T. Minh-ha, and

Cornel West (New York: New Museum of Contemporary Art; Cambridge, Mass.: MIT Press, 1990), 302.

30. Attention to complex subjectivity and the body work in a variety of ways, even with respect to atheistic forms of practice and to pedagogy. I look at the latter in "Black Theology, Pedagogy and the Black Body," *Cross Currents* 50, nos. 1–2: 196–210.

31. Paget Henry, "African and Afro-Caribbean Existential Philosophies," in *Existence in Black: An Anthology of Black Existential Philosophy,* ed. Lewis R. Gordon (New York: Routledge, 1997), 15.

32. I am grateful to Paula Cooey for this definition of essentialism.

33. Robert Birt, "Existence, Identity, and Liberation," in Gordon, ed., *Existence in Black,* 212.

34. I found the following helpful in developing this perspective: Aldo Gargani, "Religious Experience as Event and Interpretation," in *Religion,* ed. Jacques Derrida and Gianni Vattimo (Stanford, Calif.: Stanford University Press, 1998), 111–35. I also see this perspective as related to common understandings of Michel Foucault's take on religion. For an example of this, see Jeremy R. Carrette, ed., "Prologue to a Confession of the Flesh," in *Religion and Culture: Michel Foucault* (New York: Routledge, 1999), 1–47. At this point in my work on a black theology of immanence, my concern with religion involves function and form as opposed to traditional categories of belief. I address these, such as God, only as the need presents itself.

35. See, for example, Bryan S. Turner, "The Body in Western Society: Social Theory and Its Perspectives," in *Religion and the Body,* ed. Sarah Coakley (New York: Cambridge University Press, 1998), 19–20.

36. Mary Douglas, "Introduction," in *Natural Symbols: Explorations in Cosmology* (New York: Routledge, 1996), xxxi.

37. Douglas, *Natural Symbols,* 69.

38. Douglas, *Natural Symbols,* 69.

39. See, for example, West, *Prophesy Deliverance!,* and Bryan S. Turner, "The Body in Western Society: Social Theory and Its Perspectives," in Coakley, ed., *Religion and the Body.*

40. Shane White and Graham White, *Stylin': African American Expressive Culture from Its Beginnings to the Zoot Suit* (Ithaca, N.Y.: Cornell University Press, 1998), 84.

6

Immigration and Religion in America: The Experience of Judaism

Jacob Neusner

The story of the immigrant is the story of America, and it also tells the story of religion in America. For, as everyone understands, from the beginning of time to this morning's headlines, religion has constituted a defining force in American culture and politics. Indeed, the original European settlers in New England came to build a city on a hill and conceived of their new plantation in the very heart of the Protestant Reformation and its agonies. And much of the story of America is told by successive waves of migration, from Africans and English, French and Spanish, in the seventeenth century, to other Africans, other Europeans, and other Asians, in our own day. That is why it is reasonable to ask how immigration shapes religion in America.

It is no surprise to note that the story of Judaism in America is best told as the outcome of the experience of immigrants, their children, their grandchildren, and their great-grandchildren. The impact of the American experience on the immigrant and successive generations thereafter and the impact of the immigrant on America shape much of the character and conscience of this country. And so it is with Judaism. In this context, Judaism is viewed not as an ethnic culture but as a religious tradition of power and vitality.

People use the word *Judaism* to mean pretty much everything and its opposite: the Torah revealed by God to Moses at Sinai, surely a religious view of "Judaism," and the ethnic culture of Jews from Eastern Europe, surely an ethnic view of "Judaism." These are readily differentiated: The one is religious and involves theology; the other is ethnic and involves culture. Much then depends on the story Jews tell themselves to explain who they are. If they begin with the Exodus from Egypt, it is not secular history but a religious narrative, religious truth in narrative form; if they begin with anti-Semitism, Holocaust, and persecution, it is the ethnic history of the Jews as a distinct social entity. And this brings us to the story of the immigrants Jewish in ethnic origin, Judaic in religious conviction, as a great many of them were. The tale is best told by Oscar Handlin in *The Uprooted*, where he created a composite biography of the immigrants and their children's experiences, covering the entire range of experience of the nineteenth- and twentieth-century newcomers. Handlin drew a composite out of the memoirs of diverse groups, yet when I read it as a teenager, I thought he was writing about my grandmother, my father, and me. She represented the first generation, the immigrant; he, the second; and I, the third—and I was convinced that that third generation was the goal of it all: The entire history of the Jewish people was directed at my three best friends and me. Having produced a fourth and a fifth generation, I now understand, it is a story without an ending, one that tells of families and their continuities over changing places and periods, of what endures and how change takes hold not only of the immigrant but also of the America that receives him.

When we deal with immigration history, we deal with cohorts: large populations, defined by common experience in a determinate period of time. American Judaism conventionally divides its history into three periods, each characterized by a different immigrant group and its normative experience: Jews of Sephardi origin, coming in small numbers from Western Europe and elsewhere in the Western Hemisphere; Jews of German or, more generally, central European origin; and Jews from Polish and Russian, Romanian and Hungarian, and other East European countries. The Sephardi immigrants founded synagogues in the major eastern seaports where the American population was centered from 1654 in New York City onward. They carried forward their own liturgical traditions and established themselves as a permanent religious community outside the Christian framework. They were forerunners and precursors, but they did not produce a continuing leadership cadre for American Judaism. They were too few in numbers to start rabbinical schools, for example, and the Jewish community practiced Judaism in the United States for 200 years before the first rabbis arrived on these shores. There were no rabbinical schools, and schooling in Judaism was minimal. So while people practiced the faith, they tended to keep it less and less strictly, violating the Sabbath, disregarding the dietary laws, managing their affairs in accord with the instinct of the hour, not with the law of Judaism. That meant it was an essentially lay community, with slight access to the religious virtuosi that had the intellectual resources to sustain an ongoing religious tradition. Like the Irish who came to the United States without priests in the eighteenth century and who faded into the Protestant majority in the Appalachians and the South more generally, so the Sephardi migration, such as it was, produced no enduring population of Judaism. A study of Philadelphia failed to turn up a single descendant of the eighteenth-century community still active in the practice of Judaism in the twentieth century.

The German Jewish migration of the mid-nineteenth century brought sizable numbers and produced the organization of Judaism in America in synagogues in many cities, particularly in the South and Midwest. That is because the immigrants went to the areas of economic opportunity and expansion, bringing their distinct métier in trade and commerce. In the years before the Civil War, Jews settled in the then-expanding world of the river cities of the Midwest and the trading villages and towns of the South. These migrants encompassed in their numbers rabbis and other religious functionaries—writers and theologians, for example. So issues of theology and religious practice were debated by knowledgeable people, responding to the imperatives of Scripture and tradition.

The immigrant rabbis included numbers of highly educated and articulate Reform rabbis. They brought with them the critique of Orthodoxy that had already taken shape in Germany. The immigrant peddlers and storekeepers found the New World a challenge to the religious customs and traditions of the Old World, beginning with the prohibition of conducting business on the Sabbath day, the principal day of commerce for traders. So the theological critique of the Reform rabbis found a sympathetic hearing among the laypeople. Within a generation, the milieu-piety Orthodoxy that the German immigrants brought with them gave way to a highly articulate, intellectual Reform Judaism, represented by rabbis who interpreted the challenge of America's diverse society to represent an imperative for Judaism to change. In 1888 in Pittsburgh, these rabbis drew up a program that emphasized the universal over the particular, the moral over the ritual, and the philosophical and theological over the mythic and the narrative. With a half century or so of experience of America, they further organized national institutions: a center for educating American-born rabbis, Hebrew Union College in Cincinnati; a national union of synagogues, the Union of American Hebrew Congregations; and an association of rabbis, the Central Conference of American Rabbis.

Reform was so powerful as to define its opposition—immigrants, some German, many East European, who rejected its abrogation of the ritual laws of the Torah and its emphasis on the universal mission of Israel, the holy people, over the things that made Judaism particular. Conservative Judaism modeled its institutions after those of Reform. They too would form a seminary, a synagogue organization, and a rabbinical association, serving the local synagogues throughout the country. These reached full articulation scarcely a generation after Reform Judaism had come to its realization. The Jewish Theological Seminary of America was initially founded scarcely a generation after Hebrew Union College. Just as the Reform synagogues aimed at large congregations conducting formal worship services, not the small, intimate, informal worship services of East European Orthodoxy, so Conservative synagogues took the same model for themselves. By the end of the nineteenth century, two Judaisms had taken root in the United States, both the work of immigrants and their children: Reform Judaism and a traditional Judaism not quite Orthodox but far different from Reform.

If, then, I had to generalize through the case of Judaism in America about the relationship between immigration and the formation of religious life, I would say that the immigrants undertook the task of acculturation, of adjusting the received faith to the requirements of American life, and their children simply continued this process. A straight line joins the first and the second and following generations. But when the mass migration that followed played itself out, in a second, third, and fourth generation, what emerged was very different. Rather, each generation set the question that would confront its children, and a construction that posited a thesis, antithesis, and synthesis between the American and the Judaic would conform more closely to reality than the one just now adumbrated.

Specifically, for the East European Jews, the question of Americanization loomed far more ominously than was the case for the German Jews of the mid-nineteenth century. American society accepted difference and negotiated with it, being preoccupied with problems of politics—the relationship of the

North and the South—rather than those of culture. By the end of the nineteenth century, a massive wave of immigration from southern and Eastern Europe brought unfamiliar faces and accents in place of the more readily recognized light skins and Germanic languages of Germany and Scandinavia, not to mention Britain and Ireland, of the earlier period. Among other nativist reactions, anti-Semitism came to full expression by the nineteenth century. Anti-Semitism took a variety of forms. For the upper classes, it was a matter of social exclusion, snobbery, and disdain for Jews. For the middle and lower classes, it was a matter of hatred, dislike of the unlike. From both sources, the pressure on the Jewish immigrants to give up and repudiate the heritage of language, culture, and religion that accompanied them became intense. So the third wave of immigration had to explain itself in the American context in ways in which the first and second did not. It was a hostile context, one in which people found expedient the removal of those traits and practices, whether of religion or of culture, that made Jews different from others.

The immigrant generation that began in the early 1880s, just as Reform Judaism was making its authoritative statements, vastly outnumbered the resident Judaism of the German migration. That migration, involving people between 1880 and 1924, carried with it rabbis and teachers who, on arriving in the United States, established institutions of religion and culture comparable to those they had known in Eastern Europe: yeshivas and synagogues of various types and kosher butcher shops and other stores for proper food, all in areas of dense settlement. The Yiddish-speaking immigrants ordinarily took for granted that their life in Jewish settlements would go on for generations. But their children, educated to speak American English and think of themselves as undifferentiated Americans, had other ideas. The second generation from the immigration moved outward into neighborhoods of mixed populations and superior amenities, and the third generation, their children, found their homes in the suburbs. The pattern of settlement is matched, with important variations, by the pattern of religious identification. Many assume that the Orthodox first generation gave way to the Conservative second generation, which in turn produced a Reform third generation, which begat a de-Judaized fourth generation ready for marriage with gentiles.

That pattern, from much to little to nothing, from intense engagement with the religion in every chapter of life and through every waking hour, to desuetude, sedulous indifference, and assimilation into the undifferentiated mass of America, misconstrues what happened. That is because those who discern that pattern interpret change as evidence for dissolution. Would that matters were so simple, imagine how much work we would save for ourselves in trying to figure out what is going on. Rather, we have to recognize that in an ongoing, enduring religious tradition, some things endure, while others serve transiently and temporarily. The problem of learning, then, is to tell the difference.

To make this point stick, with your patience, let me indulge myself with an autobiographical moment. The passage of family from immigrant grandmother to American grandchildren and beyond, into the fourth and now fifth generation, tells the story I mean to convey. My grandmother was a staunchly pious Jew, and my parents embodied the second generation, ethnic assertion amid self-hatred; my father was a Zionist and an ethnic activist, and my mother was a self-hating Jew who regarded anything publicly, distinctively Jewish with embarrassment. I was raised in a Reform Temple. One moment captures the intersection of generations. At my Bar Mitzvah Sabbath, when the Torah was carried around the sanctuary, the congregation remained seated, as was its custom (contrary to thousands of years of Judaic practice). My grandmother stood up and remained standing until the Torah was returned to its place. Afterward, she asked me, "Were you embarrassed when I stood up?" I was too stupid to understand what she wanted to know or to hear.

My father was not religious, except residually. But he was a very active Jew, publishing a newspaper, a founder of the Zionist movement in southern New England, and an activist in all Jewish community affairs for his public life. He defined his mode of being Jewish in secular and political terms. He wanted me to become a journalist, like him, and from seventh grade through high school, he oversaw my education in the newspaper business. My mother was sentimentally Jewish but very uncertain about her Americanness. She was born in this country and learned Yiddish only in her adult years; her conception of Yiddish was to speak English with a Jewish accent. Thus, "vinda" meant "window." Judaism stood as a barrier between her and the world she aspired to, and the worst thing she could call something was "European," as in "European custom," by definition worthless. For her part, my mother defined for me as life's greatest reward a bacon-tomato-lettuce sandwich on white toast with mayonnaise at a department store lunch counter along with a strawberry milk shake on a Saturday afternoon outing. Anyone knowledgeable about Judaism will count on both hands and feet the number of religious obligations that were violated in that celebration. My mother wanted for me anything but Jewish—Jewish anything. Parents raise their own reward. I did not become a journalist, so my father got his, and I became a rabbi and a scholar of Judaism, so my mother got hers.

Why? Here is where Judaism's experience in America provides a model of the norms that other, more recent immigrant groups may anticipate. The experience now fully realized in Judaism is captured by the aphorism of Marcus Lee Hansen, the great immigration historian at the University of Wisconsin, writing about Scandinavians in Minnesota, not Jews in New York, Connecticut, and Massachusetts: "What the second generation wants to forget, the third generation tries to remember." The immigrant generation knows what it is and what it never can become: It is the generation of the uprooted, no longer what it was, not yet what it will become. The Jewish migrants who practiced Judaism identified the religion with the culture and the politics and the entire human existence of the Jewish people. But then any change meant nothing remained. The opposites—Jewish and American—yielded no space for compromise or, rather, defined change as compromise with de-Judaization.

That brings us to the second generation. Their children wanted very much to become Americans. They spoke unaccented American English (a "Jewish accent" of American folklore being a mixture of a New York accent with the melodies of Yiddish). They went through schools that prepared them for life in Christian America by teaching them Christmas carols and utterly ignoring whatever religious or cultural heritage the children brought from home. And they went in search of a place in American society that was exceedingly hostile—normatively hostile—to difference. And difference meant religious difference, ethnic difference, any difference. Remember, I speak of the 1920s through the 1940s, when every minority group in a country of minorities was deemed a threat to the majority group, itself fractious and fragile. So the Ku Klux Klan exercised enormous power in the white, Protestant Midwest, and something close to social war engulfed blacks in race riots, Catholics in cultural denigration and exclusion, and Jews in systematic, systemic anti-Semitism. The waves of immigration from the 1880s to the immigrant exclusion act of 1924 broke on hostile shores indeed. No wonder that, to get along, the second generation—whether Jewish or Italian, whether the black migrants from the South to the northern cities—would do its best to go along.

The third generation came to mature consciousness during and after World War II. Once more I turn to my own experience for illustration. We were fewer in numbers, the Depression babies, for example. We determined to accept what we could not change, and anti-Semitism was a reality to be avoided or dismissed, but it was very present. There were occasional, minor anti-Semitic incidents, more frequent hostile remarks about Jews. America was a Jew-hating, Jew-baiting country at that time, and West Hartford restricted Jewish residence to only certain neighborhoods (after World War II, it was mostly north of Albany Avenue, I believe). We Jews of gentile West Hartford more or less understood, moreover, that Jews did not look for jobs in insurance companies, except in sales, heavy industry (Pratt & Whitney, Colt, Pitney Bowes), the utilities, and so on. When I went to Harvard, an even 10 percent of my class was Jewish, Yale took many less, Princeton still fewer. But West Hartford was no worse than any other suburb anywhere, so I imagined. And Harvard was the deep freeze anyhow; one got used to exclusion. We were more at home than the second generation; we knew no other world than the American. So when I went to Harvard, I took for granted I would be cut off from most contact, outside of class, with gentiles, and when I was, I regarded it as the norm. But, embodying that third generation that wanted to remember and naturally identifying with my father, I wanted to reconnect with what my father had neglected and my mother denigrated, which was that religion, Judaism, that my grandmother had embodied in standing while everyone else sat, as was the custom in our Reform Temple.

What exactly I wanted to remember was dictated by America and defined by Judaism. America, by the 1950s, was explicit in accepting difference of some kinds but not others. In the crucible of the Cold War, the country could no longer tolerate internal war of group against group; the unity of World War II had to be recovered. Where difference would find acceptance was in religion, which, the elites took for granted, really does not matter very much anyhow. Where difference would not find acceptance, in the 1950s, was in most other matters. So when the third generation determined to remember what the second generation had tried to forget, the turning was toward religion. And the reversion to religious life was measurable, in the building of churches and synagogues and the vast increase in institutions of faith and religious culture of that period. Religion became the medium of ethnic assertion, the renewal of synagogue life the mode of "being Jewish," and that was for an entire generation that had known religiosity only in the most formal terms, if at all. The upshot was the idealization of the grandparents, the immigrants, but especially their place of origin. That was the age of the idealization of the shtetl, the village and its life, set forth in such classics as Mark Zborowski and Elisabeth Herzog in *Life Is with People*, and captured in the much later musical, *Fiddler on the Roof.* The generation of the great return to Judaism, therefore, drew on resources of ethnic memory on the one side and sentimentalization of Jewish existence on the other. It was a milieu piety, not a theological piety, that drew Jews into synagogue life, and the synagogues that they built and that prospered accepted the model of community center, pools with shuls we used to call them: heavy on the sweat, light on the tears. So the third generation committed an act of ethnicization of an otherworldly religious culture, turning the survival of the Jews as a group into an end in itself and preparing the way for the ethnic Judaism, the Judaism of Holocaust and Redemption, that the fourth generation produced and that today atrophies. It has turned a catastrophe into the center of life for the Jewish community, setting aside the life-affirming message of Judaism in favor of memorialization of the disaster in Holocaust museums. The Holocaust out of context transforms "being Jewish" into a lachrymose exercise and yields no positive message for the living. That is why the Judaism of Holocaust and Redemption has begun to recede from the center of Judaic existence. What the fifth generation will produce I do not know. My sons of the fourth generation take their daughters of the fifth generation to synagogue services every Sabbath, but what this all will mean I cannot begin to predict. I can only say, it makes me very happy, if slightly mystified. My father's mother, my grandchildren's great-great-grandmother, would have understood.

New waves of Jewish immigration have swept these shores since World War II, first the survivors from the displaced-persons camps of central Europe immediately after the war, then the survivors of Communism coming in ever-growing numbers from the late 1970s forward, smaller number of immigrants from South Africa and Latin America (including my daughter-in-law from Montevideo), and very large numbers of immigrants from the state of Israel through the first fifty years of the state's history. At this time it is not easy to characterize their experience within the framework of Judaism. It is clear that

no religious movements are now emerging from the Israeli or the Russian migration, equivalent to Reform Judaism in the nineteenth century, Conservative
Judaism in the early and mid-twentieth century (the Judaism of the second
area of immigrant settlement, as Marshall Sklare showed in his Conservative
Judaism), and the renewal of segregationist–Orthodox Judaism by part of the
post–World War II migration of survivors of the Holocaust. So if with the third
and fourth generations of the East European migration of 1880–1924 I stop my
story of the experience of Judaism within the larger immigration history of
America, it is because I do not know how the chapter written by the immigrants of the post–World War II half century (with the stated exclusion of the
Holocaust survivors) is going to record.

A few comments on the American Judaism that is taking shape in the beginning of the twenty-first century may prove pertinent. While among the
new waves of immigrants are large numbers of Russian and Israeli Jews, as
well as smaller but significant numbers of South African and Iranian Jews and
some from the Muslim world and from Latin America, the new migration of
Jews has added to the size of the Jewish community without materially affecting its Judaism. American Judaisms, Orthodox, Reform, Conservative, New
Age, Reconstructionist, and other are native; they speak unaccented American
English. Four points deserve some attention.

First, renewed interest in religious observance has taken over the several
Judaisms, so that Reform Jews have begun to adopt traditional practices,
and moving from there, the other Judaisms have undertaken a more intense level of observance than prevailed before and after World War II.
Whether or not that tendency toward greater observance is numerically
significant, it has made the Jewish community appear more observant than
in the time of the first, second, and third generations of American Jewry
from the nineteenth-century migrations. But that tendency competes with
the contrary one. As Jews have entered the mainstream of American life,
they also find mates among other Americans than Jewish ones, and the intermarriage rates, variously estimated to be sure, certainly rise over those
of the previous generations.

Second, feminism has made a profound impact on American Judaisms of
all streams. The obvious effect has been the opening of the rabbinate to
women. Women make up the larger part of the rabbinical student bodies at
the Reform, Reconstructionist, and Conservative seminaries, and the rab-

binate is rapidly becoming a woman's calling. The first woman ordained as a rabbi joined the Reform rabbinate in the early 1970s, so a generation has passed, and women are now fully accepted as rabbis. But no counterpart development of women as scholars of Judaism, the religion, has yet taken shape. Only a few women teach at the rabbinical schools, and no woman has attained prominence, let alone preeminence, in scholarship on Judaism and its classical sources.

Third, engagement with the affairs of the state of Israel continues to form an important medium of Jewish self-expression in the United States and Canada. Just now, major philanthropists have determined that the way to nurture identification with "being Jewish" is to bring every Jewish youth for a visit to the state of Israel, and that project has taken shape. Its effect on participants, its promise of securing long-term engagement with the Jewish community and with Judaism the religion, has yet to be clarified. But the general agreement that a visit to the state of Israel makes a positive impact on young Americans' self-understanding as Jews obscures the answer to the question, Precisely how is such a transient visit effective in defining an everyday existence somewhere other than in the state of Israel? Since from World War II forward it was Reform Judaism that most fully "Israelized" itself, investing much of its emotional energy in Israeli issues (and the long series of wars made such a focus natural), recent trends in Reform Judaism point in a different direction. First, Reform Judaic leadership has reacted to Orthodox control of Judaism in the state of Israel by calling into question the philanthropic support, coming in large proportion from Reform Jews, for Orthodox institutions and programs in the state of Israel. Second, Reform Judaic leadership has certainly identified tradition and religion as its focus for the coming generation.

If I may close with a message for the newest population of Americans, the Immigrants and their children, it is a very simple one. There is nothing to fear in the changes and challenges of America to religion. Religion, being what God has given to us all (though in a variety I cannot explain), endures through time and through change, ever able to renew itself, in ways we must find mysterious—if also a bit rich in humor, for God has the best sense of humor of us all. Muslim immigrants and their children face challenges familiar to generations of Jewish Americans. Thus far, their response to those challenges tracks that of Jews over the preceding century. One thing is certain: While Muslim immigrants aspire to keep the faith as they have always known it, their children and grand-children will have their own opinions as well. Islam will flourish in America, as Judaism has flourished, but it will speak with a very American accent. At home, American Jews are distinguished by being Jewish. But overseas, they are perceived first and foremost as Americans. And so it is with all Americans, whatever their race, religion, or ethnic identification. At home we see difference. But overseas everyone knows what we really are: Americans all.

7

American Jews in the New Millennium

Jonathan D. Sarna

Prophecy is a dangerous assignment for a historian of American Judaism. A cursory examination of the history of prophecies about Jews, whether in America or elsewhere, discloses that a great many of them through the years have proved wrong. The oldest recorded mention of the name Israel is, in a sense, such a prophecy. It is included in an Egyptian hymn of victory dating to Pharaoh Mer-nep-tah (about 1230 B.C.E.), and it reads, "Israel is laid waste, his seed is not [i.e., his offspring is wiped out]."[1] We know that things worked out rather differently; in fact, the pharaohs were eventually wiped out, while Israel lived on. The second mention of Israel, 400 years later in the so-called Mesha Stone, is of the same order: "I have triumphed . . . ," Mesha king of Moab declared, "while Israel hath perished for ever."[2] Again, things worked out rather differently. Except for the Hebrew Bible, who would ever even have heard of Mesha?

In 1818 in America, one of the nation's wisest leaders, the nation's then attorney general, William Wirt, predicted that within 150 years Jews would be indistinguishable from the rest of humankind.[3] Today, Wirt is himself indistinguishable and long forgotten; again, Jews live on. Still more recently, *Look* magazine, in a famous cover story in 1964, wrote of "The Vanishing American Jew."[4] Today, *Look* itself has vanished—not just once but twice—and again the Jewish people live on. In short, as someone once said, "prophecy is very difficult, especially about the future." This may be worth bearing in mind as we proceed.

In this spirit, I want to point to four transformations affecting American Jewry in the twenty-first century. And then I want to point to three areas of uncertainty concerning the community's future—areas where it seems to me that the evidence is not yet in, visions are contested, and the future is being shaped (even as we speak) by the actions of contemporary American Jews. As we look ahead into the twenty-first century, these are some of the challenges that the Jewish community confronts.

The first transformation that is impacting on Jewish life in the United States is demographic. In the twenty-first century, it is safe to predict, the American Jewish community will shrink both absolutely (the number of Jews will decline) and also relatively (the percentage of Jews within the total U.S. population will also decline). The latest *American Jewish Year Book* estimates the current American Jewish population at somewhere between 5.5 and 6 million.[5] This means that Jews form between 2.2 and 2.4 percent of the national population; 22 to 24 out of every 1,000 Americans are Jewish. As a percentage of the population, this represents a substantial decline since the 1940s, when Jews were almost 3.7 percent of the nation's population (37 out of every 1,000). Relatively speaking, then, the Jewish population has already been in decline for half a century. Because the U.S. population is growing and the Jewish population is not, Jews will almost undoubtedly form a smaller and smaller percentage of America's population, falling below 2 percent in the twenty-first century. Still, the absolute number of American Jews has until now not declined. Thanks to immigration and conversions to Judaism, that number has remained fairly constant for forty years.[6] Yet given the low Jewish birthrate (below zero population growth), the now-declining rate of Jewish immigration, and the burgeoning effects of nonmarriage and intermarriage, it seems likely that America's Jewish population will decline in the twenty-first century. This would mark the first time since the colonial period that America's Jewish population has moved downward.

The Jews of England have already witnessed such a decline. Since 1967, Anglo Jewry's population is estimated to have dropped from more than 400,000 to less than 300,000.[7] The diaspora Jewish population as a whole has also been dropping, by about 0.8 percent (65,000) a year.[8] There is no reason why American Jewry should be immune from this trend. While no one can predict how great the future decline will be, I suspect that the American Jewish population will fall substantially below five million in a few decades.[9]

At least one scholar, Steven M. Cohen, professes to be unconcerned by this development. He argues that the American Jewish community will become, in effect, "leaner and meaner." It "may shrink numerically," he admits, but those who remain will be "stronger qualitatively"—better educated Jewishly and more committed Jewishly—than before.[10] To some this may sound like the ideal corporate scenario for the twenty-first-century: downsize in order to become stronger and more effective. But I am not so sanguine. All evidence suggests, at least in the world of religion, that when faith communities cease to grow—when their numbers decline both in absolute and in relative terms—pessimism takes hold, and they lose their vitality and spiritual freshness. Look at Christian Science in America, the Quakers, or the mainline Protestant denominations that have been in decline for decades and have to a great extent lost the spark that once made them attractive. Continuing cutbacks in the size of the American Jewish population may have a similarly demoralizing impact on the American Jewish community of the future, particularly when Jews see that other faith communities, such as the Mormons, Evangelicals, and Catholics, are rapidly increasing.

This leads me to a second important transformation affecting American Jews: the likelihood that in the twenty-first century, American Jewry will shrink in significance both nationally and internationally. This claim may initially elicit surprise: A case could be made, after all, that American Jews have never been as significant politically as they are right now, with Jews occupying two seats on the Supreme Court, about 10 percent of Congress, several governors' chairs, and more. But at the same time, in other respects, the decline in Jewish significance has already taken place. For a time, particularly in the 1950s and 1960s, American Jews saw themselves and were seen by others as part of a religious triad celebrated in a best-selling book by Will Herberg titled, significantly, *Protestant-Catholic-Jew* (1955). According to Herberg, America had become a "triple melting pot," defined by three great "communions" or "faiths." "Not to be . . . either a Protestant, a Catholic or a Jew," he declared, "is somehow not to be an American."[11] Americans at that time also commonly spoke of their "Judeo-Christian" heritage, again a phrase that included Jews among religious insiders.[12] Nonbelievers, Muslims, Buddhists, and all the other non-Christian faiths, by contrast, did not feature on the nation's religious canvas in those years. They were outsiders and in many cases had no official status at all.

Today, no serious student of American religion adopts the Protestant-Catholic-Jew model. We recognize that Herberg excluded a great many significant players from his account, and we pay enormous attention to religious outsiders—and well we should: Their numbers are growing fast. Islam is reputedly the nation's fastest-growing religion. In the twenty-first century, there is every likelihood that there will be more Muslims than Jews in this country, and some would say that has already happened.[13] The result, for Jews, is a decline in status in the world of American religion, one that will only become more evident in the years ahead. Where once most Americans viewed Judaism as the "third faith" in the United States, as well as the nation's largest non-Christian faith, now Judaism is viewed as one of many American "minority faiths," and in many circles it is treated accordingly.

A revealing indicator of this may be seen in J. Gordon Melton's widely praised *Encyclopedia of American Religions*. The 1989 edition of this work divides the country's 1,588 primary religious bodies into nineteen "families" of religion, only ten of which follow Christian beliefs and practices. Remarkably, Judaism does not even rate a religious family of its own in this classification; instead, it is grouped along with Islam, Sufism, Zoroastrianism, and Bahai as part of the "Middle Eastern Family."[14] While this is somewhat bizarre, it does seem to me to adumbrate changes that lie ahead. In the twenty-first century, Judaism will be seen not as America's third or even fourth faith but as one of a great many American religious options—part of the smorgasbord of religion in the United States.

As if this change were not enough, twenty-first-century American Judaism will also have to come to terms with its diminished significance on the world Jewish stage. Within the next few decades, Israel is poised to overtake the United States as the largest Jewish community in the world. Today, the United States still is home to between 700,000 and 1,000,000 more Jews than live in Israel, but Israel's high birth and immigration rates make its ascension almost inevitable, barring a catastrophe. Indeed, already according to the *American Jewish Year Book,* there are more Jews in greater Tel Aviv than in greater New York, the first time in a century that New York has not ranked first on the list of cities with major Jewish populations. From an Israeli point of view, Israel's demographic rise marks the ultimate triumph of Zionism: the first time since the days of the Bible that Israel will truly be the single largest population center of world Jewry. For American Jews, though, the impact of downward mobility, of moving from being the greatest Jewish community in the world—the center of world Jewry—to merely second best may well prove sobering. It will surely affect the self-image of American Jews, their fund-raising, their relationship to Israel, and their sense of responsibility to the Jews around the world. Already, the American Jewish community is mired in something of a crisis of confidence concerning itself and its future.[15] The additional trauma of diminished world and national significance runs the risk of alienating some twenty-first-century Jews completely.

The third transformation is related to this change: In the twenty-first century, Jews, especially American Jews, will view the diaspora differently than they view it today. Currently, there is an enormous disjunction between the image of the diaspora in the contemporary Jewish and Christian mind and the reality of the diaspora as it now exists and likely will continue to exist in the new millennium. Jews and Christians still imagine Jews as being a global people spread from one end of the world even unto the other, a people that is, as the late Jacob Rader Marcus used to say, "omniterritorial." The reality, however, is that the combined forces of persecution on the one hand and Zionism on the other have redrawn the map of world Jewry completely. The diaspora has shrunk by more than 40 percent since 1939, and Jews in the diaspora are more concentrated today than ever before. Ninety-five percent of the diaspora Jewish population is confined to just fourteen countries today. A mere thirty-nine countries can boast communities of 5,000 Jews or more. Most of the 200 or so countries of the world, including several where Jews had lived for millennia (Iraq, Syria, and Ethiopia) are now completely barren of Jews or show tiny communities that are unsustainable. Indeed, huge areas of the world show no Jewish presence whatsoever.[16]

There is, to be sure, a silver lining in this data: The vast majority of diaspora Jews, as Sergio DellaPergola has shown, have moved to "economically affluent, politically stable and socially attractive environments" over the past fifty years.[17] They have abandoned underdeveloped countries (such as Yemen) and unstable, dangerous countries (such as Bosnia) and now live in the world's most economically advanced countries (such as America and France). Yet this benefit comes at a price. Where most of the world's great religions— Christianity, Islam, and Eastern religions—are today expanding, Judaism is contracting. Where other peoples are preaching the gospel of globalism and spreading their diasporas north, south, east, and west, Jews, who invented the very concept of a diaspora, are reducing their exposure to the larger world and practicing consolidation.

That brings me to the fourth transformation to be discussed, which concerns the changing nature of general American religious life and its impact on Judaism and Jewish life. American Judaism, of course, has always operated within the context of American religion and has always been deeply influenced—some would say too deeply influenced—by its norms and values, even when, as frequently happens, these run counter to millennia of Jewish tradition. This accounts for the extraordinary variety of Jewish religious expressions in the United States, parallel to what we find in Protestantism, and also accounts for such much-discussed phenomena as Jewish feminism, gay/lesbian synagogues, the growing interest in Jewish spirituality, and even the rising tide of intermarriages—all of them developments that parallel, albeit with elements of uniqueness, what we find in contemporary American religion as a whole.

In the twenty-first century, American Judaism is likely to resemble the Protestant denominational structure ever more closely, with the result that in Judaism, as in Protestantism, there will be burgeoning pluralism, greater focus on the individual than on the group, more permeable denominational and even interfaith boundaries, and greater emphasis on the value of consent as against the more traditional Jewish emphasis on descent. Most immediately, we see many new movements in Jewish religious life, including New Age Judaism, Havurah Judaism, humanistic Judaism, and more. About 20 percent of Jews in a 1995 Boston survey refused to categorize themselves under one of the more familiar rubrics of Orthodox, Conservative, Reconstructionist, and Reform Judaism.[18] There is also a burgeoning number of "private ordinations" outside the established rabbinical seminaries.[19] In the twenty-first century, these trends will likely continue; they parallel what is happening in American religion generally. Similarly, I suspect that we will see a growing number of one-generation Jews: Jews (converts to Judaism) who have neither Jewish parents nor Jewish children. The cultural emphasis on "consent" rather than "descent" (free choice rather than automatically following in the ways of one's ancestors) makes this well-nigh inevitable. A great many converts today assume that their children will freely choose their faith just like they did.[20]

Intermarriage reflects a similar emphasis on consent (marry whomever you choose) as opposed to descent (marry only a member of the tribe). Americans of all faiths are marrying across religious lines today in record numbers.[21]

It seems very unlikely that Jews will form an exception to this pattern. The recently published Boston Jewish population survey reveals that only one-third of unmarried Jewish adults consider it "very important to marry someone Jewish."[22] Indeed, it seems to me likely that American Judaism will come in the years ahead to resemble the pattern familiar to us from studies of Protestant denominational switching. A substantial amount of population "churning" will characterize the American Jewish community as eager newcomers enter the Jewish fold and dissatisfied veterans seek out greener religious pastures. As a result, assuming that present trends continue, Jewish "peoplehood" will become a far less significant category in twenty-first-century America, while Judaism (the religion) comes increasingly to resemble its American religious counterparts. Recent research by Steven M. Cohen suggests that this is happening sooner than anyone could have anticipated. Just 52 percent of the Jews he surveyed agreed with the statement "I look at the entire Jewish community as my extended family." Only a minority (47 percent) believed that they "have a special responsibility to take care of Jews in need around the world."[23]

So much for transformations. Let me now turn to areas of uncertainty, where it seems to me that the future is still very much up in the air and significant questions remain. The first of these questions—much discussed in American Jewish circles today—is whether the twenty-first century will be marked by assimilation or revitalization. Signs of assimilation, of course, abound, as seen in widespread ritual laxity, disaffiliation, and intermarriage. Most Jews have friends whose children have either married out or are less religiously observant than their parents. The much-publicized (although probably exaggerated) figure of 52 percent intermarriage is indicative of this trend. Efforts to promote what the organized Jewish community calls "continuity" and "renaissance" reflect the same fear that American Jews may eventually disappear.

At the same time, however, anyone even remotely connected with Jewish life is aware of strong elements of revitalization and renewal within the community. Jewish educational institutions and programs of every kind are flourishing, including Jewish day care centers, private Jewish day schools (equivalent to parochial schools), Jewish high schools, Jewish studies programs at the university level, Jewish summer educational programs, Jewish summer camps, intensive talmudical academies (yeshivas), educational institutions for women, and an array of programs of adult Jewish study. There has also been a perceptible return to religion among young people. Every Jew today knows someone whose children are far more religiously observant than their parents. Even in terms of synagogue attendance, figures point upward. In Boston, synagogue attendance rose dramatically between 1985 and 1995 among Orthodox, Conservative, and Reform Jews alike.[24]

The question as Jews witness these two contradictory trends operating simultaneously—assimilation and revitalization—is, Which one will turn out to be the dominant trend and which will be looked back on as an epiphenomenon, a historical sideshow, "static on the screen"? The answer, of course, is that no one knows. The question is being decided day by day in the hearts and minds of contemporary American Jews. At the deepest level, that is what much of Jewish communal politics in recent years has been all about: how to prevent assimilation and promote revitalization.

A second area of uncertainty concerns the question of whether Judaism in the years ahead will be characterized by religious polarization (Jews becoming, in Jack Wertheimer's memorable phrase, "A People Divided"[25]) or whether there will be a return to the "vital center" in Jewish life, isolating extremists on both sides. The case for religious polarization is easy to make not only because the level of polarizing rhetoric is so high and American culture as a whole has been embroiled in culture wars but also because there are some seemingly unbridgeable issues that divide left and right, chief among them the hundreds of thousands of Jews whom the Reform movement accepts as Jews and traditional Orthodoxy does not (including converts and children of intermarrieds where the mother is not Jewish). Israel also encourages polarization in American Jewish life in many ways. Because Orthodoxy is the only recognized form of Judaism in Israel and most Jewishly affiliated Israelis are in fact Orthodox, many leaders of American Orthodoxy view rapprochement with Conservative and Reform Jews as almost a betrayal of their Orthodox counterparts in Israel who are fighting to maintain the state's Orthodox character. Add all this together, and the case for a schism in the Jewish world seems powerfully strong.

There are, however, also significant signs of a movement back to the center in Jewish life, especially at the lay level. The vast majority of American Jews identify themselves as standing somewhere in the middle of the Jewish religious spectrum, from centrist Orthodox to centrist Reform, and it is these Jews who are most appalled by the specter of a communal schism. Most Jewish lay leaders come from this group, and they form a strong force speaking out on behalf of Jewry's "vital center." Recent years have thus witnessed the rise of "transde-nominational" Jewish schools and summer programs, intra-Jewish dialogues, and other efforts aimed at effecting communal reconciliation. America itself seems to be moving back to the center politically; might Jews follow suit? At this point, the answer to the question cannot be known. Like the assimilation–revival conundrum, the question of whether the center will reemerge or schism will result is actually being decided on the ground wherever Jews gather.

Finally, uncertainty surrounds the question of whether twenty-first-century American Jews will be able to identify a mission compelling enough for the American Jewish community to become passionate about and rally around. The great causes that once energized and invigorated American Jewry—immigrant absorption, saving European Jewry, creating and sustaining a Jewish state, and rescuing Soviet, Arab, and Ethiopian Jews—have now been successfully completed. Today, for the first time in historical memory, no large community of persecuted Jews exists anywhere in the world. Nor will twenty-first-century American Jews gain the kind of meaning from helping Israel, keeping alive the memory of the Holocaust, and fighting anti-Semitism that their twentieth-century parents did; indeed, the major themes of twentieth-century American Jewish history—fighting anti-Semitism, saving world Jewry, and establishing Israel—are essentially past.

There is, to be sure, no shortage of important secular and universal causes that American Jews can and do embrace, from environmentalism and gay rights to world hunger and animal rights, and these are all significant causes, many of them with a sound basis in Jewish tradition. But these are not, ultimately, Jewish causes in the way that Zionism and the Soviet Jewry movement certainly were. Diaspora Jews today are the poorer for not having found a well-defined, elevating mission to inspire them. It remains to be seen whether such a new and compelling mission can in fact be formulated.

Rather than concluding on this note of uncertainty, however, let us instead recall that problems, crises, and anticipated catastrophes—many of them far worse than anything that American Jews are currently experiencing—cascade through Jewish history. They are what make Jews, in Simon Rawidowicz's famous phrase, the "ever-dying people."[26] The fact that Jews have so often defied the odds and continued to survive testifies to the value of their being highly attuned to such problems. Complacency, Jews know, is a luxury that they can never afford.

NOTES

1. James B. Pritchard, ed., *The Ancient Near East: An Anthology of Texts and Pictures* (Princeton, N.J.: Princeton University Press, 1958), 231.

2. Pritchard, *The Ancient Near East,* 209.

3. Jonathan D. Sarna, *Jacksonian Jew: The Two Worlds of Mordecai Noah* (New York: Holmes & Meier, 1981), 178, 65.

4. Thomas B. Morgan, "The Vanishing American Jew," *Look* 28 (May 5, 1964): 42–46.

5. *American Jewish Year Book* 99 (1999): 209, 552.

6. Jonathan D. Sarna, *The American Jewish Experience,* 2nd ed. (New York: Holmes & Meier, 1997), 359.

7. Bernard Wasserstein, *Vanishing Diaspora: The Jews in Europe since 1945* (Cambridge, Mass.: Harvard University Press, 1996), viii.

8. See the "World Jewish Population" section of each year's *American Jewish Year Book.*

9. Compare Sidney Goldstein, "Profile of American Jewry: Insights from the 1990 National Jewish Population Survey," *American Jewish Year Book* 92 (1992): 124.

10. Steven M. Cohen, "Why Intermarriage May Not Threaten Jewish Continuity," *Moment* 19 (December 1994): 95.

11. Will Herberg, *Protestant, Catholic, Jew: An Essay in American Religious Sociology,* rev. ed. (New York: Anchor, 1960), 256–57.

12. See Mark Silk, *Spiritual Politics: Religion and America since World War I* (New York: Simon & Schuster, 1988), 40–53.

13. Carol L. Stone, "Estimate of Muslims Living in America," in *The Muslims of America,* ed. Yvonne Yazbeck Haddad (New York: Oxford University Press, 1991), 25–36; Richard Bernstein, "A Growing Islamic Presence: Balancing Sacred and Secular," *New York Times,* May 2, 1993, A1; Diego Ribadeneira, "Islam's Rising Role: Religion's Discipline Appeals to Many African-Americans," *Boston Sunday Globe,* October 20, 1996, B1.

14. J. Gordon Melton, ed., *The Encyclopedia of American Religions* (Detroit: Gale Research, 1989).

15. Jonathan D. Sarna, *The American Jewish Community's Crisis of Confidence,* Policy Forum No. 10 (Jerusalem: World Jewish Congress, 1996).

16. *American Jewish Year Book* 97 (1997): 542; 99 (1999): 578.

17. Sergio DellaPergola, "Changing Cores and Peripheries: Fifty Years in Socio-Demographic Perspective," in *Terms of Survival: The Jewish World since 1945*, ed. Robert S. Wistrich (London: Routledge, 1995), 36.

18. Sherry R. Israel, *Comprehensive Report on the 1995 CJP Demographic Study* (Boston: Combined Jewish Philanthropies, 1997), 46.

19. See Irene Sege, "A Most Unorthodox Rabbi: Moshe Waldox Turns to Buddhism and Humor to Wake Jews Up," *Boston Globe*, October 22, 1996, D1, D4.

20. See, for example, Brenda Forster and Joseph Tabachnik, *Jews by Choice: A Study of Converts to Reform and Conservative Judaism* (New York: Ktav, 1991), 107.

21. Jonathan D. Sarna, "Interreligious Marriage in America," in *The Intermarriage Crisis: Jewish Communal Perspectives and Responses* (New York: American Jewish Committee, 1991); Paul R. Spickard, *Mixed Blood: Intermarriage and Ethnic Identity in Twentieth Century America* (Madison: University of Wisconsin Press, 1989).

22. Israel, *Comprehensive Report on the 1995 CJP Demographic Study*, 94.

23. Steven M. Cohen, *Religious Stability and Ethnic Decline: Emerging Patterns of Jewish Identity in the United States* (New York: Florence G. Heller–Jewish Community Centers Association Research Center, 1998), esp. 19–20, 44.

24. Israel, *Comprehensive Report on the 1995 CJP Demographic Study*, 48–49.

25. Jack Wertheimer, *A People Divided: Judaism in Contemporary America* (New York: Basic Books, 1993).

26. Simon Rawidowicz, "Israel: The Ever-Dying People," in *Studies in Jewish Thought*, ed. Nahum N. Glatzer (Philadelphia: Jewish Publication Society, 1974), 210–24; Marshall Sklare, "American Jewry: The Ever-Dying People," in *Observing America's Jews*, ed. Jonathan D. Sarna (Hanover, N.H.: University Press of New England, 1993), 262–74.

8

"No Matter How Poor and Small the Building": Health Care Institutions and the Jewish Immigrant Community

ALAN M. KRAUT

In autumn 1654, the directors of the Dutch West India Company sent a letter to Governor Peter Stuyvesant of New Amsterdam that would in many ways shape the assimilation experience of Jewish immigrants to North America for the next 350 years. Over Stuyvesant's objections, the company had decided to permit twenty-three Jewish immigrants from Recife in Brazil to settle in New Amsterdam provided that "the poor among them shall not become a burden to the Deaconry or the Company, but be supported by their own nation." Later the company sent members of five wealthy Jewish families to New Amsterdam to add to the colony's commercial success and to "take care of their own poor." Taking care of their own, then, became a pattern of North American Jewish life from the very beginning.[1]

To Jews, taking care of their own had a dual meaning—taking care of Jewish spiritual needs, generally, and taking care of the economic needs of Jews who were too poor to fully provide for themselves and their families. In colonial North America, Jews organized congregations and purchased land so they could be buried in sacred ground, separate from non-Jews. Providing for the needs of the poor was crucial because self-sufficiency was the price of living in peace among gentiles but even more important because it was a religious injunction. *Zedakah,* or charity delivered with loving-kindness as a religious obligation, was required of all who would lead a Jewish life.

Throughout American history and in the midst of every wave of Jewish immigration, the American Jewish community built religious and educational institutions to perpetuate Judaism and to care for the needs of its poor. There is a rich historical literature that describes how wealthy Jewish philanthropists, such as Guggenheim and Schiff and Rothschild and Baron de Hirsh, offered financial support to aid and educate those less fortunate. There is a growing literature on the voluntary organizations that Jews formed so that the entire community—rich and poor alike—could be involved in aiding those who needed it. Historians, especially those dealing with the Eastern European Jewish immigration, have written on the labor unions and *Landsmannschaften* (lodges) that newcomers joined to get and give assistance.[2]

Simply being Jewish was frequently not enough to make philanthropists and the recipients of charity feel comfortable with each other. Givers and takers of different national origins who arrived in the United States at different times and took different approaches to ritual often felt awkward in each other's presence. Russian Jews, 2.25 million strong at the turn of the twentieth century, were often poorer, more Orthodox, and less acculturated to Western ways than their German coreligionists who arrived in America in great numbers half a century earlier. Many of the German Jews who were philanthropists or who ran the social agencies that aided the Russians were Reform Jews. They were middle class and well down the road to full incorporation into American society. When the Russian takers met the German givers, they often felt the assistance they sought accompanied by an icy chill. In an April 1894 issue of the *Yiddishe Gazetten*, an Eastern European Jew contrasted the efficient charity of incorporated German Jews with the ambience of the agencies formed by Eastern Europeans:

> In the philanthropic institutions of our aristocratic German Jews you see beautiful offices, desks, all decorated, but strict and angry faces. Every poor man is questioned like a criminal, is looked down upon; every unfortunate suffers self-degradation and shivers like a leaf, just as if he were standing before a Russian official. When the same Russian Jew is in an institution of Russian Jews, no matter how poor and small the building, it will seem to him big and comfortable. He feels at home among his own brothers who speak his tongue, understand his thoughts and feel his heart.[3]

If cultural sensitivity is a critical adjunct to charitable assistance, it is especially important in those institutions when the body and the spirit both need healing—namely, the health care institution, especially the hospital.

Of all the institutions that Jews in America created to defend the faith and to take care of their own as assimilation proceeded, the Jewish hospital still requires far more scholarly attention than it has received as an intersection of sacred and secular. Still needed is a thorough exploration of why Jews opened hospitals and how those hospitals helped perpetuate Judaism even as they nurtured assimilation.[4]

Until the early twentieth century, hospitals were not generally regarded as places where the application of scientific medicine by highly trained physicians and surgeons could restore most patients to health. Instead, hospitals were charitable institutions where those who had no families to care for them at home went to receive the care of strangers. Often hospitals were where the poor went to die.[5] Not surprisingly, clergy from some religious traditions saw the vulnerabilities of sickness and death as opportunities to effect religious conversions. Hospitals in the United States during the early and mid-nineteenth century became fields of religious combat as evangelically inclined Protestant clergy sought converts among sick and dying Roman Catholics and Jews. Both religious groups responded by building hospitals of their own.

The Catholic Church led the way. In 1828, the Sisters of Charity started the first Catholic hospital in the United States in St. Louis.[6] As early as 1830, high-ranking Catholic clergy in the busy port of New York expressed the need for a hospital to care for the increasing number of indigent immigrants, mostly from Ireland, who were arriving. New York's eminent bishop, John Dubois, wrote to the secretary of the Association for the Propagation of the Faith in Lyons that his diocese required "a hospital in New York, where a number of the emigrants who daily arrive and suffer for want of attention might regain both corporal and spiritual health." He regretted that at the time more than 700 ill Catholics were being cared for at an institution (probably Bellevue) that was three miles outside the city and "administered by Protestants."[7] Seventeen years later, New York's Catholics were still without a hospital. Now Bishop John Hughes published a pastoral letter attacking the intrusion of Protestant ministers on Catholic public almshouse and hospital patients. Tales of deathbed conversions of Catholics to Protestantism and testimony of priests who had been turned away by hospital administrators when they arrived to comfort the sick or hear the confession of the dying abounded. Stirred by the intensity of the war for souls between his Church and the Protestants, Hughes wrote a pastoral letter calling for the establishment of a Catholic hospital in New York to care for immigrants.[8] Finally, in 1849, St. Vincent's Hospital opened its doors in lower Manhattan, on East Thirteenth Street.

St. Vincent's was staffed by the Sisters of Charity under the direction of Sister Mary Angela Hughes, Bishop Hughes's sister, who had joined the order. The hospital identified itself as a Catholic institution but one "opened to the afflicted of all denominations who seek admission" and one where the sick might be "attended during their illness by their own ministers" whatever the denomination.[9] The hospital began modestly, having a thirty-bed capacity. However, by 1861 the institution had moved to West Eleventh Street and expanded to 150 beds. According to its annual reports, by 1900 St. Vincent's Hospital was treating more than 3,500 patients annually.[10] Although the hospital was opened to all the city's Catholics, the inability of the Sisters of Charity to speak German contributed to its becoming a very largely Irish Catholic institution. To meet the need of the city's large German Catholic population, the German Sisters of the Poor St. Francis founded St. Francis Hospital on New York's Lower East Side in 1865.[11]

To enhance patient dignity as well as to meet the growing financial needs of St. Vincent's Hospital, the institution charged even the poor modest fees rather than establishing an almshouse. However, those who could not afford the three dollars per week for board and medical treatment were received free.[12] Resources were always inadequate to the growing need. Many destitute patients needed clothing as much as they needed medical care. Catholic philanthropy to serve the hospitals was cast in the form of subscriptions. Catholic New Yorkers were encouraged to purchase "yearly subscriptions which would secure free beds, and thus afford relief to many of the poor suffering creatures."[13] By the turn of the century, the needs were still great. Of St. Vincent's 3,681 patients in 1900, 1,161 were total charity cases, 1,255 were receiving partial assistance, and 1,265 (a third) were paying for their care.[14]

The needs of the New York Roman Catholic community were not unique. In antebellum Philadelphia, too, the arrival of immigrants stirred clergymen, laity, and physicians to join together to establish denominational hospitals that offered care of the body and the soul. In Philadelphia, as well as other cities, the Roman Catholic community was ethnically heterogeneous, resulting in the founding of separate institutions: St. Joseph's Hospital for the Irish and St. Mary's Hospital for the Germans.[15]

The Jewish community in the United States was not far behind the Catholics in responding to the need for separate hospitals. There had been Jewish hospitals in Europe for a long time. Evidence suggests that as early as the eleventh century, but perhaps even earlier, synagogues in cities such as Cologne had one room reserved for the care of sick itinerants. It was called a *hekdesh*. By the eighteenth century, little had changed in most communities other than location of the *hekdesh* outside the town, often near a cemetery. Rarely were there more than two rooms with a few beds in each room. However, in larger Western European cities, more elaborate facilities were erected by the eighteenth century. In these *Krankenhausen* (houses for the sick), modern, scientific medicine was offered to patients. A 250-bed hospital opened in Breslau in 1726. Two decades later, London's Sephardic community opened one. And by the end of the century, Berlin and Vienna did, too. Elsewhere, Jewish facilities were not built until the nineteenth century. The first Jewish hospital in Paris opened its doors in 1836. Four years later, Dutch Jews in Amsterdam opened one, followed by Hamburg in 1841. The first such hospital in Jerusalem was the Mayer de Rothschild Hospital, which was established in the Old City in 1854. Jewish hospitals appeared in Eastern Europe as well. By the first third of the twentieth century, there were forty-eight hospitals in Poland that identified themselves as Jewish, with a 1,000-bed facility in Warsaw alone.[16]

In 1850, the first Jewish hospital in the United States was opened in Cincinnati, Ohio, a commercial city populated by German Jewish merchants and craftsmen, many of whom were committed to reform Judaism. The cholera epidemic of 1849 hit Cincinnati hard. The epidemic may well have been a catalyst because one year later the Jewish Hospital of Cincinnati opened its doors to serve the approximately 4,000 Jews who lived in the city. It also served those impoverished peddlers who moved from place to place throughout the Midwest and had no home but clung to their Jewish identities.[17]

More than a quarter of a century later, when Jews in St. Louis were contemplating founding a hospital, they sought advice and information from the Cincinnati community. An 1878 letter from Solomon Levi, a merchant and board president of the Jewish Hospital in Cincinnati, explained what Levi thought were the arguments in favor of a Jewish hospital. First, he cited the community's "pride" and historic responsibility for taking care of its "sick and needy." Second, there was the issue of dietary restrictions, or *Kashrut*. Levi observed that a "good many Israelites have religious scruples as to the food of which they may partake." Third, Levi explained that newly arrived members of the Jewish community, presumably including immigrants, were not welcome at the municipal hospital. He wrote, "The regulations of the City Hospital in this city (and most likely in any other city) prohibit the admission of any except citizens or such sick who have sojourned in the city for a period of time." Finally, Levi offered an argument not uncommon in the era before hospital care was understood in the broader context of the therapeutic revolution that took place at the end of the nineteenth century. He suggested that a hospital could serve double duty as an almshouse. He explained to his coreligionists in St. Louis, "A Jewish hospital need not to be specifically a hospital for the sick alone, it can be at the same time an infirmary for the *indigent* and *old* invalids."[18]

Solomon's letter reflects the limitations of medicine to cure. Care was more important than cure because the hospital was opened more than thirty years before the discovery of germ theory, antisepsis, or aseptic surgery. Hospitals could make the sick comfortable more often than they could make them well.

In New York, the same cholera epidemic that ravaged Cincinnati took more than 5,000 lives. During a single week in July 1849, 714 deaths were attributed to cholera. New York needed hospital facilities to aid the poor, but did it need a Jewish hospital? Bellevue accepted patients of all faiths, and the Jewish population of New York would not skyrocket until the end of the century. Led by attorney Samson Simpson, the Jewish hospital founders included English as well as Spanish and Portuguese Jews. While their motivations were never made explicit, the founding of St. Vincent's by the Catholics in 1849 and St. Luke's Hospital by the Episcopalians in 1850 may well have led wealthy Jewish philanthropists to think that they would be remiss if they did not provide for the spiritual comfort of their sick even as the other major religious communities had for theirs. Adolphus Solomons, an influential member of the American Jewish community and behind-the-scenes power broker who had even been a confidante of Abraham Lincoln, was a member of the Hebrew Benevolent Society, which investigated the need for a Jewish hospital in New York. On his return from the impressive Jewish Hospital in Frankfurt am Main, Germany, he lamented that there was no equivalent institution in the United States. "God willing, such a reproach upon my native land shall not long exist if I can do aught to prevent it."[19]

Although the hospital was chartered in 1852, it took another three years of fund-raising before Jews' Hospital of New York opened in 1855 at the corner of Twenty-eighth Street and Seventh Avenue with a forty-five-bed capacity.[20] Its act of incorporation stated that it was founded "for the purpose of affording surgical and medical aid, comfort and protection in sickness to deserving and needy Israelites for all purposes appertaining to hospitals and dispensaries, a benevolent, charitable, and scientific hospital."[21] The early directors hired four rabbis to serve patients' spiritual needs. The kitchen was kosher to meet the ritual requirements of Orthodox English and Sephardic Jews, and those women who gave birth in the hospital rather than at home had access to *Bris Milah* (ritual circumcision) for their newborn sons.

During the Civil War, Jews' Hospital accepted wounded soldiers regardless of religion. After the war, the hospital continued the nonsectarian policy and, to signal its broader appeal, changed its name to Mount Sinai Hospital. With the growing number of Reform German Jews, the hospital abandoned its kosher kitchen. To secure financial aid from New York State (funds derived from the sale of liquor licenses), Mount Sinai had to match its words to its actions. It amended the act of incorporation by adding to "needy Israelites" the words "and others." Funding from the state was desirable but not crucial because the directors could afford large gifts. Families such as the Lehmans, Guggenheims, and Lewisohns poured hundreds of thousands of dollars into coffers, as did the synagogues that these wealthy patrons attended, including such well-heeled congregations as Shearith Israel, B'nai Jeshrun, and Temple Emanuel, all of whom helped with the move to larger quarters. On May 29, 1872, the hospital moved north on the east side of Manhattan to Lexington Avenue between Sixty-sixth and Sixty-seventh Streets. Now Mount Sinai could accommodate 120 beds and, a year later, an outpatient dispensary for those who did not require hospitalization. Ten years later the number of beds increased to 200. As New York's Jewish population swelled with Eastern Europeans, medical needs escalated as well.

Mount Sinai's final move came in 1904, when the hospital dedicated a 456-bed facility at 100th Street and Fifth Avenue. New buildings have continued to be added to the structure right up to the present. By the early 1950s the hospital had 1,020 beds and served more than 20,000 patients per year. By 2000, the hospital had more than 1,100 beds, with approximately 50,000 discharges, 400,000 inpatient days, and 300,000 outpatient visits annually.

From early on, Mount Sinai earned a reputation for medical excellence. At a time when many institutions discriminated against Jewish physicians, Mount

Sinai welcomed them. Because most of the Jewish physicians and many of the non-Jewish physicians were fluent in Yiddish, Eastern European Jews flocked to Mount Sinai for medical treatment. Although the Yiddish press occasionally charged that Mount Sinai doctors, who were almost always German Jews, seemed strict and judgmental, few Jewish immigrants in search of quality care were deterred by their doctor's countenance.[22]

What did send many Eastern European Jewish immigrants in New York in search of other hospitals to serve them was the inadequacy of Mount Sinai to cope with the large numbers of poor in lower Manhattan who needed a facility close by and responsive to their poverty and to their religious orthodoxy. On December 1, 1889, forty Orthodox Jews gathered in a tailor shop to establish a hospital on the Lower East Side. Without sufficient funds for a hospital, the group opened a dispensary in the rented loft of a factory near Henry Street. Two months later they moved to a parlor on Henry Street, where the dispensary remained until May 1891, when the small group of Eastern European Jews raised sufficient funds to open a hospital at 196 East Broadway in the heart of the Jewish Lower East Side. Gradually, the hospital grew and moved uptown for more space. By 1902, the hospital was at the corner of Cherry and Jefferson Streets and consisted of 115 beds, an operating room, a surgical work area, and a laboratory. However, as many as 1,000 people were being turned away annually because of the lack of space. By 1922, Beth Israel was expanding again. The new building between Sixteenth and Seventeenth Streets on First Avenue had 322 beds. By 1951, it had 448 beds and by the 1980s more than 900 beds.[23]

The first annual report in 1893 cited three reasons for founding the hospital. First, it mentioned the need for a hospital close to the crowded tenements where most Eastern European Jews were living. Second was the need for a kosher kitchen and practice of Orthodox ritual in conduct of the hospital's affairs because so many of the Eastern Europeans were Orthodox Jews. Finally, Beth Israel pledged itself to serve immigrants who were not eligible to be seen by physicians in public hospitals because the newcomers were in the city for under one year. Implicit, though, was a fourth reason. Beth Israel's founders continued to bristle at the haughtiness of the German Jews who were in charge at Mount Sinai Hospital.[24] Those who founded Beth Israel insisted that patients be accepted by priority of application, first come, first served. After 1900, Mount Sinai had special private rooms reserved for wealthy patients.

These rooms were not used for those who could not afford them no matter how many sick newcomers had to be rejected because of lack of space in the wards. The observant wealthy who required a kosher diet might go to Beth Israel, but they did not get special accommodations.

As did Mount Sinai, Beth Israel proclaimed itself "dedicated to suffering humanity regardless of race, creed or religion."[25] However, unlike Mount Sinai, Beth Israel frequently referred to God and Judaism, invoking the "blessings of the Almighty God" on their hospital, which they characterized as "a monument to Jewish liberalism."[26] In addition to its Orthodox ethos, Beth Israel's economic condition was more precarious. Without a base of wealthy German Jewish philanthropists, Beth Israel was dependent on physicians and altruistic members of the Jewish community of modest means. Even when the membership increased to 500 subscribers, many did not pay the annual fee of three dollars. The first organized election for a board of directors occurred in January 1892. The new president, John M. Stone, observed that because directors were always asked for financial contributions, many did not attend meetings, leaving the board in the position of having to transact business without a quorum.

The panic of 1893 tested the resolve of the directors. Several, such as builder Henry Fischel and clothing manufacturer Barnett Price, kept the hospital's doors open when in 1893 the hospital finance committee could raise only $3,544, approximately half the hospital's operating expenses. Not all the directors donated money. Physicians, who often made up as much as a quarter of the board of directors, donated their services.[27] They staffed the dispensary free of charge. Rabbis who joined the board frequently conducted weekday worship services and funerals free of charge.

The directors of Beth Israel were far more diverse than those at Mount Sinai. However, they did have one common trait. All were Eastern Europeans, except for Kauffmann Mandel, who was born in France and emigrated in the 1850s to the United States, serving as an officer in the Union army during the Civil War. Later he became a bank president and served on the board of Montefiore hospital, a German Jewish institution, as well as Beth Israel.[28] Many German Jewish philanthropists donated money, including Jacob Schiff, but they were excluded from the board. Schiff and others accepted their exclusion, hoping that managing their own affairs would allow Russian Jews to develop their own responsible leadership. Annual balls and dinners were the rare occasions when German Jewish businessmen and Russian Jewish businessmen met to engage in philanthropy.

The patient population reflected differences of class and ethnicity between Mount Sinai and Beth Israel. Throughout the 1890s, more than 90 percent of those admitted were not charged. Mount Sinai's percentage hovered at 70 percent.[29] However, by the 1920s the percentages were generally equal, with Beth Israel still slightly ahead.[30] While Russian Jews entered both hospitals, German Jews never made up more than 3 percent of the Mount Sinai patient population. While both hospitals were opened to patients of all nationalities, fewer than 1 percent of the patient population was Irish, Italian, or Chinese.[31] The institutional self-perception of Beth Israel was that its popularity had to do with the fact that it served only kosher food. Many Russian Jews sought the excellent care at Mount Sinai, but those most concerned with ritual observance would go nowhere other than Beth Israel.

As the Jewish population of the United States increased in the late nineteenth century, so too did the number of hospitals, although few cities other than New York could afford to support several Jewish hospitals to serve the preferences of German and Eastern European Jews, respectively. More than sixty Jewish hospitals opened after the ones in Cincinnati and New York. More than 50 percent of these institutions were established between 1880 and 1930 during the period when the Jewish population increased from 230,000 to 2.5 million. Cities building such hospitals included Baltimore, St. Louis, San Francisco, Newark, Cleveland, Louisville, Denver, Hartford, and Boston. The need was great, and there was often little income because such a high proportion of the patients were charity cases. In New Jersey, Newark Beth Israel Hospital was opened in 1902 with accommodations for twenty-one patients. From then until 1908, a total of 854 patients were treated. Of this number, 573 were charity patients, and 281 paid at the rate of eight to ten dollars per week. Thus, about 70 percent of the patients were receiving free treatment. A new building, opened in 1908, expanded the number of beds to eighty, including wards and more expensive private rooms. Newark Beth Israel continued expansion in the 1920s as more and more of the working poor bought insurance policies or acquired union benefits that paid their way.[32] After World War II, a third and final era of construction saw Jewish hospitals being erected in Miami Beach, Los Angeles, Detroit, and Long Island.

Efforts to build an adequate Jewish hospital did not progress quickly or smoothly in all cities. In Detroit, the debate over whether to build a Jewish hospital has been characterized by one historian as "the longest-lived continuously palpable point of contention in Detroit Jewry's history."[33] The controversy was not resolved until 1953 with the establishment of Sinai Hospital. In Washington, D.C., building a Jewish Hospital was discussed well into the 1940s without result. The Washington Jewish community remained small until after World War II, and those preferring treatment in a Jewish hospital could travel the thirty-seven miles to Baltimore's Sinai Hospital. By the early 1890s, Boston was the only one of the fifteen largest cities in the United States that did not have a Jewish hospital. Indeed, as late as 1898, "only about 36 of Boston's 1,550 doctors were Jewish," and many were quite young.[34] Although Eastern European immigrants swelled Boston's Jewish population to almost 30,000 by 1902, it paled beside the size and diversity New York's Jewish population.

The Boston example suggests why Jewish immigrants believed they needed separate facilities. In addition to the need for kosher food and opportunities for ritual observance, as well as the ministrations of a rabbi, Jewish immigrants such as those in Boston often felt the sting of anti-Semitism or, at the very least, cultural insensitivity. Otherwise decent physicians who were neither conversant in Yiddish nor informed as to the customs and problems of Jewish immigrants sometimes diagnosed neurasthenic symptoms as a uniquely Jewish ailment, dubbed "Hebraic Debility."[35] Those so diagnosed were said to be highly nervous and having difficulty adjusting to life in the United States. Aside from such peculiar, culture-bound diagnoses, some physicians admitted to an almost uncontrollable repugnance at the sight of Jewish immigrant patients. Richard C. Cabot, a distinguished physician, admitted in his memoir to having treated Jewish patients as invisible men and women, much as Caucasians do African Americans in Ralph Ellison's classic novel *Invisible Man:*

> As I sit in my chair behind the desk, Abraham Cohen, of Salem Street, approaches, and sits down to tell me the tale of his sufferings; the chances are ten to one that I shall look out of my eyes and see, *not* Abraham Cohen, but a *Jew;* not the sharp clear outlines of this unique sufferer, but the vague misty composite photograph of all the hundreds of Jews who in the past ten years have shuffled up to me with bent back and deprecating eyes, and taken their seats upon this stool to tell their story. I see a Jew,—a nervous, complaining, whimpering Jew—with his beard upon his chest and the inevitable dirty black frock-coat flapping about his knees. I do not see *this* man at all. I merge him in the hazy background of the average Jew.[36]

Boston needed a Jewish facility. Initial efforts resulting in the founding of Mount Sinai Hospital could not sustain the institution, and it failed. The aloofness of the non-Jewish population and later the Jewish community's own internal bickering were barriers, but eventually even Boston built a lasting Jewish hospital, Beth Israel, which opened to its first patient on February 4, 1917.

For members of the Jewish community in the United States at the turn of the century, the debate over whether to pour badly needed philanthropic dollars into health care institutions was more than academic. Jews sought to care for their own in response to the charges of nativists that they were inferior physical specimens generally as compared to America's pioneering breed and that they were disproportionately tubercular. Nativists stoked fears that Jews might spread the "white plague," the great killer of the nineteenth century, among their hosts or that they might themselves be so debilitated by tuberculosis that the Jewish newcomers would become disproportionately dependent on public charity.

Tuberculosis (or consumption, as the disease was often called) came to be regarded as the "Jewish disease" or the "Tailor's disease" because it appeared that so many consumptives were working-class Jews. Weakened by long hours in sweatshops bending over their sewing machines, workers often contracted tuberculosis from those at the next workbench in the congested, unventilated environment. Of course, tuberculosis was peculiar neither to Jews nor to those who worked in the garment industry. Dr. Maurice Fishberg, an epidemiological expert in the early twentieth century, demonstrated statistically that the rate of tuberculosis in the Jewish wards of New York was considerably lower than in the non-Jewish wards.[37] Still, nativists such as E. A. Ross at the University of Wisconsin appropriated physical descriptions of those suffering consumption to describe the "typical" Jewish immigrant.[38] Manly Simons, medical director of the U.S. Navy and an ardent anti-Semite, wrote that Jews as a group are "very tuberculous" because of the unhealthy lifestyle they choose.[39]

Stigmatized as disproportionately consumptive and fearing that those of their brethren who did contract the disease would become a burden to Americans and evoke an anti-Semitic backlash, Jewish philanthropists and voluntary organizations bent their efforts toward creating a Jewish institutional response. The standard of care for consumptives included treatment in a sanatorium. Separated from family and coworkers, consumptives in sanatoria were exposed to such therapies as a beneficial climate, fresh air, and a supervised

nutritious diet. The sanatorium could not offer a specific cure for tuberculosis, but it reflected a revision of how the disease was viewed. If not curable, tuberculosis was treatable. Survival was possible with sanatorium care.[40]

Patricia Nelson Limerick, a historian of the American West, observes that
many places in the West were refuges for those who had trouble breathing, including victims of tuberculosis, as well as asthma and bronchitis. Denver, Colorado, became a magnet for these "respiratory refugees."[41] The Jewish sanatoria built there allowed Jewish consumptives to breathe the clear mountain air.
Differences among the institutions suggest how religious identity and ritual
requirements became the focus of religious conflict among Jews even as they
battled the same disease. As in eastern cities, the principle conflict in Denver
was between Reform Jews and their Orthodox Eastern European brethren.[42]

Under the leadership of Reform Rabbi William Friedman, a committee of
Denverites pledged $3,000 and incorporated the Jewish Hospital Association of
Denver to build a hospital for the care of respiratory diseases that, though built
by Jews, would be available to all. On December 10, 1899, the hospital opened,
and appropriately enough for an institution dedicated to serving all the suffering, the hospital's first patient was not even Jewish but a twenty-five-year-old
Swede from Minnesota, Alberta Hansen.

National Jewish was sustained by assimilationist German Jews, many of
whom practiced reform Judaism. Not all those the hospital hoped to serve
were satisfied that the institution was sufficiently sensitive to the spiritual
needs of the growing number of Eastern European Jewish tuberculosis victims. Their religious practices were Orthodox, and they needed care that
combined therapy with opportunities for traditional religious observance.
Unable to find a satisfactory synthesis of care and cultural climate at National
Jewish, some of the newcomers turned to a new facility founded by others like
themselves, the Jewish Consumptive Relief Society (JCRS).[43]

Twenty Eastern European Jewish tradespeople—including a tinner, a fur-
rier, a silk weaver, a tailor, a house painter, a cigar maker, an actor, and a pho-
tographer—all victims of tuberculosis, met in October 1903 to found an institution that would meet their needs. It was a humble beginning. Among
themselves, the twenty could raise only $1.10 for their Denver Charity for
Consumptives. However, a change of name to the Denver Appeal Society for
Consumptives to eliminate the word *charity* because of its condescending
connotations, coupled with an advertising campaign launched in Yiddish and

English, gave the idea momentum. Most contributions came from workers and their labor unions. Agents of the JCRS combed Jewish communities around the country for donations, entreating philanthropists and placing *pushkes* (collection boxes) in stores, homes, and meeting halls for whatever coins a community could spare.[44]

The guiding light of JCRS was its secretary, Dr. Charles Spivak. Spivak was born Chaim Dovid Spivakofski in 1861 in Krementshug, Russia. He was a revolutionary socialist in his youth and was forced to flee Russia in 1882 to escape being apprehended by the Russian secret police for his political activities. In the United States, he got an education, including a medical degree in 1890 from Philadelphia's Jefferson Medical College.[45]

The JCRS was formally dedicated on September 4, 1904; several days later six men and one woman became the society's first patients. They were housed in wooden tent cottages. Within a year the patient population expanded to twenty, and the tents increased to fifteen. By 1917, the patient population was 146: 115 men and 31 women. Since 1904, 2,974 patients had chased the cure at JCRS. The hospital accepted those at all stages of the disease at no charge and catered to the special religious needs of those who practiced Orthodox Judaism, including careful observance of dietary ritual.[46]

The cultural tensions that existed between assimilated German Jews and newer Eastern European arrivals characterized the tension between National Jewish Hospital and the JCRS. One example will have to suffice, namely, the debate over the observance of the Jewish dietary laws of *Kashrut*. National Jewish did not observe the dietary laws because it was believed that tubercular patients needed a combination of milk, meat, and butter at all meals to restore their health. Dr. Moses Collins, an administrator at National Jewish, had maintained that following the Jewish dietary laws was "inadvisable" for "medical reasons."[47] For many Orthodox Jews, abandoning religious law was a step toward a fate worse than dying of consumption. The JCRS contended that patients need not abandon belief and tradition to recover their health. In an article titled "Kosher Meat in Jewish Hospitals and Sanatoria," JCRS's Dr. Adolph Zederbaum argued that *Kashrut* and better health were consistent: "It is mere nonsense to claim that a sick person cannot thrive on Jewish meat and delicacies . . . at the Sanatorium of the JCRS dairy articles never appear together with meat." Moreover, he observed that by forcing patients to forsake dietary laws, "more damage might be done to their health and general welfare than any positive nutritional value that might result by violating the laws."[48] National Jewish finally did establish a kosher kitchen. However, the cultural tensions embodied in the debate over *Kashrut* continued to chafe administrators at Jewish hospitals throughout the country. The conflict between competing tuberculosis sanatoria in Denver, each representing a different religious and cultural perspective within the Jewish community, suggests that illness not only precipitated struggles between natives and newcomers but also irritated existing tensions within ethnic groups over assimilation. Beyond that, it often widened the abyss between institutions and the individuals those institutions purport to serve.

If wards in Jewish hospitals were sometimes battlefields for coreligionists seeking to reconcile science and faith, they were also portals for many young Jewish immigrants seeking careers in medicine. Jewish medical students were often met with hostility, subjected to admissions quotas in medical schools, denied residencies in non-Jewish hospitals, and sometimes even refused hospital privileges so they could continue the care of patients requiring hospitalization. One of the main reasons for the rise of the Jewish hospital in America was the need for a place where Jewish physicians could train and practice medicine. In 1923, the progressive journal *Survey* said that Jewish hospitals were needed "to obviate the discrimination against Jewish physicians in non-Jewish hospitals." In Hartford, Connecticut, Dr. J. J. Goldenberg, glancing at the photographs of men and women on the walls of Hartford's Mount Sinai Hospital, recalled that "they founded this hospital for the Jewish doctors who were unable to get staff privileges at the other hospitals in town." He bitterly remembered the indignities suffered by Jewish physicians at the hands of non-Jewish hospital administrators. "Jewish doctors had to put their patients on a list for elective admission to the hospital. Usually a week or two would pass before a gentile colleague would admit your patient and turn over the care to you, if you were lucky!"[49] Catholic St. Francis Hospital took a few Jews on staff, but not until Mount Sinai opened its doors in 1923 could Jewish physicians be certain that they would not fall victim to discrimination. Dr. Arthur Wolff, the future chief of staff at the hospital, observed that Mount Sinai was critical "for the younger medical men of our city who for years have been hampered in the accomplishment of their surgical work."[50]

In Detroit, physician Harry August cited the difficulty of obtaining internships and residencies at hospitals.[51] While some of Detroit's Jewish physicians worked in clinics that had been built and sustained with philanthropic contributions, the *Survey* article was critical of such clinics. The author of the report, S. S. Goldwater, thought such clinics "isolated" and capable of providing only "discontinuous medical services" because they could not follow clinic treatment with hospital care, while the physicians who practiced there did not benefit an environment enriched by research and teaching. From the perspective of physicians, clinic work usually meant providing free medical care to impoverished immigrants. Such service, while noble, offered no path to professional development for physicians, no possibility of research opportunities to those drawn to the laboratory, and no advancement derived from offers of positions from more prestigious and wealthy medical institutions.

Not all Jewish physicians supported the creation of Jewish hospitals. Those Jewish physicians, largely German Jews, who had managed to achieve positions on the staffs of non-Jewish hospitals were not supportive. In Detroit, some of Detroit's most prestigious physicians opposed the idea, including Drs. Hugo Freund, David Levy, Norman Allen, and Max Ballin. Dr. Freund served as chief of medicine at Harper Hospital from 1928 to 1945. He also sat on the board of health and on the board of public welfare. Ballin labored tirelessly in clinics to help the poor, but he managed to become chief of surgery at Harper Hospital. Others, such as Emil Amberg and David Levy, who were also on hospital staffs, claimed the real issue to be the poor qualifications of most Jewish physicians entering the profession to be on staff at a hospital. A survey commissioned by the North End medical staff in 1929 concluded that Jewish doctors were indeed underrepresented on hospital staffs. Their absence was especially marked in private hospitals, where many Jews, especially the more affluent, went for treatment. The thrust of the data seemed to suggest that non-Jewish physicians agreed with those Jews who were critical of their coreligionists entering the medical profession, especially those of Eastern European background.

The Detroit physicians who opposed building a Jewish hospital were not without self-interest. Jewish physicians who needed hospital care for their patients were forced to send referrals to one of the physicians who had such privileges. In addition, Freund, Ballin, Levy, Amberg, and several others had the attention and loyalty of Detroit's wealthiest Jewish families, most of them German Jewish, such as the Winemans and the Butzels. Members of such families may have found physicians of Eastern European background and hospitals that had kosher kitchens uncomfortable reminders of their ethnic ties to those they now regarded as their social inferiors.[52]

Ironically, despite the prejudice, Jewish immigrants and the children of newcomers poured into medical schools. Jewish immigrants to the United States, whether from Germany or Eastern Europe, held medicine in the highest esteem. Russian arrivals especially craved careers in medicine because of the prestige and mobility. In Russia, physicians had been able to leave the pale, where most Jews were confined, and migrate to cities. In the United States, young Russian Jews saw in medicine social advantages as well.[53]

Prior to the 1920s, there had been relatively little discrimination against German Jewish medical school applicants. However, with the arrival of millions of Eastern European Jews at the turn of the century, quotas were imposed on medical school admissions much as they were on undergraduate admissions at many colleges and universities. In 1934, the secretary of the Association of American Medical Colleges documented that more than 60 percent of the 33,000 applications on file that year were from Jews. Historian of medical education Kenneth Ludmerer quotes one Harvard Medical School officer who described himself as feeling "overwhelmed by the number of Jewish lads who are applying for admission."[54]

By the late 1930s, rigid medical school quotas were fully functioning. How was the door to medical school closed against Jews, especially Russian Jews? As historian of medicine Leon Sokoloff observes, "A variety of indirect methods were employed to establish the Jewishness of candidates in the first place." An initial pass through the applications was to identify Jewish names, especially in those geographic areas known to have high concentrations of Jewish residents. In some cases there were data from applicants' colleges. Personal interviews allowed admissions officers to see the faces behind the names as they sought to identify those visibly Semitic in appearance. Eventually, applications were changed to require submission of a photograph and answers to questions concerning the applicant's religion and place of birth of father and mother. When Jewish groups raised objections to the question concerning religion, the schools substituted questions about the "racial origin" of the applicant, the mother's maiden name, or whether the applicant had ever changed his or her name.[55] By the early 1940s, three out of every four non-Jewish students were accepted but only one out of thirteen Jewish students.[56] In New York City, where the concentration of Jewish applicants was highest, the restrictive measures had their most dramatic results. At Columbia University's College of Physicians and Surgeons, the enrollment of

Jewish students between 1920 and 1940 declined from 47 percent of the class to 6 percent and at Cornell from 40 percent to 5 percent. At the renowned City College of New York, known for its largely working-class Jewish student body, acceptances to medical school declined from 58.4 percent in 1925 to 20 percent in 1941.[57] As Kenneth Ludmerer observes, those who were themselves the target of quotas did not always practice solidarity. Woman's Medical College of Pennsylvania, too, had a Jewish quota.[58]

According to one study using data from 1933 to 1934, a decade after the end of the peak period of Jewish immigration, of 22,000 medical students enrolled at seventy-six "approved" medical schools, 4,000, or 18 percent, were Jewish.[59] Such data sent chills up the back of assimilationist Jewish leaders such as Rabbi Morris Lazaron, who so feared an anti-Semitic backlash within the medical community that he conducted a survey to see how medical school deans felt about the influx of young Jewish students. He sent questionnaires to the deans of sixty-five medical schools. From the forty-four responses he received, he drew the somewhat problematic conclusion that "while there is limitation of Jewish enrollment [usually through quotas] there is no anti-Semitism involved in the admission of Jewish students to medical school." However, the deans' letters suggest that at least some had their doubts.[60] Dean Burton Meyers of the Indiana University School of Medicine deplored the "anti-Jewish reaction in Germany" but thought it might be echoed in the United States if "forty percent of the Doctors of Medicine were Jews."[61] Dr. C. C. Bass, dean at Tulane, said their teachers thought Jewish medical students had a "disagreeable manner and attitude in their classes" while being "less acceptable to patients with whom they come in contact in their studies," though, he conceded, "some of the most distinguished members of our faculty are Jews. Some of our best students are Jews. Some of our most distinguished alumni are Jews."[62] For still others, the "problem" was not the Jewishness of Jewish students but the manner and style of those who were themselves immigrants, the sons of a "recently immigrated" Russian Jewish family who is "intensively aggressive and presents other personality difficulties," or students "who were born in Europe, or whose parents have recently migrated from Europe," and who "are apt to be an entirely different type, sometimes radical, sometimes asocial, often unstable."[63]

The perceived personality traits that were used as excuses for excluding Jewish students from medical schools were also used to exclude or at least curb the presence of Jews on medical faculties.[64] Prior to the publication of Abraham Flexner's scathing denunciation of the state of American medical education in 1910, Jews held places on medical faculties in such midwestern cities as Cleveland, Cincinnati, and St. Louis. In each city, senior physicians at the local Jewish hospital contributed their efforts to medical education. The Flexner report inadvertently reduced the number of Jews involved in medical education as these small medical schools were absorbed by large private Protestant-dominated universities with restricted personnel policies.[65] The trend spiraled downward. By 1927, Dr. S. M. Melamed lamented that of the 4,000 to 5,000 Jewish physicians in New York City, there was not one that held the position of a "full-fledged" professor in any medical school that was part of a university.[66] The same complaints made about the manners and comportment of Jewish medical students were often leveled at those Jews seeking faculty appointments or upward mobility as chair of a department. As Leon Sokoloff observes, "A concern with personality can also be a cloak for prejudice."[67] Those with liberal or socialist political views were vulnerable. So, too, were those whose educational background included a city or state institution rather than an elite Ivy League university. A profession that had a long history of valuing gentility, according to historian of medicine Gert Brieger, often used a scale that included a classical premedical education at an elite university to determine a student's suitability for the medical profession.[68] Moreover, the success of a handful of Jews in achieving prestigious appointments did not always pry open doors for others. Insecurities fostered by discrimination left a residue of fear that successful Jews who helped other Jews might be the targets of a backlash that would undo their accomplishments. Such is the explanation that his daughter offered in behalf of brilliant pathologist Dr. Milton C. Winternitz, who was the dean of Yale Medical School from 1920 to 1935 but had the well-earned reputation of being "almost a caricature of the American Jew striving to become part of Gentile society."[69] Winternitz's daughter, writer Susan Cheever, believes that her father, who so prided himself on his ascent from working-class Baltimore, would not have prospered in his career if he had chosen to ignore the anti-Semitism that surrounded him and made it his mission to mentor other Jews.[70]

Not until the 1960s did the barriers in medical schools and hospital residencies begin to fall. Now Jews had little difficulty getting hospital privileges, and those on staff had few obstacles to becoming chiefs of their respective services.

However, by this time Jewish hospitals were well established, although most were no longer serving primarily Jewish patients. In 1966 there were sixty-four major Jewish hospitals in the United States. Many had international reputations for their research, such as the Denver hospitals known for their research on tuberculosis and other respiratory diseases, Newark Beth Israel for research on the Rh factor in blood, or Mount Sinai's work on diphtheria, led by Hungarian-born Dr. Bela Schick. Although these hospitals now had patient populations that were only 10 to 20 percent Jewish, their existence was sustained by Jewish philanthropic dollars donated out of a desire to serve the urban communities that had nurtured Jewish immigrants several generations earlier.

By the 1990s, Jewish hospitals began to lose their importance as extensions of the Jewish religious presence in the United States. According to one account written in 1992,

> The typical Jewish hospital today is large (about 470 beds), inner-city, affiliated with a medical school, and not getting rich. According to statistics gathered by Premier Hospital Alliance, a Westchester, Illinois-based cooperative owned by 49 large teaching hospitals, in 1989, U.S. hospitals had an average profit margin of 2.6 percent, compared to the Jewish hospital margin of less than one-half of one percent.[71]

Though still top-drawer medical institutions, Jewish hospitals now treated fewer and fewer Jews; especially reduced were the number of observant patients requiring kosher meals and services. In Cleveland, only 15 percent of Mount Sinai's patient population was Jewish by the 1990s.[72] Large numbers of Jews, the immigrants' children and grandchildren, had moved to suburbia, leaving the old neighborhood and local hospital behind. Jewish hospitals in many inner-city neighborhoods treated more African Americans or Latinos than Jews. Jewish hospitals also sought to minister to special needs of inner-city populations. New York's Beth Israel Medical Center runs one of New York's largest substance abuse programs, serving 8,000 addicts annually, mainly publicly assisted patients in methadone programs. Beth Israel also has a full-time Cambodian translator to serve the latest wave of immigration.[73] Nevertheless, Wayne Lerner, president of the Jewish Hospital of St. Louis in the early 1990s, contended that

> the [dwindling Jewish] community would feel a great loss if we were to disappear. . . . Not just because of the [loss of] health care, but because of the

psychic contribution, the feeling of investment in the community. If you talk to people in the community, they say, "Oh, Jewish Hospital, I was born there."[74]

The strong commitment to service kept many Jewish hospitals in business until the high cost of medical technology, combined with empty beds (a product of outpatient services), and dramatic declines in reimbursements left many institutions vulnerable. The latter hurt all hospitals during the 1990s, especially hospitals that served large numbers of elderly and poor patients, as the Jewish hospitals often did, fulfilling a moral commitment to those who resided in the decaying inner-city neighborhoods that often surrounded them. By the mid-1990s, a Republican Congress mandated lower Medicare reimbursements for the treatment of the elderly and reduced Medicaid reimbursements for the care of the poor. In states such as New Jersey, Republican governor Christie Todd Whitman pushed to reduce state reimbursements to hospitals for the care of those who could not pay at all and were uninsured. Finally, managed care embodied in for-profit health maintenance organizations (HMOs) reduced hospital income by pegging reimbursements for in-hospital care, such as expensive surgical procedures, well below their actual costs. Global fees paid by HMOs in compensation for all the expenses incurred by the performance of heart bypass operations, for example, routinely forced hospitals to lose needed revenue.[75]

The siren call of mergers grew ever louder from the late 1980s to the end of the century. Jewish hospitals struggled with the choices. In Chicago, the Jewish community had mixed results in trying to save the city's two Jewish hospitals. The Michael Reese Hospital, founded in 1881, sought to survive by positioning itself as a world-renowned medical research institution, pursuing lucrative grants and researchers at the cutting edge in their fields. The strategy failed, and Michael Reese was sold for an undisclosed sum to the Humana Corporation, a for-profit company based in Louisville, Kentucky. While the sale was prudent financially, many Jewish contributors who had extended themselves to Michael Reese over the years were bitter. Ironically, the less prestigious of the two Chicago institutions, Mount Sinai Hospital, founded in 1919, survived. Mount Sinai's strategy was grounded in operating on a very tight budget. Describing the strategy in 1992, one Mount Sinai administrator said, "We operate as one of the lowest-cost teaching hospitals in the U.S. . . . . That's very difficult. But as hard as it is, the staff works well at getting things

done." To maintain the revenue flow, Mount Sinai struggled to keep an 80 percent occupancy rate at a time when the average occupancy rate for all Chicago
hospitals was 57 percent. In part, the high occupancy rate was linked to Mount
Sinai's close relationship to the largely non-Jewish residents in the community. The hospital participated in the construction of housing projects near its
site in partnership with the local building industry. It also contributed to community employment projects and established a dozen sites outside the hospital where neighborhood residents could get primary care. Still, Mount Sinai
might not have survived had it not been for subsidies exceeding $1 million an-
nually from Chicago's Jewish Federation.[76]

In other cities, mergers proceeded apace during the last two decades of the
twentieth century. Mount Sinai in Hartford merged with St. Francis. Mount
Sinai Hospital of Milwaukee merged with Good Samaritan Medical Center
and became part of Aurora Healthcare. Mount Zion Hospital and Medical
Center in San Francisco affiliated with the University of California, San Francisco, under an agreement by which the university operates the hospital. Montefiore of Pittsburgh was sold to the University of Pittsburgh. Mount Sinai
Medical Center in Minneapolis merged with Metropolitan Medical Center,
owned by Health One Corporation, to become Metropolitan–Mount Sinai
Medical Center. In New Jersey, the St. Barnabas Health Care System purchased
Newark Beth Israel Medical Center.

Sales and mergers often left some institutions with less than Jewish-sounding
names, such as Boston's Beth Israel Deaconess Medical Center. Still, there remains in many of these institutions evidence of a Jewish heritage both in ritual
and in values. There is the mezuzah, the small case containing Hebrew text (the
first two paragraphs of the Shema) written on parchment scrolls that are affixed
to doorways, fulfilling the commandment that God's words be written on the
doorposts of one's house. There is often a Star of David under the hospital's
name or cast in metal and resting on the front lawn. A condition of the sale of
Newark Beth Israel Medical Center to the St. Barnabas Health Care System was
that the Beth Israel name and the Stars of David on buildings and lawn remain.
Some institutions have elevators that stop at every floor to allow the Orthodox to
avoid operating machinery on Shabbat. Members of the boards of these hospitals are usually Jewish by custom if not by contract. Moreover, as the chief executive officer of the Premier Hospital Alliance, Alan Weinstein, has observed, Jewish values prevail even when ritual has been abandoned. Jewish values to

Weinstein means commitment to education and first-rate care provided to all who come regardless of their faith.

Today, Jewish hospitals are truly a dying breed. As recently as March 2000, the *Cleveland Jewish News* announced that Cleveland's Mount Sinai, opened since 1903, was closing its doors. Of the twenty-two Jewish hospitals that existed as recently as 1990, only about half still operate under Jewish auspices. Only seven or eight cities still have Jewish community-owned hospitals, including New York City, Louisville, Baltimore, Philadelphia, Los Angeles, Miami, and Chicago.[77]

The Jewish hospital played a central role in the assimilation of Jewish newcomers to the United States. During the peak period of Jewish immigration at the turn of the twentieth century, Jewish hospitals allowed patients to continue religious observance in traditional ways as they negotiated the transition from alien to American. The training grounds for generations of Jewish physicians facing prejudices and discriminatory barriers erected by the American medical establishment, Jewish hospitals became a refuge for doctor as well as patient. Finally, Jewish hospitals allowed the American Jewish community to continue to make good on the promise that the first Jewish arrivals made so long ago that in return for a safe haven they would always take care of their own.

NOTES

1. There are many accounts of the first settlement of Jews in North America and the encounter with Peter Stuyvesant. See Howard M. Sachar, *A History of the Jews in America* (New York: Alfred A. Knopf, 1992), 14–15, and Arthur Hertzberg, *The Jews in America, Four Centuries of an Uneasy Encounter: A History* (New York: Simon & Schuster, 1989), 22–23. See also Eli Faber, *A Time for Planting: The First Migration, 1654–1820* (Baltimore: The Johns Hopkins University Press, 1992), 29–32.

2. For a study of the issues involved in providing for the large Jewish immigration of the late nineteenth and early twentieth centuries, see Boris D. Bogen, *Jewish Philanthropy: An Exposition of Principles and Methods of Jewish Social Service in the United States* (New York: Macmillan, 1917; reprint, Montclair, N.J.: Patterson Smith Publishing, 1969). Many overviews of that migration offer a description of the social services available because of Jewish philanthropy. See Moses Rischin, *The Promised City: New York's Jews, 1870–1914* (Cambridge, Mass.: Harvard University Press, 1962), 95–111, and Irving Howe, *World of Our Fathers: The Journey of the East European Jews to America and the Life They Found and Made* (New York: Harcourt Brace Jovanovich, 1976), passim. Some excellent recent studies of Jewish voluntary

organizations include Daniel Soyer, *Jewish Immigrant Associations and American Identity in New York, 1880–1939* (Cambridge, Mass.: Harvard University Press, 1997); Shelley Tenenbaum, *A Credit to Their Community: Jewish Loan Societies in the United States, 1880–1945* (Detroit: Wayne State University Press, 1993); and Hyman Bogen, *The Luckiest Orphans: A History of the Hebrew Orphan Asylum of New York* (Urbana: University of Illinois Press, 1992). The desire of German Jews to relieve the pressure of teeming urban neighborhoods resulted in plans to disperse the Jewish population across the United States at the expense of German Jewish philanthropists. See Jack Glazier, *Dispersing the Ghetto: The Relocation of Jewish Immigrants across America* (Ithaca, N.Y.: Cornell University Press, 1998).

3. *Yiddishe Gazetten* (April 1894), as quoted by Rischin, *The Promised City,* 104.

4. The best overview is Ethan Bridge, "The Rise and Development of the Jewish Hospital in America" (rabbinical thesis, Hebrew Union College, 1985). There have been a number of individual hospital studies. Two of the best published volumes are Dorothy Levenson, *Montefiore: The Hospital as Social Instrument, 1884–1984* (New York: Farrar, Straus & Giroux, 1984), and Arthur J. Linenthal, *First a Dream: The History of Boston's Jewish Hospitals, 1896 to 1928* (Boston: Beth Israel Hospital, in association with the Francis A. Countway Library of Medicine, 1990).

5. The single most comprehensive volume on the evolution of the hospital in the United States is Charles E. Rosenberg, *The Care of Strangers: The Rise of America's Hospital System* (New York: Basic Books, 1987). Two other volumes that describe the hospital as a charitable institution that cared for the impoverished but often served as a venue where those without families went to die is Morris J. Vogel, *The Invention of the Modern Hospital, Boston, 1870–1930* (Chicago: University of Chicago Press, 1980), and David Rosner, *A Once Charitable Enterprise: Hospitals and Health Care in Brooklyn and New York, 1885–1915* (Princeton, N.J.: Princeton University Press, 1982).

6. Ann Kathryn Webster, "The Impact of Catholic Hospitals in St. Louis" (Ph.D. diss., Saint Louis University, 1968).

7. A letter from Right Rev. John Dubois, D.D., Bishop of New York, to Rev. ———, secretary of the Association for the Propagation of the Faith, Lyons, March 16, 1830, in United States Catholic Historical Society, *Historical Records and Studies* (New York: United States Catholic Historical Society, 1907), 1, 5, 228.

8. *Freeman's Journal and Catholic Register,* February 20, 1847.

9. *First Annual Report of Saint Vincent's Hospital under the Charge of the Sisters of Charity for the Year Ending January First, 1859,* 4. The best history of St. Vincent's

Hospital is Marie De Lourdes Walsh, *With a Great Heart: The Story of St. Vincent's Hospital and Medical Center of New York, 1849–1964* (New York: St. Vincent's Hospital, 1965).

10. *Fifty-First Annual Report of the St. Vincent's Hospital of the City of New York for the Year 1900* (New York: Meany Printing, 1901), 8.

11. *Fifty-First Annual Report,* 22.

12. *First Annual Report ,* 4.

13. *First Annual Report,* 4.

14. *Fifty-First Annual Report,* 22.

15. Two fine articles have treated the Catholic hospitals in Philadelphia: Gail Farr Casterline, "St. Joseph's and St. Mary's: The Origins of Catholic Hospitals in Philadelphia," *Pennsylvania Magazine of History and Biography* 108 (July 1984): 289–314, and Judith G. Cetina, "In Times of Immigration," in *Pioneer Healers: The History of Women Religious in American Health Care,* ed. Ursula Stepsis, C.S.A., and Delores Liptak, R.S.M. (New York: Crossroad, 1989), 86–117.

16. Samuel S. Kottek, "The Hospital in Jewish History," *Review of Infectious Diseases* 3 (July–August 1981): 636–39.

17. Bridge, "The Rise and Development of the Jewish Hospital in America," 18.

18. Solomon Levi to Jacob Furth, October 22, 1878, as quoted in David A. Gee, *216 S.K.: A History of the Jewish Hospital of St. Louis* (St. Louis: Jewish Hospital of St. Louis, 1981), 9.

19. Adolphus S. Solomons, "Some Scraps of History Concerning Mount Sinai Hospital," *Jewish Messenger* 3 (December 17, 1875): 1.

20. For the history of Mount Sinai Hospital, see Joseph Hirsh and Beka Doherty, *The First Hundred Years of the History of Mount Sinai Hospital of New York, 1852–1952* (New York: Random House, 1952). See also Jeremy Hugh Baron, "The Mount Sinai Hospital: A Brief History," *Mount Sinai Journal of Medicine* 67 (January 2000): 3–5.

21. Jews' Hospital of the City of New York, *Act of Incorporation and By-Laws,* 1852; Hirsh and Doherty, *The First Hundred Years of the Mount Sinai Hospital of New York.*

22. Rischin, *The Promised City*, 106.

23. Tina Levitan, *Islands of Compassion: A History of the Jewish Hospitals of New York* (New York: Twayne, 1964), 89–106. See also *Beth Israel Hospital Proudly Marks 75 Years of Service to the Community* (Beth Israel Hospital, New York, 1965, pamphlet).

24. *Annual Report of the Directors of Beth Israel Hospital* (January 1894).

25. *Annual Report of the Directors of Beth Israel Hospital* (January 1905).

26. *Annual Report of the Directors of Beth Israel Hospital* (January 1905).

27. Undated pamphlets in the Beth Israel Hospital Archives (BIHA). Letter from Harry Fischel to Dr. Maxwell S. Frank, Beth Israel Hospital medical director, BIHA, and letter from Maxwell S. Frank to Robert Smith, publicity director, Federation of Jewish Philanthropies, July 29, 1953.

28. Henry Whittemore, *Progressive, Patriotic, and Philanthropic Hebrews of the New World* (New York: Henry Whittemore and Company, 1907), 143–45.

29. *New York Times*, September 25, 1917.

30. *Hospital Situation in Greater New York: Report of a Survey of Hospitals in New York City by the Public Health Committee of the New York Academy of Medicine* (New York: G. P. Putnam's Sons, 1924), 125. Beth Israel was second only to Columbia Presbyterian.

31. See data in *Annual Reports of the Directors of Beth Israel Hospital* (1894–1920s).

32. Bridge, "The Rise and Development of the Jewish Hospital in America," 92–93, 155. See also "Report of the Newark Beth Israel Hospital and Dispensary, from Jan. 1, 1901 to Jan. 1, 1906" (Beth Israel Hospital, Newark, N.J., 1906), 8–9.

33. Sidney Bolkosky, *Harmony and Dissonance: Voices of Jewish Identity in Detroit, 1914–1917* (Detroit: Wayne State University Press, 1991), 412–13.

34. Linenthal, *First a Dream*, 19–21.

35. Linenthal, *First a Dream*, 20.

36. Richard C. Cabot, *Social Service and the Art of Healing*, 2nd ed. (New York: Dodd, Mead, 1931), 4–5.

37. For a full discussion of the stigmatization of Jewish immigrants as disproportionately tubercular and Dr. Maurice Fishberg's efforts to dispel the

mythology, see Alan M. Kraut, *Silent Travelers: Germs, Genes, and the "Immigrant Menace"* (New York: Basic Books, 1994).

38. Edward Alsworth Ross, *The Old World in the New: The Significance of Past and Present Immigration to the American People* (New York: Century, 1914), 289–90.

39. Manly H. Simons, "The Origin and Condition of the Peoples Who Make Up the Bulk of Our Immigrants at the Present Time and the Probable Effect of the Absorption upon Our Population," *The Military Surgeon* 23 (December 1908): 433.

40. Valuable historical studies of tuberculosis are Rene and Jean Dubos, *The White Plague, Tuberculosis, Man, and Society* (1952; reprint, New Brunswick, N.J.: Rutgers University Press, 1987); J. Arthur Myers, *Captain of All These Men of Death: Tuberculosis Historical Highlights* (St. Louis, Mo.: Warren H. Green, 1977); Guy P. Youmans, *Tuberculosis* (Philadelphia: W. B. Saunders, 1979); and Barbara Bates, *Bargaining for Life: A Social History of Tuberculosis, 1876–1938* (Philadelphia: University of Pennsylvania Press, 1992). For social and cultural approaches to tuberculosis, respectively, see Sheila M. Rothman, *Living in the Shadow of Death: Tuberculosis and the Social Experience of Illness in American History* (New York: Basic Books, 1994), and Katherine Ott, *Fevered Lives: Tuberculosis in American Culture since 1870* (Cambridge, Mass.: Harvard University Press, 1996).

41. Patricia Nelson Limerick, *The Legacy of Conquest: The Unbroken Past of the American West* (New York: W. W. Norton, 1987), 89. On the Jewish community in Denver, see James Richard Giese, "Tuberculosis and the Growth of Denver's Eastern European Jewish Community: The Accommodation of an Immigrant Group to a Medium-Sized Western City, 1900–1920" (Ph.D. diss., University of Colorado, 1979).

42. For an account of the conflict between Reform and Orthodox Jewish sanatoria in Denver, see Kraut, *Silent Travelers,* 204–6.

43. Jeanne Lichtman Abrams knows more about the JCRS than anyone else. Jeanne Lichtman Abrams, "Chasing the Cure: A History of the Jewish Consumptives' Relief Society" (Ph.D. diss., University of Colorado, 1983). She has also written on Anna Hilkowitz, one of the female volunteers for the JCRS, in "*Unsere Leit* ('Our People'): Anna Hilkowitz and the Development of the East European Jewish Woman Professional in America," *American Jewish Archives* 37 (November 1985): 275–89. Jewish consumptives in Denver often also suffered family dislocation. See Jeanne Lichtman Abrams, "'For a Child's Sake': The Denver Sheltering Home for Jewish Children in the Progressive Era," *American Jewish History* 79 (winter 1989–1990): 181–202.

44. Howe, *World of Our Fathers,* 149.

45. Abrams, "Chasing the Cure," 11–15.

46. *The Sanatorium* 12 (May–August 1918): 54–55. This JCRS publication was located in the JCRS papers in the collection of the Rocky Mountain Jewish Historical Society at the University of Denver.

47. *Jewish Outlook* 1 (October 7, 1904): 6.

48. Dr. Adolph Zederbaum, "Kosher Meat in Jewish Hospitals and Sanatoria," *The Sanatorium* 2 (November 1908): 275.

49. J. J. Goldenberg, as quoted in Barry A. Lazarus, "The Practice of Medicine and Prejudice in a New England Town: The Founding of Mount Sinai Hospital, Hartford Connecticut," *Journal of American Ethnic History* 10 (spring 1991): 21.

50. Arthur Wolff, as quoted in Lazarus, "The Practice of Medicine and Prejudice in a New England Town," 35.

51. Bolkosky, *Harmony and Dissonance*, 413.

52. Bolkosky, *Harmony and Dissonance*, 434–35.

53. Leon Sokoloff, "The Rise and Decline of the Jewish Quota in Medical School Admissions," *Bulletin of the New York Academy of Medicine* 68 (November 1992): 498.

54. Kenneth M. Ludmerer, *Time to Heal: American Medical Education from the Turn of the Century to the Era of Managed Care* (New York: Oxford University Press, 1999), 64.

55. Sokoloff, "The Rise and Decline of the Jewish Quota in Medical School Admissions," 500–1. Sokoloff derives much of this information from a report compiled by an investigating committee of the New York City Council in 1946.

56. Sokoloff, "The Rise and Decline of the Jewish Quota in Medical School Admissions," 500–1.

57. Ludmerer, *Time to Heal*, 64.

58. Ludmerer, *Time to Heal*, 64.

59. Max Danzis, "The Jew in Medicine," *American Hebrew and Jewish Tribune*, March 23, 1934 (photocopy located in Morris Lazaron Papers, American Jewish Archive, Cincinnati).

60. Morris S. Lazaron, "The Jewish Student in Medicine" (draft located in Morris Lazaron Papers, American Jewish Archive, Cincinnati).

61. Burton D. Meyers to Rabbi Morris S. Lazaron, October 30, 1934, in *Jews in Medicine: Survey of Medical Schools, 1930–1934,* collection no. 71, file 37/16, American Jewish Archives, Hebrew Union College, Cincinnati.

62. C. C. Bass, M.D., to Rabbi Morris S. Lazaron, March 8, 1934, in *Jews in Medicine,* collection no. 71, file 37/16, American Jewish Archives, Hebrew Union College, Cincinnati.

63. A. C. Bachmeyer to Rabbi Morris S. Lazaron, February 24, 1934, and Arthur C. Curtis, M.D., to Rabbi Morris S. Lazaron, February 20, 1934, in *Jews in Medicine,* collection no. 71, file 37/16, American Jewish Archives, Hebrew Union College, Cincinnati.

64. Leon Sokoloff, "The Question of Antisemitism in American Medical Faculties, 1900–1945," *Patterns of Prejudice* 31 (1997): 43–54.

65. Sokoloff, "The Question of Antisemitism," 47.

66. Sokoloff, "The Question of Antisemitism," 45.

67. Sokoloff, "The Question of Antisemitism," 53.

68. Gert H. Brieger, "Classics and Character: Medicine and Gentility," *Bulletin of the History of Medicine* 65 (spring 1991): 88–109.

69. Dan Oren, *Joining the Club: A History of Jews at Yale* (New Haven, Conn.: Yale University Press, 1986), 136.

70. Susan Cheever, *Treetops: A Family Memoir* (New York: Bantam Doubleday Dell, 1991), 49. In a footnote, Leon Sokoloff observes that after World War II, Winternitz may have reassessed his position because he cochaired a commission to help refugee physicians and mentored the first Jew to become a professor at Yale Medical School after 1945. See Sokoloff, "The Question of Antisemitism . . .," 50. See also Joseph S. Fruton, *Eighty Years* (New Haven, Conn.: Yale University Press, 1994), 82.

71. Christina Kent, "Jewish Hospitals: Staying When the Getting Gets Tough," *Faulkner & Gray's Medicine & Health* 46 (September 14, 1992): 1–4.

72. Marilyn N. Klarfeld, "End of an Era," *Cleveland Jewish News,* March 3, 2000, 1.

73. Mary Wagner, "Jewish Hospitals Yesterday and Today," *Modern Healthcare* 21 (February 14, 1991): 33.

74. Kent, "Jewish Hospitals," 1.

75. The complex reasons for reimbursement reduction are discussed clearly, intelligently, and in historical context by Ludmerer, *Time to Heal,* 349–99.

76. Ludmerer, *Time to Heal,* 349–99. See also Klarfeld, "End of an Era."

77. Ludmerer, *Time to Heal,* 349–99. See also Klarfeld, "End of an Era."

9

Islam in America: The Mosaic

AMINAH BEVERLY MCCLOUD

The American Muslim community is at once a mosaic, and a tattered quilt. Orthodox, heterodox, Sunni, Shi'i, and Sufi all make claims of Islam in the United
States. Because there is no official or state-sponsored Islam, all find sanctuary and
voice. Exiled princes and authors, refugees, and asylum seekers from the Muslim
world jockey for a platform to represent Islam along with first-, second-, and
third-generation converts of African and European American descent. The ca-
cophony of voices raised is dynamic, if sometimes deafening. The variety of discourses is as wide as the many ethnicities in the Muslim community. The latest
estimates of the number of Muslims in the United States range from six to ten
million. There is much debate over the accuracy of any projected numbers, and
since the census does not record religion as a category of identification, it is
doubtful that we will ever be able to do more than make an educated guess.
Whatever the size of the community as a whole, we do know that in the United
States the largest community of immigrant Muslims is South Asian (about 35
percent), followed by Arabs (about 20 percent). There are also small numbers of
Africans, Iranians, Bosnians, Somalians, and Chinese Muslims, along with many
others. Immigrant Muslims find the heterogeneity of the Muslim community almost as overwhelming as the diversity of America itself.

All Muslims who are citizens of America live a minority existence but with
the benefits that citizenship brings. Though they may experience the frustra-
tions of being unfairly stereotyped and sometimes even ridiculed, they are

nonetheless free to practice the fundamentals of worship, to avail themselves of the opportunities America offers, and to live reasonable lives. Muslims in America behave like all other religious groups—they divide along racial, class, and ethnic lines. Unlike some of the major religious traditions, however, they worry a great deal about these divisions and engage in endless conversations about how to seam the divide. This chapter examines 1) the process of the formation of the Muslim community; 2) the religious landscape of America to which immigrant Muslims came and the inherent discriminations they encountered; 3) issues of integration, assimilation, and anonymity in the process of becoming American; 4) the development of Islamic institutions; and 5) relationships between indigenous and immigrant Muslims.

FORMATION OF THE COMMUNITY

The Muslim community is very much in process in the United States. The very first Muslims came unwillingly to the American continent several centuries ago as slaves brought from West Africa. The research of scholars such as Allan Austin and Sylvaine Diouf provide evidence of a substantial Islamic presence throughout the Atlantic slave trade, among them both professionals and religious scholars. Hard evidence of the practice of Islam among the slaves is meager. A few apparently were able to build Qur'an schools and teach the reading and writing of Arabic; for a time, some left artifacts for their descendants. For the most part, however, slaves were not allowed to practice the faith of Islam and were forced to convert to Christianity. Since the end of the slave trade, which lasted illegally until the 1930s, researchers have been trying to trace Islamic retentions in some areas of the southern states. As Diouf affirms, "What is clear is that [African Muslim slaves] introduced a second monotheistic religion into America. Islam was also the first revealed religion freely practiced—as opposed to imposed Christianity—by the Africans who were transported to the New World."[1]

The first immigrant Muslims to come to the United States of their own volition arrived in the mid- to late nineteenth century. Mainly Arabs from rural areas of greater Syria, Lebanon, Jordan, and Palestine, for the most part they came with the hope of earning money quickly and then returning home. Often lacking in both skills and education and usually with inadequate knowledge of English, they worked as peddlers, as petty merchants, in factories and mines, and in railroad construction.[2] Arab immigrants were soon joined by fellow religionists from many other parts of the world, including Indians (Punjabis) who settled in California, Albanians in the Midwest, and Tatars on the East Coast.[3]

Substantial communities of Muslims could not form in these early days of American Islam because of the restrictions of U.S. immigration laws. Therefore, in the nineteenth century there was really no impetus to begin the process of religious community formation. For the most part, these early Muslims came for better opportunities to enhance their personal fortunes, not to build Muslim communities in America or to proselytize. As it turned out, of course, many who expected to return home never did so, and as time passed they were joined by members of their families and by other Muslim immigrants.

The actual process of community building began in the twentieth century in both of the two major and distinct groupings that have come to constitute American Islam: the immigrants and those who have chosen to convert to the religion (or some interpretation of it). In the small immigrant community at the beginning of the twentieth century, the majority of Arabs tended to practice their faith, if at all, in private rather than in public and to deemphasize to whatever extent possible the fact that they were members of a "non-American" religion. They lived quietly, often turning to each other for social relationships and forming small groups and associations for companionship. Many sought complete assimilation into American culture, to the point of changing their Arab names to sound more like those of other Americans. The few South Asian immigrants went about the business of finding a home in the American environment in somewhat different ways than the Arabs. Some spent time working through the legal system trying to validate their Aryan ancestry so as to "prove" that they were part of mainly white Western culture.[4] Others actually did come to proselytize and in doing so illustrated a very different approach to Americanization. Each of these approaches to "being American" illustrates alternatives that have continued, along with many others, to be seen as possible ways for Muslims to exist in the American milieu. Converts to Islam at the beginning of the twentieth century, mainly African Americans, all embraced Islam as the "true" religion. While some of them looked to Islam as a means of aiding their nationalist goals of fighting against racism in the United States, others were drawn to a "color-blind" Islam that transcends ethnicity and culture.

The civil rights movement of the 1960s opened the doors for Muslim immigrants as it did for other non-European immigrants of color. In the movement's aftermath, the immigrant community initially established itself along two lines: students and "true" immigrants, the latter being those who came seeking employment. After 1965, immigrant Muslim students established Muslim student associations on almost every university campus across America. While some of these students did return home, influenced by their time abroad and in turn often themselves becoming influential in their own countries, others remained and assumed the leadership of Muslim professional and social organizations in the United States. By this time in American history, the "typical" Muslim immigrant looked very different from his or her earlier counterpart. Muslims on the whole were better educated, more economically advantaged, and generally competent in English. Often recruited to study and work in this country, they came as professionals in the fields of medicine, engineering, and other sciences prepared to join American middle and upper middle classes of the professionally successful. As students graduated and as the professionals established themselves, community was formed. Both Arab and South Asian immigrants began to build mosques, schools, and community centers in suburbs around many major cities.

Many Muslims have found themselves in a quandary when trying to decide how to participate in this society or whether it is even lawful for Muslims to take active part in a non-Muslim form of government. Sometimes they have seen their continued existence in the United States as a kind of abdication of leadership "at home." These debates continue today, although, particularly in the past several years, many American Muslims have determined that it is part of their responsibilities as Muslims, as well as U.S. citizens, to play as active a role as possible on the various levels of American society and politics. In other parts of the West (e.g., in Europe), Muslims have already answered many of these questions and are empowered by their participation in European governance. The resolution of these issues is intimately bound to the process of community formation.

Communities are presently still finding their American seating. By this I mean that they are still debating the positives and negatives of life in America. For immigrants, this ambivalence is heightened by American stereotypes of Muslims and Islam. The majority of the stereotypes relate specifically to the image of Islam in the Arab community since most westerners seem automatically to equate "Muslim" with "Arab." South Asian Muslims do not escape stereotyping, of course, but generally fall under a different set reserved for "Hindus." Even within the Muslim community in America itself, stereotyping is an issue, and Muslims often find themselves divided over racial/ethnic distinctions.

Many South Asian immigrant Muslims tend to be both politically liberal and religiously conservative, exhibiting a conservative tendency regarding social programs. Others are openly secular in orientation. These religious positions have dictated how mosques are built, who is permitted in, and what activities are available. In the conservative mosques, women are more or less out of sight, holding no leadership positions, although they may teach in the Islamic schools, and generally the mosque administration is not welcoming either to non-Muslims or to other Muslims of a different ethnicity. The more liberal community mosques, on the other hand, are more likely to have many classes for both believers and non-Muslims, and while women may be separated in the prayer areas, they often play active roles in the running of the mosque.

Arab immigrant Muslims have had more incentive to hold outreach forums for members of other religions. They have also had the Arab Christian community's expertise in dealing with media stereotypes. Generally, the mosques established by Arabs prior to the 1960s are liberal and have women on their administrative boards. Mosques established by Arabs in the past three decades tend to be conservative, and women often participate primarily as teachers in women's classes or in associated schools.

Immigrant Sunni Muslims have been faced with the diversity of Islam in America in other ways. Communities that have been deemed "heretical" in the Muslim world are present in America. The Ahmadiyyah movement, for example, has been responsible for almost all the Qur'ans, other Islamic literature, and knowledge about Islam in the first decades of the twentieth century as part of its *da'wa*, or missionary activity. This movement, which had its beginnings in India in the last decade of the nineteenth century and subsequently was banned in India and declared heretical in the Muslim world, is still active in the United States.[5] Sufism, though not declared heretical but nonetheless looked on with disdain by more legalistic Sunni Muslims (particularly in its more "popular" dimensions), is alive and well in the United States. Major Sufi orders, such as the Naqshabandis and the Tijanis, have organized themselves both inside and outside mosques. Their communities are increasing in number and size as they invite men and women to share equally in spiritual worship. Many of these communities also provide a number of activities for young adults, such as skating parties and bowling events.

Among the other immigrant Muslims who make up the balance of the community in America are Sunni refugees from East Africa and the Balkans, Shi'a Muslims who fled Iran or were expelled, and Shi'a (many Isma'ilis) from East Africa. Those refugees who were formally U.S. collaborators or who worked for American institutions in their home countries naturally have been given the most attention; their settling, in terms of housing, food, and jobs, has been relatively easy, as many of them are well educated and speak English. For most refugees, however, such has not been the case, and they have suffered severely through dislocation. Some, such as the Somalians and the Bosnians, have been forced to find residence in shelters and other places in which facilities are at a minimum. Fathers and husbands are often without work, and the language barrier has made getting around a traumatic adventure. Christian groups have been the primary agencies in securing their transport to the United States. Since they generally run the shelters to which the refugees are brought, there have been some complaints about the constant proselytizing. Though Muslims do not run social agencies, various mosques have tried to assist. Without the resources of the system, however, their aid usually is in the form of donations of food and clothing rather than making the connections that could provide needed housing and employment.[6]

All immigrant communities are obviously in the process of community building. Some funders have sued administrators over rising costs of ornate buildings, and some members have sued other members over slander. In most cities, feuds and differences that may characterize life in general are put aside when it is time for major celebrations. Even then, disagreements may emerge, such as when Arabs want to celebrate the end of Ramadan (the month of fasting) and the hajj (pilgrimage) at the same time as the rest of the Arab world, South Asians prefer to rely on American calendar calculations, and the smaller communities celebrate with the largest group. While there are strong movements within American Islam as a whole to resolve these differences, they can lead to misunderstandings both within the Muslim community and on the part of other Americans.

One of the most significant issues facing Muslims in America today is the integration of the many varieties of immigrant Islam with the Islam of the indigenous American community. The religion of Islam is dedicated to the ideal of one *Ummah*, or overall community, with no boundaries of race or ethnic identities. Because American culture continues to discriminate and to segregate, immigrant communities feel the tension between a religious imperative and a social norm. They are coming to realize that the idea of an integrated *Umma* is in reality a difficult goal to achieve in the American environment. Often it is easier for immigrants to try to maintain as much of the homogeneity of their home culture as possible in order to avoid this dilemma, although that too is difficult both because of the pressures of conformity in the United States and because the Muslim community in the United States is, in fact, so overwhelmingly diverse.

AMERICA AS HOST

Substantial Muslim immigration to the United States began with the change in American immigration law in 1964. This change came about as a direct result of the civil rights war waged by African Americans. Their fight for the right of person, property, and vote included the struggle for special legal rights for minorities who had been disenfranchised. Three avenues opened up for immigrant Muslims: 1) The United States began recruiting persons with skills in professions such as medicine, pharmacy, and engineering; 2) students were able to obtain visas for study, especially in the sciences; and 3) special programs for minorities provided seed monies for businesses that enabled those immigrants without professional training to have both the opportunity for and the realization of employment. Immigrants as well as American disenfranchised minorities formed "distinct identities" to take advantage of government funding. As Raymond Brady Williams observes, when the role of government in racial and ethnic relations underwent this kind of change, it encouraged the formation of communities along distinct ethnic lines. Thus, today, he says, most immigrants are classified as members of minority groups so that they can conform to affirmative action requirements of schools and businesses.[7] It is interesting to note here that the professional middle-class immigrants often have voted against these very programs that have assisted them in the process of making a viable community under the presumption that for them to show a stake in America, they too have to be "against minorities" despite their own minority status.

As a Christian nation whose terrain is still defined mainly by Protestant Christianity, along with a Constitution guaranteeing the freedom of religion, the United States is at once a place of freedom and a place of confusion. For many immigrant Muslims, the freedom to believe and practice their Islamic understandings or, if they choose, to break away from those Islamic under-standings is a kind of paradise. On the other hand, the need for a religious hi-erarchy in order to function as a religious community has led to tension and confusion. Since Islam technically does not have a clergy, positions of religious leadership have had to be created in the United States appropriate to the new context. Immigrant imams (religious leaders) imported to teach the Qur'an and/or Hadith literature find themselves playing roles that would never have been part of their responsibilities in Muslim countries. Once in the position of imam, these immigrant men often have found themselves in alien spaces. Many are thrown into roles as counselors, community activists, and partici-pants in interfaith dialogue, fund-raisers, and spokespersons for all Muslims when in fact they have little or no training and/or experience with American institutions and public space.

Religious leadership is thus one of the most significant issues facing the Muslim community in America today. Imams who are imported from Mus-lim countries need time to experience America and to understand the differ-ent kinds of expectations that may be placed on them here. They also need teachers to educate them about American strategies for discourse in the pub-lic space and about American issues and concerns. And they need support from other religious communities. American religious (largely Christian) leadership has not made a concerted effort to dispel hostility against Islam and Muslims in their congregations. It is only recently that some churches are beginning to recognize the importance of inviting scholars and/or members of local mosques to speak with their congregations about Islam. Until this changes, the landscape will continue to have many land mines as far as Mus-lims are concerned.

What is clear is that for one part of the community, there is tension about what becoming American means and what it costs, while for significant oth-ers, the tension relates to what Islam is and how they understand their iden-tity as Muslims. Since the process of community building is less than a cen-tury old and has not begun with real seriousness until fairly recently, it is not anywhere near completion. Given the religious and ethnic landscape of Amer-ica today, however, it is certainly dynamic. The two original strands in the im-migrant community—Arab and South Asian—have multiplied as newer immigrants have come with a range of new political and philosophical posi-tions. The limitless possibilities for "being" in America have served as the impetus for the formulation of new and unprecedented ways of understanding what it means to be an American Muslim/Muslim American.

Almost every movement in the Muslim world is present in the body of immigrant American Muslims. There are those who have been educated in either the United States, Canada, or Europe who consider themselves "modern" and are indeed westernized in their opinions of Islam. There are also those whose Western education has led them to very conservative Islamic understandings, almost as a backlash against Western stereotypes of Islam and Muslims. Some use their American freedom of speech to join the Western chorus on the backwardness of their homelands, while still others use their American opportunities for wealth to aid causes and to influence politics at "home." Immigrant Muslims are still very much in the process of seeing themselves as Americans and focusing on American concerns. Issues of assimilation, acculturation, segregation, and anonymity are very much priorities and command prominence in texts, articles, e-mail conversations, and other forms of communication.

Another serious problem facing all immigrant Muslims, and particularly Arabs, is that of persistent hostility and unfair discrimination due to the prevailing stereotypes. When the first large numbers of immigrants came to the United States, they were treated "special"—like all minorities of color. Letters were written home about the shock many immigrants experienced when they found themselves the victims of discrimination and segregation. Egyptian feminist Nawal El-Saadawi talks about the confusion of trying to figure out which bathroom to enter—white or colored. While obviously there have been many changes in the American environment in terms of consciousness raising, affirmative action, and other attempts to meet the challenge of racism, stereotyping of Muslims and Arabs has continued with little abatement. Much of this seems to be due to the efforts of the media and film industries, which since the late 1970s and the Iranian Revolution have often been especially guilty of presenting a negative picture of Islam and Muslims.

In the epic films of the first few decades of the twentieth century, Muslims and/or Islam were often the subject of fantasy and wild flights of imagination. Much more damaging has been the more recent activity of the film industry, which, when treating the Muslim world or Muslims in interaction with the West, all too often has painted Islam as a fanatical religion with violent followers. As the media define for the general American public who Muslims are and what Islam is, Muslims find themselves under siege in public spaces, in school, and at work. But Muslims have been fighting back using American tools. When movies such as *Executive Decision, Under Siege, Savior,* and *The Mummy* were in production, Muslim organizations, such as the American Muslim Council and the Council on American Islamic Relations, jumped into action. They have attempted to assist directors and producers in thinking about the image of Islam and Muslims they are portraying. These interactions have been somewhat successful in eliminating the more outrageously negative portrayals of Islam and Muslims, though the film industry on occasion continues to make movies that present some objectionable aspect of Islam.

Print media have provided another source of angst in the Muslim community as journalists persist in writing articles focused on veils, Islam, and terrorism. While some journalists write sympathetically about the need for a better understanding of Islam, others are presenting statistics about the rapid growth of Islam in America today in such a way as to strike terror in the hearts of readers. The focus on the violence in the Muslim world has devastating consequences for members of the American Muslim community who are connected by ethnicity and religion. Muslims have been held suspect when they have tried to give financial aid to orphanages in the West Bank or hospitals in Gaza, being accused of supporting Hamas or some other "terrorist" group. While the "media terrorism" has remained directed largely to the Arab world, Muslims of different backgrounds experience hostility in a variety of ways based on either their ethnicity or their citizenship status. Black African Muslims experience the same discrimination as black Americans. South Asian Muslims experience the consequences of the stereotypes reserved for "Hindus."

ISSUES OF INTEGRATION, ASSIMILATION, AND ANONYMITY

Early immigrants to the United States, as has often been observed, generally did not arrive with the idea that they were remaining permanently. They came for the purpose of earning some money and returning home and thus made little effort to learn English or become members of the community. Those that did see the United States as their final destination began the process of Americanization. They assimilated and largely disappeared into the landscape by changing or Anglicizing their names, marrying non-Muslim women, and abandoning Islamic practices though not always Islamic belief. Some of the immigrants who came in large numbers after the change in immigration policies also did not initially think they would stay in the United States, resisting assimilation insofar as possible. As the time for departure gets more and more indefinite and they realize that they probably will not return home, these immigrants find themselves in tension between resisting assimilation and accepting the acculturation that in varying degrees has already taken place. It is difficult for them not to want the "American dream" of wealth and happiness for their children.

Many immigrant Muslims, of course, know that they came intending to stay and are trying to find ways in which to have the best of both worlds. Those who are middle-class or wealthy professionals have assimilated but have fought acculturation by spending a significant amount of time in their old "home" culture. Immigrant Muslims are acutely aware of the possibility of losing touch with Islamic beliefs and practices. Given the legacy of the "free-love" era in the West (which enshrined free choice in matters of sex, sexual preference, recreational drug, and alcohol use) and other practices seen as antithetical to Muslim belief and practice, Muslims have been justifiably fearful for their children in American society. Many have enjoyed a relative anonymity that has permitted them to remain more or less untouched by the "goings-on" in American life, even though their children have been exposed to most everything. As the profile of Islam and Muslims was heightened in the media and the numbers of immigrant Muslims increased, including significant numbers of refugees in the past decade, anonymity has become virtually impossible. The tensions between assimilation and acculturation remain issues in the process of community building. Acculturation is hotly debated in the community and is a special concern when it comes to the building of mosques and schools, which suggests permanence. Most immigrants favor a blend of assimilation and acculturation where they can benefit from the luxuries and educational and financial opportunities that America provides and become mainstream Americans in their political and social attitudes.

Assimilation, for those who can afford it, has often meant moving into all-white suburbs, making sure that children receive the "best" education, go to the "right" universities, claim the "right" profession, and eschew any political and social activism that has its seating among the poor and/or disenfranchised. Energies are to be directed toward finding marriage partners, forming professional organizations, and engaging in political and social activism only insofar as it affects Muslims in their ethnic community.

Those immigrants who are blue-collar workers populate the cities in clus-
ters. Many are resigned to "just making a living" and sending a little money
back home. Second-generation Muslims are generally assimilated and acculturated to a significant degree. These young adults have been schooled in
America and for the most part accept American values, though they are keenly
aware of their ethnic Islamic heritage. They represent a kind of "American Islam with a foreign tint," comfortable for the most part with this identity although frequently reminded that they are still somehow different from mainstream American society.

Despite the relative success of their general efforts at acculturation and/or
assimilation, Muslims continue to face obstacles in the path of their acceptance in America. Americans often find it difficult to accept immigrants who
come from countries that are not considered friends of this nation, and relations are highly conditioned by the government's attitude toward the Muslim
world. Many non-Muslim Americans believe that Muslim immigrants are taking jobs meant for them, that they want to impose Islamic fundamentalism on
American society, that they are somehow linked to or supportive of terrorism,
and that their existence in this country constitutes a serious societal threat to
an accepted way of life. While immigrants have been successful in some areas
(e.g., in combating blatant housing or employment discrimination), experiences of hostility and sometimes even hate crimes against themselves or their
mosques remind them that they have some distance to go before acceptance.
Meanwhile, immigrant Muslims continue to build institutions along the lines
of other religious communities.

INSTITUTIONS

One of the clear determinants of the extent to which a group has successfully
"Americanized" is the number and quality of institutions they have been able
to build. Immigrant Muslims have sought to put their stake in the land in the
time-honored fashion. Arab and South Asian Muslim immigrants have introduced into the American landscape a synthesis of architectural styles from all
over the Muslim world. Millions of dollars have been and are being spent in
the attempt to replicate the splendor of mosques in the Muslim world. The
number of Islamic schools has increased over the past decade with a significant number expanding their curriculum to include high school. Nearly 500
schools across the nation are listed on the Web. Both mosques and schools are

facing a number of challenges, both expected and unexpected, and most are meeting those challenges. Many mosques were built with large spaces available for prayer but with inadequate room for educational facilities or for community activities. Where possible, these problems have been remedied by additions. Communities have learned that they need space for activities for youth, teens, and young adults and that those activities are expanding in variety. One *masjid* (mosque) in Chicago has recently increased its classes to include counseling for married couples and tutoring for children in grades 7 to 12.

African immigrant Muslims, often with less substantial resources than some other immigrant groups, are buying buildings and restoring them rather than buying land and then building. Interestingly, among the immigrant groups, these communities are the most diverse, as Muslims from a variety of different nations all worship together. Many African Americans have also joined these communities.

Institutions of other kinds are also being built as Muslims provide facilities for political action groups, refugee centers, and social work groups. In areas where buying residential complexes is possible, Muslims are availing themselves of the opportunities. In Orange County, California, the largest mosque provides housing for Bosnian refugees on its grounds. Muslims from the country formerly known as Champus (now a part of Cambodia) have bought a housing complex in Santa Ana to house refugees and immigrants from that region. The number of shelters for abused women is also increasing with facilities in Chicago, Atlanta, New York, Philadelphia, and Los Angeles. Institution building is being done in American ways, though each has both its own ethnic flavor and an Islamic overlay.

THE RELATIONSHIPS BETWEEN INDIGENOUS AND IMMIGRANT MUSLIMS

Interaction, cooperation, and exchange between immigrant and indigenous Muslims have always been a sensitive subject. On the one hand is the post-/neocolonial personality of the immigrant and on the other the denigrated personality of the indigenous Muslim (African American, Native American, Hispanic, and other). Both are oppressed and fighting for recognition from the majority community, and both know that America is fertile ground for some acceptance by mainstream America if they are first to present an American Islam. Immigrants who have suffered in the Muslim world from colonial

and then Muslim oppression "just want to get along" and support their families. It is those immigrants whose families were wealthy and/or professional or
who have been educated in America who seem to be the accepted voices of Islam in America. Even though their education has been Western, their ethnic
version of Islam is pushed as a remedy for America's ills and as the only "true
Islam." Immigrants in this category have laid out what Islam is and have offered their definition to indigenous Muslims without recognizing that American Muslims whose families have converted to Islam also think they have a
definition of Islam that is not ethnically bound.

African Americans have had a more tortuous experience with Islamic definition. They are now learning the history of Islam in this country as they reflect on the permutations that Islamic representations have undergone in the
twentieth century. Though there were both Sunni and non-Sunni Islamic
presences in the United States in the first few decades of the twentieth century
and a significant presence of indigenous Muslims by 1965, when most of the
immigrant Muslims were let into the United States, immigrants have tended
to assert that there were no Muslims until they arrived. The tension between
the two groups is now growing at a rapid pace. There are several significant
arenas of contention, including the definition of Islam and who has the right
to contribute to that definition, who is authoritative in Islamic discourse, and
the constantly recurring reality of racism.

The immigrant community has at least ten times the wealth of the African,
Hispanic, European, and Native American community. They therefore have the
best facilities, including those for providing Islamic schooling, and can take advantage of ready access to the Muslim world. Many immigrants have attempted
to share this knowledge with the indigenous community, but their efforts have
been hampered because they have failed to respect the learning accomplished
in the indigenous community about Islam and America. A vivid example of the
tension between the groups presented itself in the 2000 presidential election
when the immigrant community, which was just beginning to pay some attention to the political process, came out for George W. Bush without any consultation with other Muslim constituents. The arrogance displayed in projecting
the image that the entire Muslim community favored Bush, discounting indigenous Muslims as if they did not exist, has forever left a mark of distrust.

The political concerns of immigrant Muslims have consistently focused on
events and circumstances overseas, with little or no attention paid to the

plight of the oppressed communities in America to which many of the indigenous Muslims belong. The racism and class/status consciousness of immigrant Muslims is felt keenly by African American Muslims who feel that they count only when someone wants to know how many Muslims there are in this country or when some overseas donor wants to know about Islam in America. The divide only widens when a researcher looks at the process of diversification in the communities. The fact is that most indigenous Muslims feel unwelcome at immigrant mosques and at immigrant celebrations. Indigenous Muslims worry that the "color blindness" of Islam is slowly slipping away and giving in rapidly to American racism. This was brought home especially to African American Muslims at the time of the arrest in March 2000 of Jamil Al-Amin in Atlanta. Imam Al-Amin was widely sought after for lectures at immigrant-sponsored conventions because of his reputation as "an excellent Muslim who had been converted to Islam from the violence of the Black Power movement." At the time of the incident that eventually led to his arrest, however, several prominent groups who had recruited him to sit on their boards turned their backs and circulated rumors speculating that he was possibly guilty and should turn himself in. These same organizations, however, have asked the African American Muslim community to rally behind any effort to support Arab Muslims arrested on "secret evidence" and Palestinian, Bosnian, and Somalian issues. African Americans have shown their support financially and by their presence at rallies. The case of Imam Al-Amin may prove to be another great divide in the future.

While clearly there are many difficult aspects to the experiences of American Muslims both within the Islamic community and between Muslims and the rest of American society, there also are many hopeful indications. While some Americans continue to fear and sometimes even resent or hate Muslim presence in this country and while prejudicial representations have not fully abated, much of American society acknowledges and even accepts the growing plurality of this culture. Efforts of major Muslim organizations and institutions, often assisted by individuals and organizations outside the community, are bringing results in addressing incidents of prejudicial treatment and in providing more accurate information about Islam and its adherents.

Within the Muslim community itself, there are also significant changes occurring. As second- and third-generation immigrants increasingly find their identity as Americans (and not necessarily hyphenated Americans), ties to the "old country" weaken, and efforts to affirm a common American Islam are given new impetus. Both immigrant and indigenous youth provide bright lights on the horizon of this emerging American Islam. Many of the immigrant youth, though not completely disassociating themselves from their cultural Islamic heritage, are rejecting the efforts of their parents and grandparents to define Islam in culture-specific terms. They also understand the dangers of racist assumptions and are working to create an American Islam that meets the challenges of its own egalitarian ideology. This author prays that the perspective and balance of these young American Muslims will prevail.

NOTES

1. Sylvaine Diouf, *Servants of Allah: African Muslims Enslaved in the Americas* (New York: New York University Press, 1998), 1.

2. Yvonne Haddad and Adair Lummis, *Islamic Values in the United States: A Comparative Study* (New York: Oxford University Press, 1987). Many studies have been done on this early phase of immigration by scholars building on Haddad and Lummis's work.

3. Information taken from Gutbi Mahdi, "Muslim Organizations in the United States," in *The Muslims of America,* ed. Yvonne Y. Haddad (New York: Oxford University Press, 1991), 11–12.

4. According to Kathleen Moore, ignorance on the part of U.S. immigration officials led to arbitrary classification of regions of the world where people of color lived and thus the world of Islam. Some immigrants from the Arab Muslim world were classified as "Turks from Asia," while all Muslims from India were classified as "Hindus." Who was "white" depended on popular opinion, and thus most Muslims were rejected in the early decades of the twentieth century. Moore also informs us that there were a few cases of Muslims declaring they were indeed "white" because of their "Aryan ancestry." Kathleen Moore, *Al-Mughtaribun* (Albany: State University of New York Press, 1995).

5. For more information, see Jane Smith, *Islam in America* (New York: Columbia University Press, 1999), 74–75.

6. Interview with Imam Nur in St. Louis, Missouri, 1999.

7. See Raymond Brady Williams, *Religions of Immigrants from India and Pakistan* (New York: Cambridge University Press, 1988), 21–22.

10

Constructing the American Muslim Community

M. A. MUQTEDAR KHAN

Identity formation is a complex process that allows for the intervention of both historical and material forces and human agency. In the specific case of the Muslim community in North America, one can clearly see that both historical forces and political agencies are shaping the emerging identity of American Muslims, the political forces both local and global in nature. In this chapter, I identify and examine the historical and political forces that are constructing the American Muslim.

It is important to understand identities, for they shape the interests and determine the actions and interactions of human agents. Identity is essential to understanding society and politics insofar as human actions and behavior are often geared toward representation of themselves. Identity is often the driving force behind politics and cannot be overlooked.[1] I take identity seriously. I believe that politics and identity are inseparable, and thus the process of identity construction is political and has political consequences.[2]

In seeking to examine how a particular community transforms as well as reproduces itself in a foreign environment, this chapter ventures into the realm where identities compete, clash, and impact each other at several levels. When we ask how Muslims are becoming American Muslims, we are essentially inquiring how the demands of being American and being Muslim coexist within a singular self. Care must be taken to understand some of the philosophical dilemmas inherent to such an undertaking. What do we mean when we use a double adjective such as "American Muslim"? Are we describing an American who is a Muslim, a Muslim who lives in America, or someone essentially distinct from the two?

There is a large group of Americans who are Muslim by conversion. We are here referring to individuals whose first identity, chronologically and not necessarily politically, is American (Islam came later). A large section of the African American community would fit this description. There are hundreds of thousands of white Americans who have converted to Islam, but they do not really constitute a distinct community.[3] In the literature on Islam in America, African American Muslims are referred to as "indigenous Muslims" and sometimes fondly as "Al-Ansar." Indigenous Muslims are roughly 25 to 30 percent of the entire Muslim population in the United States. In a sense, most indigenous Muslims can be described as Americans who are Muslims without prejudice toward American or Muslim identity.[4]

The immigrant Muslims, who constitute about 70 to 75 percent of Muslims in America, are a diverse lot. Roughly one-third of them are from the Middle East and Africa and two-thirds from South Asia. These Muslims do form a cohesive community, and a large section of this community sees itself as Muslims who live in America. Nostalgia for the countries they left behind and ideological alienation from the West have contributed to a great extent to the self-perception of the members of this community as Muslims in America. Even though they maintain that Islamic identity alone is of primary importance, they do not resist the ethnic associations of their origins. Thus, for instance, one encounters several institutions that affirm Arab American and Pakistani American identities.[5]

It is the central thesis of this chapter that a third identity, the American Muslim identity, is rapidly emerging.[6] Political as well as historical forces are constructing it. The interplay between American values and Islamic values and the mutual reconstitution of each other is leading to a liberal understanding of Islam more in tune with dominant American values such as religious tolerance, democracy, pluralism, and multicultural and multireligious coexistence. It is in an attempt to create a uniquely American interpretation of Islam that the Muslims of America are giving expression to their American experience.

AMERICA A MOVING TARGET

Identities are not only constructed but are constantly produced and reproduced through social practices and identity discourses. In relatively stable environments, where there is a widespread consensus on notions of the collective self and what is to be valued, identities remain relatively stable. However, when values are continuously questioned and challenged, identities become contested and remain constantly in flux.[7]

The American social and cultural environment is highly dynamic. It is constantly challenged from within as new social movements arise to question established cultural and moral norms and destabilize social equilibrium. It is also challenged from outside as new immigrants flood it, bringing with them competing social, religious, and moral values. While it is beyond the scope of this chapter to try to map the fluctuating contours of American society, it must be noted that who or what is an American is not a stable or uncontested notion.

The substantive meaning of being American varies across race, religion, and ethnicity and is also evolving over time. Becoming American for individuals as well as communities is like hitting a moving target. Over a million new immigrants every year continue to add to the cultural richness of America, and the ever-expanding demand for civil rights and freedoms is opening America wider to new lifestyles and cultural manifestations. Thus, even as immigrant and emerging countries fight for acceptance and adjust to America's mainstream, the idea of who is an American has become increasingly unstable and contested.[8] I once remarked to a Muslim friend, a Caucasian woman from the backwaters of Florida, that "a love affair with the university and the discovery of my liberal self" best describes my American experience. When I asked her to describe her American experience, she replied that it was "discovering Islam and becoming a Muslim." It is safe to claim that "discovering the other" has in a sense become the essence of the American experience.

There are several trends in American society. The explosion of liberalism in the past three decades and the resurgence of conservatism in the 1990s are suggestive of the dynamic character of the American social milieu. The steady movement toward cultural pluralism has resulted in a completely radical reconceptualization of America as a multicultural society rather than a melting pot. The oversold idea that America is now a multicultural society has opened up social spaces to create cultural ghettoes secure from any guilt of isolation and free of any criticism for not getting with the program.

Muslims have flirted with notions of building an Islamopolis, a city where Muslims could live according to Islamic laws and culture within the United States. But a comparison of the so-called Mormon model of physical isolation with the Jewish model of political and cultural integration as ways of coping with America has led most Muslims to reject the former in favor of the latter. In fact, the Mormon option really does not exist anymore. There is no "uninhabited Utah" to which the Muslims could go. Besides, most Muslims came to America to partake in its vitality and prosperity, not to get away from it.

The decision to participate in the mainstream of American life was unconsciously made by a large section of the community.[9] There have been a few attempts here and there to create Muslim enclaves, but they failed. Some prominent areas in Chicago and Detroit are predominantly Muslim, but they are not independent of America's day-to-day existence. But to participate in American life, Muslims in America had to have a conception of what it means to be an American. Thus, defining America became the first step in the process that has led to the Americanization of life.

TWO IMAGES OF AMERICA

There are clearly two images of America—"America the democracy" and "America the colonial power"—that exist in Muslim minds. Muslims who focus on the "inside" are fascinated and excited by the political freedom available to its citizens. They understand and appreciate the vitality of its economy, its culture, and its ethics of competition and free enterprise. Most of all, they are deeply enamored of what they call "Islamic values in action," such as consultative governance (democratic processes), religious freedom, and cultural and political pluralism. For these Muslims, the relative opportunity to practice Islam and build Islamic movements and institutions in America, when compared to the presently autocratic Muslim world, remains the most thrilling aspect of American life. And it is to this aspect that they respond. For them, America is liberal, democratic, tolerant, and multicultural.

There is also a competing image of America. Muslims who focus primarily on U.S. foreign policy see America as an evil force—a colonial power dominating the Muslim world, stealing its resources, and depriving it of its freedoms and right to self-determination. Many Muslims also believe that the United States is anti-Islam and seeking to globalize its immoral culture. They find America's uncritical support of Israel, even as Israel oppresses the Palestinian population and massacres its young people, to be proof of its evil motives. The complete devastation of Iraq and the incredible hardships caused by the U.S.-sponsored sanctions are seen as further evidence of American intentions to destroy and eliminate Islam and Muslims. These Muslims have trouble reconciling America's benign attitude toward Muslims at home with the consequences of its malevolent foreign policy.[10]

The leaders of Islamic organizations such as the Islamic Society of North America (ISNA) and the Islamic Circle of North America (ICNA); of Islamic political institutions such as the Council on American Islamic Relations (CAIR), the American Muslim Council (AMC), and the American Muslim Alliance (AMA); and of Islamic intellectual initiatives such as the Association of Muslim Social Scientists (AMSS) and the North American Fiqh Council all share the first image of America. It is not that they are indifferent or blind to American foreign policy excesses. They recognize it and are critical and frequently voice their displeasure and condemnation of unqualified support to Israel and the inhuman sanctions against Iraq. But they also understand the need to build a strong, vibrant, and thriving Islamic community in America. And in the interest of establishing Islam in America, they focus more on the "inside" than the "outside." In defining the goals and interests of Muslims in America, these institutions have emphasized "America the democracy" identity over "America the colonial power."

The difference between these two images is often directly related to where Muslims imagine their homes. Those who still see the countries of their origin as "home" are more focused on U.S. foreign policy and are resentful toward and distrustful of America. Those Muslims who imagine the United States as their home and the homeland of their progeny are more concerned with establishing Islam in America and are excited by the opportunities they see. Muslims who wish to make America their homeland dominate American Muslim leadership. Largely because of this group, Islamic activism in the area of politics and in the realm of religious life is well on its way toward what one may call Americanization.[11]

Henceforth in this chapter, when I refer to the American identity or use a phrase such as "becoming American," I am referring to "America the democracy" identity. That is the target on which Muslims in America have focused. They wish to partake in American democracy as an equal constituent. Indeed, they even imagine themselves as playing a morally significant role in making America a better, more God-fearing and tolerant society.

ASPIRATIONS OF THE AMERICAN MUSLIM COMMUNITY

Muslims who entertained a negative image of America before arriving often have been surprised by the relative freedom they enjoy in the United States.

Muslim immigrants who started coming to the United States from the early 1960s on had already tasted the elixir of Islamic revivalist fervor and also tasted the brutality and autocracy of their own governments who were interested in either crushing or co-opting emerging Islamic movements. When those belonging to various Islamic movements (e.g., the Muslim Brotherhood and the Jamaat-e-Islami) came to America, they soon discovered the opportunity that America provides.

In a society where there is political and religious freedom, Muslims could quickly organize and freely establish the kinds of Islamic movements that are constantly repressed in the heartlands of the Muslim world. While many Americans clearly evidence hostility and prejudice toward Islam and Muslims, it is nothing compared to the stifling character of despotic regimes in Egypt, Iraq, Iran, Saudi Arabia, Libya, Sudan, and Palestine (under Israeli colonialism). The easiest and often the only way for these Muslims to come to America was through the route of higher education. They came, they got their doctorates in natural and social sciences, and they stayed to create a critical mass of intellectual Muslim elite in the United States. The nature of the immigration became a filtering process allowing only the better-educated and intellectually sophisticated individuals to enter from the Arab world. Within this flow of Muslim professionals and scholars escaping poverty and poor economies from India, Pakistan, and Bangladesh came a Muslim leadership capable of articulating enlightened self-interest and formulating a far-reaching vision for the revival of Islam and Islamic values.[12]

The Islamists who have found themselves in leadership positions in the emerging American Muslim community have had one overriding goal: to revive the Islamic civilization.[13] They strongly believe that the key to reviving Islamic civilization is the intellectual revival of the *Ummah*, or Islamic, community. Intellectuals such as Ismail al Faruqi and his Islamization of Knowledge project and Seyyed Hossein Nasr and his Islamic philosophy and Islamic sciences project are illustrative of this thinking. The establishment of the AMSS[14] was one of the first steps in structuring this kind of revivalist thinking within an institutional setting. The freedom to rethink the Islamic civilizational project and to indulge in serious rejuvenation of the stagnant Islamic sciences has not been available in the Muslim world.

The freedom available in the West led to further institutional development of this revivalist agenda and specifically to the establishment of the Interna-

tional Institute of Islamic Thought (IIIT) in Virginia and the Islamic Foundation in Leicester, United Kingdom. Both are think tanks dedicated to intellectual revival of Muslims. The idea was simple. Freedom of religion and thought
in the West and in America in particular would be utilized to produce Islamic
ideas and ideologies. These would then be exported back to the Muslim world,
where they would be tested or introduced in hopes of stimulating and galva-
nizing social and religious reform. Both centers produce prolific literature in
the forms of books and journals on various aspects of Islamic sciences and social sciences. The most spectacular of such endeavors was the establishment of
the International Islamic University (IIU) Malaysia.

IIU Malaysia is a product of American Muslim expertise and Malaysian resources. The president of IIIT, who was also a founder member and president
of AMSS, Abdul Hameed Abu Sulayman, left the United States to take over as
the rector of IIU Malaysia. He took with him not only the ideas of Ismail al
Faruqi (i.e., the Islamization project) but also many Muslim social scientists
and intellectuals who had bloomed in the free and challenging environment
of American academia. There he sought to unite the so-called secular and sacred sciences in an attempt to create a generation of Muslim students well
versed in modern as well as traditional knowledge, the essential ingredient for
the reconstruction of a thriving Islamic civilization.[15]

Muslim leaders of this generation also created Islamic political organizations such as CAIR, AMC, AMA, the Muslim Political Action Committee
(MPAC), the Kashmiri American Council (KAC), and American Muslims for
Jerusalem (AMJ),[16] using the resources of the American Muslim community
to fight for freedom, democracy, and self-determination in the Muslim world.
These organizations are trying to increase their political and economic influence in the United States in the hope that it can be leveraged to improve the
condition of the Muslim world.[17]

In the United States, the emerging leadership realized that the single most
important goal was not to assimilate and disappear into the great melting pot,
like those who had come before them, but rather to defend and consolidate Islamic identity. Muslims were not here to assimilate. They were here to be accepted. Thus, the development of the American Muslim community in the
past three decades, at least among the immigrants, can be divided into two
phases. The first phase entailed consolidation of the Islamic identity, and the
second phase entailed making an impact on American society.

To realize these goals, an extensive network of Islamic centers and Islamic schools and institutions have grown up within the past three decades. Several Islamic movements, such as ISNA, ICNA, and the Islamic Assembly of North America (IANA), emerged to galvanize momentum and fervor in adherence of Islamic practices so that the Islamic identity of the immigrant community did not dissipate. Traditionalist movements, such as the Tablighi Jamaat, focusing on ritual purity and revival, have taken roots along with the Sufi movements, such as the Naqshbandis.[18]

The leadership of the intellectual elite, the resonant echo of the Islamic revivalist fervor of the Muslim world, the gradual transformation of America from melting pot to a multicultural society, and the rapid rate of conversion of Americans, both white and black, all provided energy and momentum for the sustenance of Islamic practices in America. Unlike other ethnic immigrant and religious communities, the Islamic community has enjoyed the great advantage that comes from conversions. When the Italians and the Greeks and others came to the United States, they too struggled with the issue of assimilation and identity. But unlike the Muslim community that wins new converts, there was no such case of American Greeks or African Americans converting to Italian ethnicity or Anglo-Saxon Americans becoming Greek American. Even as assimilation took many away, reversion and conversion to Islam brought many new believers within the fold and kept the critical mass of the community sufficiently large to preclude complete assimilation.[19]

Thus, we can summarize the aspirations of American Muslim leadership as follows:

1. Defending the Islamic identity of Muslims in America against assimilation
2. Developing intellectual and political resources capable of making significant social and political changes in the Muslim world

In the pursuit of these goals, the American Muslim identity has gradually emerged as the community coped and adjusted to challenges within and without.[20]

INTERNAL AND EXTERNAL CHALLENGES

The American Muslim leadership realized that the challenges to becoming fully accepted and respected participants in American democracy were two-dimensional. First, there were barriers to acceptance posed by an ignorance of Islam and prejudice toward Arabs and Muslims widespread in American society and nurtured meticulously by its political leadership and media.[21] There was also resistance to adjustment within the community itself that would pose a major barrier to engagement with the American mainstream. Both challenges, internal and external, impacted the goals that the American Muslim community had set for itself.

Resisting Assimilation

Prejudice against Islam in the American mainstream has presented a significant barrier to the practice of Islam. Every time there is a major political development in the Middle East, American newspapers and television programs unleash attacks on Islam and its values. Islam has been and is still presented as an irrational, undemocratic faith opposed to equality, freedom, and peace. The Western imagery of Islam as antithetical to Western values has made it difficult for Muslims in the past to declare their commitment to Islam in public.

The demonization of Islam in the media and the prejudice, hatred, and intolerance it bred has sometimes made practicing Islam in the public arena a dangerous prospect. Muslim women wearing head scarves have often been discriminated against in the workplace, screened out at the interview stage, refused promotion, or even let go. In the public schools, some administrators have sent Muslim girls home for wearing the head scarf. Girls have suffered consequences for refusing to wear revealing clothes in gym classes or in the swimming pool. Social interactions in the workplace, which often takes familiarity between people of different gender as given, is alien to many Muslim women. Ignorance of Islamic gender practices also has led to deliberate or unintended discrimination of Muslims. Work environments that lack sensitivity to Muslim needs tend to become hostile.[22]

Men have faced discrimination for wearing beards or caps and for wanting a longer break on Fridays to offer the congregational Friday prayers. Both men and women have had trouble getting days off for Islamic festivals. Many Muslim scholars and intellectuals have faced discrimination while seeking jobs in higher education, particularly if they write about politics, especially in the Middle East, from an Islamic perspective. The pressure to "become normal"—to consume alcohol at parties, to eat non-*halal* food, or to participate freely in mixed environment—remains very high. Muslim men in responsible positions have found that their careers can be jeopardized because Islamic etiquette and dietary laws marginalize them socially.

Ignorance about and hostility toward Islam continue to present several challenges. The pressure to assimilate (i.e., to "normalize") was and still remains very high. Early Muslim immigrants often adopted Americanized versions of their names to hide their Islamic identity and even their "foreignness." "Muhammad" became "Mo," and "Ali" became "Al." (As the size of the Muslim community in America has grown, such practices have become less common.) Schooling of children has raised particular problems as Muslim families recognized that American public schools offered reasonable education at no cost but did not inculcate Islamic values. The food was not *halal*, and the stories and the lessons were based on either Christian folklore or secular ethos. Children found it difficult to resist wanting to be like their peers. And most parents struggling to establish themselves in their careers found that they had little time to provide their children with the religious and cultural education that they needed.

Many Muslims were neither disturbed nor concerned with this. They were happy with their material success and tried to gain acceptance within the mainstream culture by distancing themselves from Islam and Islamic practices. For those who were not keen on defending their Islamic identity, life in America was wonderful. Many had realized the American dream and all that was left was to enjoy the prosperity and freedom available in America. Many of these Muslims, however, began to reaffirm their Islamic identity and values as their children grew up and were subject to the social ills of American society, such as sexual promiscuity, drugs, moral indifference, and other negative behaviors. Some still remain assimilated, finding themselves on the fringe of both the Islamic society in America and the American society.

But many Muslims who came to America for political and economic reasons are determined to resist assimilation. They answered the call from the Islamists and Muslim intellectuals and *Dawah* workers to join the various Islamic movements that mushroomed in the 1970s and 1980s. The first thing that Islamists did was to take over the National Arab Students Association and dissolve it. They replaced it with the National Muslim Students Association (MSA). The National MSA and its branches in various campuses started working with local communities to establish small Islamic *Halaqas* (study circles) and *Musallahs* (prayer centers) in classrooms or rented apartments.

Gradually, with the help of the Muslim leadership that was graduating from schools and outgrowing the MSAs, these small communities started establishing Islamic centers. Fortunately for them, in the late 1970s the Gulf states had become cash rich with the rise in oil prices. Many of them gave generously to Muslim communities all over the world seeking to establish mosques and Islamic schools. Some of the most important Islamic centers, such as those in Washington, D.C., and New York, were built with such generous donations.[23]

With some foothold in communities and universities, Islamic movements began to fight against the pressure to assimilate. In the 1970s and 1980s, the response was purely defensive, as the primary focus was to build large numbers of Islamic centers and Islamic schools. Islamic centers and their activities kept the adults in touch with their beliefs and their heritage, and Islamic schools taught Islamic values and inculcated Islamic practices among the young. Now there are more than 2,000 Islamic centers and 1,200 Islamic schools in North America.[24]

These centers also became the hubs for activities by Muslims who in their countries of origin belonged to various Islamic movements. For example, the Tablighi Jamaat, an Islamic movement focused on Islamic rituals, quickly took root in many mosques, especially in Florida, Chicago, upstate New York, and New York City. This apolitical and mildly spiritual movement is one of the biggest Islamic movements in North America with more than 100,000 participants. It is a loose network of activists who encourage each other to pray regularly.

Similarly, ISNA and then ICNA expanded, centering their activities on Islamic centers. Gradually, all the Islamic movements began holding annual national and regional conventions bringing scholars from North America and the Muslim world to large convention centers where thousands of Muslims converge every year to listen to lectures on Islam and participate in various community- and faith-related workshops. Currently, the annual convention of ISNA attracts more than 35,000 participants and 1,000 scholars. The regional Tablighi *ijtimas* (gatherings) attract anywhere between 10,000 and 15,000 attendees. The ICNA averaged between 10,000 and 12,000 participants at its annual conventions. At all these conventions, Muslim scholars and intellectuals from North America and the rest of the Muslim world mingle with American Muslims and one another, providing a kind of sneak preview to the Islamic civilization that Muslims dream about.

Fighting Prejudice

By the beginning of the 1990s, the community as well as the leadership became more confident.[25] A new generation of American Muslims had grown
up. Some were lost, but many of the young American Muslims have done their
senior generation proud. They are confident, successful, and deeply committed to Islam and the well-being of the Muslim *Ummah*. The American landscape is now dotted with Islamic landmarks. American Muslims believe that it
is time to have the same impact on American culture.[26] While the senior generation was content to defend, the new generation is eager to be more proac-
tive. They are not satisfied with the mere preservation of Islamic identity.
They want it accepted and recognized as a constituent element of the American identity itself.

The increase in confidence has resulted in three major changes. The first is
the emergence of CAIR and the culture of "action alert activism." CAIR is a
watchdog organization seeking to combat prejudice against Islam. It specializes in fighting negative stereotypes of Muslims and demonization of Islam in
the media and discrimination in the workplace. Now when employers fire
Muslim women for wearing head scarves, they are likely to face the ire of
CAIR. From public exposure of discrimination to lawsuits, CAIR is ready to
take every available legal action to fight discrimination. It also helps organizations by providing sensitivity training. CAIR's biggest contribution, however,
is the education it provides to the community on how to fight discrimination
and prejudice. In the past few years, CAIR has enjoyed much success in restoring jobs and getting compensation for Muslims suffering from discrimination. CAIR continues to fight the anti-Islam bias in the media. In this area, it
has not been as successful as in the workplace. Following CAIR's success, several other organizations now use the action alert tool made popular by CAIR
to mobilize the community whenever and wherever prejudice and discrimination surfaces.

The second significant change is in the operating styles of the MSAs. When
the senior generation was in charge, the MSAs were focused on Muslims and
in sustaining their faith and Islamic practices. But with the new generation at
the helm, the MSAs are outwardly focused. They are at ease with their Muslim identity and more interested in presenting a positive image of Islam. Unlike the *halaqas* of the past, the biggest activity of the MSAs is the Islam
awareness week they organize each year on hundreds of campuses in North

America. Lectures on Islam, art exhibitions, and cultural events are organized to introduce America to the true dimensions of Islam. This is the new form of *Dawah* developed by the new generation of American Muslims. The Islam awareness weeks are as American as coke and burgers.

The third major development in the 1990s is the explosion of Islamic media on the Internet. The Internet has provided American Muslims an excellent opportunity to share information and provide news and views services with other Muslims. Muslims have long complained about the bias in the Western media. Now at least the Internet allows Muslims to put out the news that concerns them. Websites such as Iviews.com compete with CNN and other major global news providers. They also are able to advance opinions and views on current events from an Islamic perspective. The Internet has facilitated fund-raising, networking, and discussions and dialogue among Muslims from various perspectives and has helped build consensus among Muslim activists in the United States. It is also eliminating duplication of effort, saving precious resources, and, most important, enabling Muslims in collective learning.[27]

All these developments indicate that American Muslims are now ready to influence American culture and politics. Muslims have never lacked in commitment or zeal. Now they not only have a base to work from but also have developed the "know-how" to effectively resist assimilation and defend their identity from the social pressure to conform. This newfound confidence has influenced a new trend in the institutional development of the Muslim community of America. Muslims have stopped spending all their resources, both human and material, on institutions for identity preservation, such as mosques and schools.

The 1990s have seen the emergence of the previously mentioned organizations (AMC, MPAC, AMA, and AMJ) as well as the Center for the Study of Islam and Democracy (CSID). The explicit purpose of these organizations is the political mobilization of American Muslims to accumulate power that can be used to affect change in the Muslim world. These organizations are involved in educating American Muslims in the nuances of democracy, pluralism, and interest-group politics. They are mobilizing them to participate in American politics at every level, from voting in elections to running for office. They are actively lobbying Congress and the president to change American foreign policy toward Palestine, Iraq, Pakistan, and Kashmir in particular and the rest of the Muslim world in general. Hundreds of seminars and workshops have been conducted in Islamic centers all over the country and at regional and annual conventions of Islamic movements, such as ISNA and ICNA, to encourage Muslims to participate in the American political process.

There is an upbeat mood in the community as it is beginning to flex its political muscles, which in reality are still in the infancy stage and need a lot of steroids and vitamins before they can match the powerful lobbies of American Jews and Cuban Americans. Small successes—such as the appointment of the first Muslim as a U.S. ambassador (to Fiji), the appointment of the first Muslim federal judge, a Muslim as deputy secretary of agriculture, and the appointment of a Muslim activist to the Congressional Commission on International Religious Freedom—have fueled Muslim enthusiasm. These successes have also given credence to the claims of Muslim leaders that participation will bear fruit. In the 2000 presidential election, Muslims decided to take the plunge. They endorsed and voted in block for the eventual winner, George W. Bush. It is too early to assess the payback from this bold gambit. But for the first time, Muslims gained recognition as a domestic force in mainstream American media.[28]

THE BATTLE AGAINST "AMERICAN ISLAM"

The transition of American Muslims from a fragile group focused on defending its identity to an intrepid community determined to make an impact has not been without contention. There is still no consensus in the community over a number of issues. To understand the political dynamics and the various contentions, it is important to return to the two images of the West that Muslims currently entertain: America as a democracy and America as a colonial power. For the purpose of this discussion, I will use the term "Muslim democrats" to describe Muslims who pay more attention to American democracy. Those who give American imperialist tendencies overseas greater significance in conceptualizing American identity will be identified as "Muslim isolationists."

The relationship between the two groups, Muslim democrats and Muslim isolationists, can best be described as a love–hate relationship. On practical issues concerning the defense of Islamic identity, such as establishing and maintaining Islamic centers and schools, these two groups cooperate fully, and the community appears to be seamless. But on political issues, they break apart and seldom see eye to eye. It is safe to say that while on preserving belief and rituals these two groups have common ground, they clearly entertain different conceptions of the role of Muslims in America.

MUSLIM ISOLATIONISTS AND AMERICA

Muslim isolationists view the United States as an evil empire dedicated to global domination. They have seen the United States benefit from the Iran–Iraq War and then destroy the most advanced Arab nation in the Persian Gulf War, making billions of dollars in profit by billing Muslims for that war. They have seen how the U.S.-led sanctions have gradually squeezed the life out of Iraq, killing hundreds of thousands of Muslim children. Recently, they watched in horror as the Israeli military killed more than 350 protesting Palestinians using a war machine that has benefited from U.S. aid, which is about $4 billion to $6 billion every year and has exceeded $80 billion in total.

They could not believe their senses as they read report after report in the media blaming the Palestinians for dying and listened in amazement as the United States, the so-called defender of human rights, refused to blame or admonish its ally Israel. Muslim isolationists are incensed with the United States for having an utter disregard for Muslim lives and Muslim society. The media demonize Islam, everyone gets away with defamation of Muslims, and when the president needs to divert attention from his private life, he chooses to fire cruise missiles at Muslim nations.

Most important, Muslim isolationists are not impressed with America's democracy or its values of freedom and pluralism. They point to the secret evidence act, used only against Muslims, which violates both these values by not allowing defendants full access to due process of law. They see American society as immoral, sexually decadent, greedy, and exploitative of the weak at home and abroad. Philosophically, they do not appreciate the value of freedom and tolerance; ideologically, they disagree with democracy as a means of political governance. For them, democracy is an institution that legitimizes the basic instincts of humanity and is an affront to divine laws. They describe the American system as *kufr* (a system against the laws of Allah or the Islamic Shariah) and reject it totally.

The frustration and animosity that they feel as a consequence of American foreign policy excesses is translated into a rejection of all that is American and Western, including democracy and so-called religious tolerance. The hostility toward America is also extended toward people of other faiths and makes them suspicious and paranoid even when they see the United States doing something right, such as intervening against a Christian state to protect Muslims in Bosnia and Kosovo. Some of the isolationists are disingenuous in their explanation about religious freedom in America. They argue that all the positive things that are happening to Muslims in America are from Allah and that American values of tolerance, freedom, and democracy have nothing to do with it since they are just empty slogans. They of course do not apply the same determinist approach in explaining the misfortunes of Iraqis or the Palestinians. The bad things that are happening to them are not from Allah but are a consequence of American and Israeli colonialism.[29]

There is an element of hypocrisy, too, in the manner in which the isolationists conceptualize their own role in America. They maintain that the American system is not divinely ordained and is not geared toward realizing the Islamic Shariah, ignoring the fact that in theory both the American Constitution and the Islamic state are designed to promote justice, protection, and the moral and material well-being of their citizens. Thus, they say, participation in that system constitutes a violation of Qur'an 5:45, which says that Muslims shall not rule by anything other than what Allah has decreed. Participation means endorsement of the system; therefore, they are opposed to Muslim participation in American politics. Even though isolationists reject the entire system, however, they have no qualms about participating in the American economy. They take jobs and pay taxes (to support the system), and some of them even start businesses in the system in which the economy is also un-Islamic. When queried about this inconsistency and pressed further by suggestions that since they disapprove of the system they should migrate (which is an Islamic thing to do), the isolationists resort to accusing Muslim democrats of being agents of the State Department in league with the enemies of Islam.

Isolationists argue that American Muslims must participate in an effort to revive the institution of the *Khilafah* (caliphate), which will magically take care of all Muslim problems. Some have organized themselves under the banner of Hizb-ul-Tahreer, a fringe political movement that advocates a narrow and harsh interpretation of Islam. Tahreer has been shut down in most Muslim countries, recently in Pakistan. The only places where they are free to pursue their activism in the open and without any fear of state reprisal is in the West: the United Kingdom, the United States, and Canada. Ironically, Tahreer condemns the West for its belief in democracy and freedom, yet it is this very belief in freedom that has helped them escape political extinction.

In the past few years, the isolationists have focused their attention on preventing the Muslim democrats from bringing Muslims into the American mainstream. However, their attempts to create intellectual and political ghettoes has failed as more and more Muslims are participating in the American political process.[30]

MUSLIM DEMOCRATS AND THE AMERICAN MUSLIM IDENTITY

Muslim democrats, on the other hand, have transformed American Muslims from a marginal, inward-looking immigrant community to a reasonably well organized and coordinated interest group able not only to fight for its rights but also to begin asserting its interests at the national as well as international level. The key to the success of Muslim democrat success has been their understanding of the West and their liberal vision of Islam.

Muslim democrats were quick to grasp the significance of the constitutional guarantee of religious freedom in the United States. They used this in the beginning to organize institutions and movements focused solely on preserving the Islamic identity of Muslims. They were aware that Muslims who had come before them had been culturally assimilated and had lost all connection to Islam. But as more and more Muslims came to America and answered their rallying call, they began to see a dream. It was of a "model Muslim community" practicing Islam as well as playing a role of moral leadership, guiding not only other Muslim communities but also Western societies toward a life of goodness and God consciousness.

What Muslim democrats see in America is not just the imperialist impulse but also the respect for law and fellow human beings. They are aware of the double standards that Western nations employ while treating their own citizens and others differently. But this is not new to them. They have witnessed their own societies employing separate standards while dealing with people. They are frustrated with the United States when it does not fulfill its commitments to democracy and human rights in the Muslim world but are quick to acknowledge that Muslims are better treated here than in their own countries. They have seen democracy, pluralism, and cultural and religious tolerance in action and are fascinated by its ability to resolve political differences peacefully. They admire the American state for its commitment to consultation and desire to rule wisely through deliberation. They wish that Muslim societies, too, would be able to escape the political underdevelopment from which they currently suffer and rise to manifest Islamic virtues, presenting the world with a model worthy of emulation.

Muslim democrats have had several successes. First, they have been able to quickly assume leadership positions in nearly every avenue of American Muslim activism. Whether it is in the political arena or in religious affairs, Muslim democrats hold sway. Second, they have been able to advance a vision for the American Muslim community that makes American Muslims proud of themselves and galvanizes them to contribute their money and time in the pursuit of this vision. Their greatest achievement has been their liberal interpretation of Islam.

Through thousands of seminars, persuasive articles in monthly magazines and Islamic center newsletters, and lectures at regional and annual conventions, workshops, and leadership retreats in the past thirty years, as well as in Friday *Jumma* prayers across the nation, Muslim democrats have campaigned to alter the way Muslims think about America and about Islam itself. They have fought for the legitimacy of their ideas against traditional scholars and battled against the siege mentality that had prevented Muslims from opening up and, from their new location, taking a fresh look at the world as well as themselves.

In the past three decades, Muslim democrats have shifted the focus of the Muslim communities from fighting against the West to building bridges with it. They have rejuvenated the tradition of *ijtihad* (independent thinking) among Muslims and now openly talk about *fiqh al-aqlliyatt* (Islamic law, or interpretation of the Shariah for places where Muslims are in the minority).[31] They have emphasized Islamic principles of justice, religious tolerance, and cultural pluralism. They have Islamized Western values of freedom, human rights, and respect for tolerance by finding Islamic sources and precedents that justify them. A very good example of this tendency is the establishment of the CSID that explores common ground between Islamic governance based on the Shariah and *shura* (consultation) and democratic governance that emphasizes rights and consent.

In the battle for American Islam, Muslim democrats have enjoyed a resounding success. They have gradually marginalized the isolationists and rendered their arguments and positions illegitimate. There are still pockets of resistance, confined largely to Internet-based discussion groups or web-sites. In the run-up to the 2000 presidential election, the struggle between the two types of Muslim elite in America had intensified. But the isolation-ists indeed have been isolated. Muslim democrats succeeded in mobilizing Muslims to register to vote. They did so in large numbers, making a differ-ence in the crucial state of Florida. Today, American Muslims are not only eager to participate and make an impact but also recognize that they have made an impact already.

The isolationists do not have any program or vision that would attract Muslims. Their call to establish *Khilafah* is without substance and lacks credi-bility. They themselves spend their resources in attacking Muslim democrats for "inventing an American Islam," in conjunction with American scholars such as John Esposito and Yvonne Haddad, that emphasizes the "softer side of Islam." Their activism is now limited to harassing Muslim activists and trying to place hurdles in their paths.

As a new generation of Muslims joins the community, the influence of Muslim democrats is consolidated. While the new generation is familiar with the problems of the Muslim world and its bill of complaints against the West, life as they know it is in the West, with all its pluralities and inconsistencies. They are strongly in the corner of the democrats and truly manifest that "third identity": American Muslims. They are proud to be Muslim and American.

These young people are not Americans who are Muslims or Muslims who are born in America. They are American Muslims. They believe in Islam, they are democratic, they respect human rights and animal rights, and they share a concern for the environment. They are economic and political liberals and social conservatives. They believe in the freedom of religion and the right of all peoples, ethnic as well as religious, to be treated equally. They are aware of their economic and political privileges and grateful to Allah for them. They dream of making changes in Muslim attitudes as well as Muslim conditions so that their fellow Muslims can also learn the bliss of practicing Islam by choice, without any fear of the state or a dominant group.[32]

THE CONSTRUCTION OF THE AMERICAN MUSLIM COMMUNITY

In the past three decades, historical and social forces and human agency have together crafted the American Muslim identity. American Muslims today are as Islamic as any Muslim and as American as any American. The social forces that shaped the American Muslim identity are those that contributed to the transformation of American society from a melting pot to a multicultural milieu. This social change helped Muslims maintain their distinctiveness without having to sacrifice too much of themselves in order to become acceptable and be included in the American mainstream. Being different is the new trend of the American mainstream and has helped American Muslims sustain their difference.

Another force that has helped the emergence of an American Muslim identity is the historical force of Islamic resurgence. *Tajdeed* (renewal) is an Islamic tradition that has helped Islam resuscitate and empower itself in wave after wave of renewal movements over the centuries. This historical force galvanized the Islamic fervor of Muslims and resulted in spectacular events, such as the Islamic revolution of Iran in 1979. The fervor of Islamic resurgence is contagious and has spread to the Muslim diaspora. American Muslims energized by the call of revival put their efforts behind peppering the American landscape with mosques, Islamic centers, and Islamic schools and have succeeded in defending their Islamic identity. Islamic movements seeking revival in North America have also contributed by keeping the flock within the fold.

Finally, another force that helped construct the American Muslim identity is the activism and the ideas of the Muslim elite. By educating the community in new ways of thinking about the West and Islam, they have been successful in transforming them and their relationship with the West. In the process, they have highlighted the liberal dimensions of Islam, marginalized bellicose tendencies, and helped construct a liberal Muslim self that revels in its Islamic and American identity. The emergence of the American Muslim identity and community indicates how historical and social forces can be marshaled by human agency to have transformative consequences.

NOTES

1. See the essays in Craig Calhoun, ed., *Social Theory and the Politics of Identity* (Cambridge, Mass.: Blackwell Publishers, 1994).

2. For a comprehensive analysis of the distinctions between rational choice and identity-based approaches to political choices and behavior, see M. A. Muqtedar Khan, "Rationality and Identity in International Relations: A Constructivist Theory of Agency and Choice" (Ph.D. diss., Georgetown University, 2000).

3. For a discussion of conversion, see Jane I. Smith, *Islam in America* (New York: Columbia University Press, 1999), 65.

4. The most widely used demographic survey of American Muslims is the one conducted by the American Muslim Council in 1992. This is the best available report on the ethnic and racial composition of American Muslims. The report is outdated for sure. A recent survey of mosques in America by Ihsan Bagby has suggested that the ratio of indigenous to immigrant Muslims may be around thirty to seventy. See Fareed H. Numan, *The Muslim Population in the United States* (Washington, D.C.: American Muslim Council, December 1992).

5. See Numan, *The Muslim Population in the United States.*

6. For similar arguments, see M. A. Muqtedar Khan, "The Case for an American Muslim Identity," www.beliefnet.com/story/35/story_3508_1.html, and "Barriers to American Muslim's Political Cohesiveness Is Largely Internal," *Washington Report on Middle East Affairs* 19, no. 5 (July 2000): 70. See also M. A. Muqtedar Khan, "What Is the American Muslim Perspective?" *Washington Report on Middle East Affairs* 19, no. 10 (December 1999): 82.

7. See Kathryn Woodward, ed., *Identity and Difference* (London: Sage Publications, 1997). To explore the contested and constructed nature of identities, compare the essays in Stuart Hall and Paul Du Gay, *Questions of Cultural Identity* (London: Sage Publications, 1996).

8. See Conrad P. Kottak and Katherine Kozaitis, *On Being Different: Diversity and Multiculturalism in the North American Mainstream* (New York: McGraw-Hill, 1998); John J. Miller, *The Unmaking of Americans: How Multiculturalism Has Undermined America's Assimilation Ethic* (New York: Free Press, 1998); and Ernest R. Myers, *Challenges for Changing America: Perspectives on Immigration and Multiculturalism in United States* (New York: Austin & Winfield, 1995). See also a short but excellent essay by Dennis Wong, "Adversarial Identities and Multiculturalism," *Society* 37, no. 2 (January/February 2000): 10–15. See also Peter Skerry, "Do We Really Want Immigrants to Assimilate?" *Society* 37, no. 3 (March/April 2000): 57–62.

9. To get a sense of this mood, see Shamim A. Siddiqi, "Islamic Movement in America—Why?" in *Muslims and Islamization in North America: Problems and Prospects,* ed. Amber Haque (Beltsville, Md.: Amana Publications, 1999), 355–62.

10. See M. A. Muqtedar Khan, "Islamic Identity and the Two Faces of the West," *Washington Report on Middle East Affairs* 19, no. 6 (August/September 2000): 71.

11. Yvonne Yazbeck Haddad and John L. Esposito, eds., *Muslims on the Americanization Path?* (London: Oxford University Press, 1998).

12. For historical accounts of how the American Muslim community emerged over the years, see Sulayman S. Nyang, "Islam in America: A Historical Perspective," *American Muslim Quarterly* 2, no. 1 (spring 1998): 7–38. See also Omar Altalib, "Muslims in America: Challenges and Prospects," *American Muslim Quarterly* 2, no. 1 (spring 1998): 39–49.

13. A review of the main themes in the works of some of the most prominent Islamic thinkers in North America (Fazlur Rahman, Ismail al Faruqi, Seyyed Hossein Nasr, and Taha Jabir Al-Alwani) and the desire to revive the Islamic civilization will be the dominant themes. A recent issue of *Islamic Horizons* (March/April 1999), the main journal of ISNA, dedicated an entire issue to the memory and ideas of Hassan Al-Bannah, the founder of the Muslim Brotherhood of Egypt and a prominent figure in the twentieth-century Islamic revivalist movements.

14. Omer Bin Abdullah, "A Forum Rebuilds: AMSS Serves as a Platform for Discussion of Issues Facing Muslims," *Islamic Horizons*, January/February 1999, 17.

15. For a review of IIIT's endeavors, see Jamal Barazinji, "History of Islamization of Knowledge and Contributions of the International Institute of Islamic Thought," in Haque, ed., *Muslims and Islamization in North America*, 13–33.

16. To learn more, visit CAIR at www.cair-net.org, AMC at www.amconline.org, AMA at www.amaweb.org, MPAC at www.mpac.org, KAC at www.kashmiri.com, and AMJ at www.amjerusalem.org.

17. See M. A. Muqtedar Khan, "Collective Identity and Collective Action: Case of Muslim Politics in America," in Haque, ed., *Muslims and Islamization in North America*, 147–59.

18. To learn more about the Islamic movements of North America, visit ISNA at www.isna.net, ICNA at www.icna.org, IANA at www.iananet.org, Tablighi Jamaat at www.almadinah.org, and Naqshbandi Sufi movement at www.naqshbandi.org.

19. See Smith, *Islam in America*, 65–71.

20. Defense of Islamic identity and the well-being of the Muslim world are the dominant themes in the American Muslim discourse. Examples of articles expressing these sentiments are Yvonne Haddad, "The Dynamics of Islamic Identity in North America," in Haddad and Esposito, eds., *Muslims on the Americanization Path?*, 19–46, and Fahhim Abdul Hadi, "Protecting the Future of Islam in America," *Islamic*

Horizons, March/April 1999, 30. See also Sarvath El Hassan, "Educating Women in the Muslim World," *Islamic Horizons,* March/April 1999, 54–56, and "Muslim in the West Serving Muslim Worldwide," *Islamic Horizons,* January/February 1998, 47. See also Altaf Hussain, "Youth and the Emerging Islamic Identity," *The Message,* June/July 1999, 21–22.

21. See Edward Said, *Covering Islam: How the Media and the Experts Determine How We See the Rest of the World* (New York: Pantheon Books, 1981). See the following chapters in Haque, ed., *Muslims and Islamization in North America:* Ahmadullah Siddiqui, "Islam, Muslims and the American Media," 203–30; Jack Shaheen, "Hollywood's Reel Arabs and Muslims," 179–202; and Ibrahim Hooper, "Media Relations Tips for Muslim Activists," 231–56. For the most recent examples of media bias against Islam, see M. A. Muqtedar Khan, "Public Face of Bigotry," *Washington Report on Middle East Affairs* 20, no. 1 (January/February 2001): 73.

22. See Ambereen Mirza, "Muslim Women and American Choices," *Islamic Horizons,* May/June 1999, 50, and Kathleen Moore, "The Hijab and Religious Liberty: Anti-Discrimination Law and Muslim Women in the United States," in Haddad and Esposito, eds., *Muslims on the Americanization Path?,* 105–28. For more on the positive role played by Muslim women in America, see Ghazala Munir, "Muslim Women in Dialogue: Breaking Walls, Building Bridges," in Haque, ed., *Muslims and Islamization in North America,* 337–41.

23. I am grateful to Dr. Ahmad Totonji, secretary-general of the International Institute of Islamic Thought, for filling me in on the early history of the MSA. Dr. Totonji was the general secretary and president of the National MSA in its formative years in the late 1960s. He has also played a major role in its development over the years and is still one of its major patrons.

24. See Abu Sameer, "Some Milestones in Islamic Education in North America," *The Message,* May 2000, 33–35. See also Mohamed Ismail, "Islamic Education in the Weekend and Full-Time Islamic Schools," *The Message,* May 2000, 41–42, and Nassir Ali-Akbar, "Challenges Faced by Islamic Schools," *The Message,* May 2000, 29–30.

25. See the editorial "Muslims Strive with Increasing Confidence," *Islamic Horizons,* January/February 1999, 6.

26. Azam Nizamuddin, "What Muslims Can Offer America," *Islamic Horizons,* March/April 1998, 35.

27. See, for example, www.iviews.com, www.mediamonitor.com, www.ijtihad.org, and www.glocaleye.org. Some of the discussion lists that help the community

explore its differences are political.islam@listbot.com and msanews at
http://msanews.mynet.net.

28. See Julia Duin, "U.S. Muslims Use Growing Numbers to Flex Political Muscles,"
Washington Times, July 11, 2000, A2; Michael Paulson, "Muslims Eye Role at US
Polls," *Boston Globe,* October 23, 2000, A1; John Chadwick, "American Muslims Gain
a Political Voice," *The Record,* September 24, 2000, A1; Dean E. Murphy, "For
American Muslims Influence in American Politics Comes Hard," *New York Times,*
October 27, 2000, A1; and Abu Amal Hadhrami, "Muslims Gain Political Rights,"
Islamic Horizons, January/February 1999, 24–25.

29. Because the isolationists are not as well organized as the democrats and lack
scholars participating in mainstream scholarship, it is not easy to refer to any of their
published works as indicative of their values. A book by Ahmad Ghorab, *Subverting
Islam: The Role of Orientalist Centers* (London: Minerva Books, 1996), is often used
as a major source book by the isolationists. However, one can easily learn about their
views by the discussions they carry out over the Internet. Some of the archives of
their views can be found at http://political.islam@listbot.com and
http://islam.guardian@listbot.com.

30. See also Abdul Basit's critique of the isolationists in Abdul Basit, "How to Integrate
without Losing Muslim Identity," *Islamic Horizons,* March/April 1998, 32–34.

31. See Yusuf Talal Delorenzo, "The Fiqh Councilor in North America," in Haddad
and Esposito, eds., *Muslims on the Americanization Path?,* 65–86. See also, for
example, Yusuf Talal Delorenzo, "Fiqh and Fiqh Council of North America,"
http://islam.org/Politics/SHARIAH.HTM#S2.

32. See M. A. Muqtedar Khan, "The Manifest Destiny of American Muslims,"
Washington Report on Middle East Affairs 19, no. 8 (December 2000): 68. This article
was published in several periodicals and websites. For a fascinating accompanying
discussion of American responses to this article, see the version in FreeRepublic.com
at www.freerepublic.com/forum/a39f129590fe4.htm.

11

How Muslims Use Islamic Paradigms to Define America

INGRID MATTSON

Muslims who immigrate to the United States are a vastly diverse group. Most Muslim immigrants to the United States, however, come from the historically majority Muslim lands of Asia and Africa. Still, the cultural, linguistic, and economic diversity of this group is vast, and in these respects, many Muslims may share more with the non-Muslim American majority than with other Muslim immigrants. Some will have been educated in the English language, while others will know no English at all. Some Muslim immigrants coming from large cities will be very familiar with modern technology and business culture; others will have lived in isolated villages, subsisting mostly on local agricultural production. All Muslim immigrants, however, have in common the fact that they do not share the Christian religious tradition of the majority of Americans. Being part of a religious minority will be a new experience for most of these Muslims and will necessitate, or at least stimulate, some thoughts about the relationship between state, society, and religion. Even those generally uninterested in religious matters may be pressed to articulate a position on this subject by the questioning of non-Muslim Americans, who assume that religious identity is paramount for all Muslims. Stereotypes about Muslims being hostile to "the West" will force many Muslim immigrants to explore their religious texts and traditions to counter or, perhaps, support such assumptions.

Of course, attempts to define the relationship between Muslim and non-Muslim communities began with the birth of the first Muslim community in seventh-century Arabia. The Qur'an, the sacred text of Islam, mentions a number of different religious and political communities that were in existence at the rise of Islam. Some of these communities, such as those of the polytheists and the unbelievers, are characterized as having been irreconcilably opposed to the message of Islam and the existence of a Muslim polity. This stance necessitated a particular response from Muslims—that of resistance and opposition. Other communities, such as those of the Christians and the "People of the Book" (a broader category that also includes Christians), are characterized as sharing important beliefs and values with Muslims. With such communities, the Qur'an seems to encourage interaction and cooperation. Consequently, the Qur'an plays an important role in defining the limitations and possibilities for a shared identity between Muslims and other faith communities and political entities. Other normative sources for defining such interaction include the biography of the Prophet (*sirah*), independent reports about normative statements he made on this topic (*hadith*), the decisions of early Muslim rulers, and the legal arguments of jurists over the century.

For theologians, legal scholars, and political scientists concerned with the place of Muslims in the contemporary world, the need to understand and define the proper relationship between Muslims and other faith communities has assumed a sense of urgency. No one engaged in this process of definition and categorization is indifferent to the implications of their efforts, and each is aware that their definitions, if accepted, would yield a particular kind of society. Coming from historically predominant Muslim areas of Asia, Africa, and Eastern Europe, people such as Abdel Wahhab El-Affendi, Farid Esack, Abdullahi an-Naim, Sayyid Qutb, Rashid Ghannouchi, Prince Hasan of Jordan, and Alija Izetbegovic, as well as other politicians, activists, human rights advocates, and scholars, argue for a specific social/political order through their definitions.[1] Whatever definition these individuals offer, they know that it must at least appear to be authentically grounded in the Qur'an and Islamic tradition. Without this, the majority of Muslims will be unconvinced.

It should not be surprising, given the importance of defining communal identity in Muslim history, that this process of definition and categorization is being applied to America itself. In order to understand their role in America, Muslims need to define not only Islam but also America. Muslims need to place America in its proper theological and legal category so they can determine what kind of relationship is possible and desirable for them to have with this country. Whether or not integration initially seems like a desirable goal, this process will be affected by the immigrant's race, ethnicity, financial means, linguistic ability, and, most important for our study, what religious paradigms are available to them to interpret their particular experience with America.

Prior to categorizing and defining, however, is knowing. Even before immigration, any Muslim man or woman will know something about America. Such knowledge is dependent largely on their level of education, their facility with the English language, and their level of access to modern communication technology. Satellite dishes and the Internet permit access to American self-presentations to augment or even undermine official depictions of news events in countries where communications are state controlled. Although this is not a new phenomenon—the Voice of America has been operating for this purpose for decades—there is no doubt that new technologies are far more popular, accessible, and effective. At the same time, even the most sophisticated American self-promotion pales beside the visceral and intense firsthand encounters Muslims in many countries have had with American military might. "Smart bombs" and U.S. Marines carry powerful messages that usually outweigh the effect of CNN and Peace Corps volunteers.

So how might Muslims define America? Is it a hegemonic state with a will to power that knows no boundaries in international relations? Or is it a Judeo-Christian country, a country founded on strong religious and moral principles? Is America a secular nation-state in which religion is marginalized? Is it a hedonistic, materialistic culture that destroys family and community values? Any one of these definitions may seem accurate to certain individuals, and each definition demands a different response from the Muslims to whom it is presented.

Muslim communities are scattered across the United States, and each one is in a constant state of transition. Although we can identify different waves of immigrants into various communities and trace some continuity over generations, every day brings new Muslim immigrants to the United States. Of course, changes in attitude are found not only between generations but within individuals as well. Muslims, like all other human beings, are engaged in a continual process of positioning and defining themselves in relationship to others. People need to choose and to choose again, as long as they live, how they will be in the world. Continual self-definition is one of the distinct needs of the human condition. The definitions of America that will be reviewed in this chapter, therefore, should not be considered fixed and unchangeable for any particular Muslim community, much less for any particular Muslim individual.

I also need to stress that the paradigms I discuss may be effective at very different levels. Obviously, religious paradigms will have a minimal effect on Muslims who have had little contact with religious discourse or for those who have an explicitly secular orientation. For others, particularly those who have sustained high contact with a religious discourse, these paradigms may have great import. Further, we should not belittle the role that non-Muslim Americans and political developments play in defining America to Muslims. The way Muslims define America will necessarily depend on what aspects of this country non-Muslim Americans promote and endorse ideologically, both in public policy and in their everyday encounters with Muslims.

Given the diversity of the Muslim community and its varied experiences, it is no surprise that there is no singular understanding of its relationship to America. However, the different responses can be grouped into three general categories: paradigms of resistance, paradigms of embrace, and paradigms of selective cooperation. Although I have chosen to group the paradigms according to the position in which they place Muslims with respect to America, it must be understood that the bases for taking similar positions can vary greatly. This will depend primarily on what is considered the essence of American identity. For example, a definition of America can be based, among other things, on its Constitution, on its body of positive laws, on its leadership, or on its culture and customs. The appropriate Islamic paradigm for understanding America consequently may be historical, juridical, or theological. This is important because a historical paradigm, for example, may be more or less open to revision than a theological or juridical paradigm.

PARADIGMS OF RESISTANCE

Most traditional seminaries in the Muslim world place a great deal of emphasis on the study of the sacred law, the *shari'ah*. In the Arab world, such seminaries, such as al-Azhar in Cairo, have been affected by modernist Islamic movements and teach from textbooks that, although rooted in classical thought, were written in the modern period. In other areas of the Muslim world, particularly in South Asia, many seminaries rely on "classical" texts written hundreds of years ago. In some of these texts, Muslim jurists used the term "abode of peace" to signify those geographical areas in which the sacred law of Islam was applied.[2] In opposition, the term "abode of disbelief" signified a place governed by any other system of law. According to some jurists, such a place was also an "abode of war," that is, a state or region that must eventually be brought under Islamic sovereignty. In traditional Islamic seminaries, there has been a tendency to apply this medieval definition to modern nation-states. Since by these definitions America cannot be considered an abode of Islam or peace, the natural conclusion is that it is an abode of disbelief. Whether or not America is also an abode of war is a matter for Muslim states to decide, for warfare is the prerogative of the state. For individual Muslims, however, travel to an abode of disbelief can legally be undertaken only when it is absolutely necessary, and the individual should return to Islamic territory as soon as possible. Those Muslim immigrants to America who are influenced by these medieval juridical concepts will obviously strongly resist integration, for America can be defined only in absolute negative terms.

This medieval bifurcation of the world, however, does not have great relevance for most Muslim immigrants to America. Many are probably not even aware of these concepts, and others certainly do not consider the lands they fled to have been abodes of peace. Nevertheless, although many Muslim immigrants may not be pleased with the lands they left behind, some regret having been compelled, by political or economic circumstances, to come to America. This is because, for some of these Muslims, American culture is seen through the very negative paradigm of the *jahiliyyah*.

The term *al-jahiliyyah* occurs in the Qur'an and was used by Muslims of the Prophet's generation to designate the pre-Islamic Arabian society whose customs and practices they were rejecting in favor of a new religious and social order. Linguistically signifying both "ignorance" and "impetuosity," *al-jahiliyyah* was used in the sense of "the bad old days" of paganism, lawlessness, and the oppression of the weak by the strong. In the modern era, the term has been revived by Muslim activists who apply it both to political regimes they consider oppressive and to cultures they consider pagan and hedonistic. *Jahili* society is irreconcilably opposed to a society based on obedience to God's commands, that is, an Islamic society.

Sayyid Qutb, an Egyptian writer who was executed in 1966 by the Nasser regime for his political opposition, was particularly influential in popularizing the notion that all modern political systems are completely dominated by *jahili* concepts, practices, and institutions. He believed that any interaction with such a system will inevitably force a believer to compromise his faith and to collaborate with forces opposed to godliness. The only choice for believers, therefore, is to isolate themselves from such a system. In Qutb's words,

> We must . . . free ourselves from the clutches of jahili society, jahili concepts, jahili traditions and jahili leadership. Our mission is not to compromise with the practices of jahili society, nor can we be loyal to it. Jahili society, because of its jahili characteristics, is not worthy to be compromised with.[3]

The ultimate aim of such isolation is to strengthen the Muslim so that he or she is able to change the *jahili* society "at its very roots." Any compromise with this type of a society will result only in superficial changes to a system that is essentially corrupt and misguided.

Qutb does not provide many details about the nature of *jahili* society in modern times or many details about the structure of a pious or Islamic society. His language is most powerful because it emotively evokes a cosmic struggle between good and evil and enrolls Muslims into a diverse project aimed at creating a just world order. The struggle between *jahili* society and Islam remains today a compelling paradigm for many Muslims.

When Muslims immigrate to America, this paradigm of *jahili* society, combined with the common immigrant pattern of seeking out those from one's homeland, can create a strong tendency toward isolationism. Some Muslim immigrants feel no need to even venture outside their religious communities to be convinced that they must avoid interaction with the dominant culture. Not only is it enough that they are Muslim in a country that lacks an Islamically oriented political and juridical system (many Muslims would say that most historically Muslim countries also lack this in the contemporary world), but America does not even have the ameliorating influence of a dominant Muslim culture. For Muslim immigrants with a superficial knowledge of American constitutional principles, the vulgarities of popular American political culture alone are enough to prove the truth of Qutb's words and sentiments. Other immigrants, uninterested in politics, have only to look to popular culture in general to be convinced that American society is thoroughly *jahili*. The attack on the American entertainment industry from a religious standpoint by non-Muslim Americans is further proof for Muslims who otherwise would be uninterested in the opinions of such persons.

Another Islamic paradigm that is used as a basis for resistance to participation in American politics and society is the story of Pharaoh. In the Qur'an, Pharaoh is the archetypal ruler whose will to power knows no bounds. In his arrogance, Pharaoh rejects the idea that he is accountable to any morality, law, or god, and he follows only his desire. The worldly effect of his refusal to submit to God is the oppression of believers. The Qur'an states, "He was arrogant—he and his armies—on the earth without a right. Did they think that they would not have to return to Us (God)?"[4]

For asylum seekers from Iraq, forced to flee their homeland after it had been devastated by relentless American bombing, and for refugees from Palestine, who see billions of American dollars behind the might of the Israeli army, these words assume a powerful meaning. However, their American experience may temper such an understanding, especially when on arrival in the United States they begin new lives and start to benefit from educational and social services. They find jobs, buy homes, and even make friends with Americans. Their view of America might begin to change, or they may at least begin to distinguish between American foreign and domestic policies. At this point, the neighborhood in which they live and their economic opportunities greatly affect how their definition of America evolves.

If such Muslim immigrants come to know and understand the grievances of many African American Muslims with the history and domestic policies of the United States, they may continue to see this country as hostile toward Muslims. This is not to say that all African American Muslims see more bad than good in this country. Indeed, there are many African American Muslims who make great efforts to highlight the benefits of American constitutionalism and democracy to their immigrant brothers and sisters. However, some African American Muslims, like some non-Muslim Americans, have well-grounded and sophisticated critiques of the American political and economic system. The long history of slavery and racism under which African Americans suffered is an experience that some Muslim immigrants relate to their own history of European colonialism and imperialism. These immigrants may well understand Samory Rashid's argument that such oppression must be faced by Muslims with resistance.[5]

We should expect such arguments to be reinvigorated after the recent rapprochement between the Muslim American Society of W. D. Mohammed and the Nation of Islam under Louis Farrakhan. Farrakhan's characterization of racism, however, with its emphasis on black/white duality, seems to repel those immigrant Muslims who are more concerned with cultural and religious oppression. Nevertheless, immigrant Muslims need only look back to the early days of the Prophet Muhammad's mission to find a paradigm of black struggle against oppression in the name of righteousness. African slaves were among the earliest Muslims who suffered for their faith. The story of the African slave Bilal being tortured by the rulers of Mecca for his conversion to Islam is one that all Muslims learn in childhood.[6] Consequently, as long as many African American Muslims continue to feel that the American political system fails them, it will be difficult to convince many immigrant Muslims otherwise.

PARADIGMS OF EMBRACE

There is no doubt that many Muslim immigrants come to see the United States as their new home and their adopted country. For many, the theological and legal implications of their dual loyalties to their religion and to their country are never brought to consciousness. Muslim leaders in the United States are only beginning to seriously examine the theoretical bases for Muslim American identity. This examination has been necessitated by the claims both of some non-Muslims, such as Steve Emerson, the notorious public critic of Islam and Muslims, and of some Muslims, such as members of the caliphate revivalist group Hizb ut-Tahrir,[7] that a real Muslim believer can never honestly express loyalty to the American Constitution. Muslims, these critics claim, can never agree to follow any law other than Islamic law. The Qur'an states very clearly, "Whoever does not judge on the basis of what God has revealed, they are rebellious transgressors."[8]

In response to such claims, many Muslim leaders point out that the Prophet Muhammad himself not only allowed emigration but even sent some of his followers to live in a non-Muslim country and required them to obey that country's ruler. This ruler was a Christian, the negus of Ethiopia, who gave refuge to a group of early Muslim converts fleeing the persecution of the chiefs of Mecca. The story of this flight and the refuge offered to the Muslims is an important and often-told episode in the life of the Prophet Muhammad.[9] As a paradigm for cooperation between Muslims and Christians, it therefore has a strong emotive effect. Further, the fact that many Muslim immigrants to American have taken flight from oppressive governments or situations of conflict and are welcomed by kind and tolerant Christians makes this an exceedingly suitable precedent for Muslims in America.

Nevertheless, although America can be embraced as a haven by virtue of the Ethiopian paradigm, the story also imposes limits on how deeply Muslims can assimilate to American society. The Muslim refugees to Ethiopia were guests of the ruler; they were not his loyal subjects, and there is no evidence that they participated in state institutions.

Another example cited as evidence that Muslims can participate in the ruling apparatus of a non-Muslim country is the Qur'anic story of the Prophet Joseph's experience in Egypt. Joseph himself asks the king of Egypt to place him in charge of the country's grain storehouses, and God says, "In this way we gave power to Joseph in the land."[10] This is clear evidence to some Muslims that there is no obstacle to their participation in American political and administrative institutions as long as they believe that they can effect some benefit. Others argue that this example is not normative for Muslims because the Prophet Joseph lived before the Prophet Muhammad delivered God's final message to humans. Although the theological message of all prophets was the same, their involvement in worldly affairs and the legislation they were required to enforce differed. Consequently, the Prophet Joseph remains a contested paradigm for Muslim integration to American society.

Among the most interesting efforts to permit Muslims a full embrace of American identity is the attempt to show that the constitutional democratic structure of America is almost equivalent to the political structure of an ideal Islamic state—in other words, a dialectic in which a redefinition of Islam meets a particular definition of America so that American democracy is identified with Islamic *shura* (consultation) and freedom of religion is identified with the Qur'anic statement "there is no compulsion in religion."[11] From a pragmatic standpoint, advocates of such a position might argue, "If the goal of an Islamic state is to allow Muslims to freely practice and propagate their religion, but not to force others to convert, and the American Constitution allows and ensures precisely these things, then is there any state more 'Islamic' in this respect than America?"

Bolstering such arguments are attempts to show not only that the American Constitution is concordant with Islamic principles but also that it may have been based on Islamic principles. Azizah al-Hibri, an American Muslim of Lebanese origin and professor of law at the University of Richmond, makes this argument in her article "American Constitutional Law: Borrowing Possibilities or a History of Borrowing."[12] Although she cautions that further research needs to be done on the historical links between Islamic and Euro-American political theory, her attempt to draw such links demonstrates her understanding that if Muslims are convinced that certain political concepts are "authentic" to their tradition, they will easily embrace those concepts.

PARADIGMS OF SELECTIVE ENGAGEMENT

Despite creative and scholarly attempts to define America in such a way that its interests can be shown to coincide with those of an Islamic state, it is unlikely that most ordinary Muslims or their religious leaders will soon be convinced by such arguments. Rather, most Muslims are striving to understand what place they should occupy, as religious minorities, in a country that they acknowledge allows great religious freedom. Many of these leaders, who are discussed later in this chapter, do not define America in much depth. Perhaps this is because they do not find any of the existing Islamic paradigms to be suitable for defining the American context and want to avoid having to rely on older models of engagement. Instead, these leaders focus on defining the character of an authentic Muslim community, emphasizing that it must make a positive societal impact whatever its size and wherever it might be.

A widely cited religious justification for the social engagement of Muslims in American society is the Qur'anic command "Let there arise out of you a group of people calling others to good, enjoining what is good and forbidding what is wrong"[13] and the frequent description of the true believers by the Qur'an as those who "enjoin the good and oppose what is wrong."[14] A widely quoted statement of the Prophet Muhammad also commands believers to take action; it is reported that he said, "Whoever sees an evil action, let him change it with his hand; and if he is not able to do so, then with his tongue; and if he is not able to do so, then with his heart—and that is the weakest of faith."[15] This statement clearly requires Muslims to change evil by whatever legal means are available to them. Although some Muslims believe that they can fulfill this by creating independent Islamic communities and institutions in the spaces that American freedom of religion permits, others believe that this duty is not fulfilled by creating ghettoes or isolated utopias within America. The dilemma for such Muslims is how to correct wrongs within American society generally without compromising their beliefs and allegiance to Islam by participating in the system without reservation. In other words, what these Muslims would like to do is to engage selectively in those organizations and institutions through which they can effect societal change but also bring an Islamic perspective to the issues and not compromise their essential religious principles.

The areas of engagement most comfortable for these Muslims to undertake, as a result, are social causes, grassroots activism, and "alternative" forms of activism: environmentalism, social justice movements, neighborhood associations, and so on. We find Muslims increasingly participating in such movements and organizations in all levels of American society. The problem is that the tolerance extended to Muslims by the non-Muslims involved in such groups is usually also extended to groups many Muslims have difficulty working with, for example, anarchists, atheists, and gay-rights activists. Consequently, a number of independent Muslim activist groups have formed across the country. In general, however, the cherished Islamic values of such groups do not prevent them from working with non-Muslim groups toward a particular shared goal.

Two such organizations, from different regions of the United States, are examples of this trend in Muslim communities. Interestingly, each of these organizations, as with many other American-Muslim groups, carries meaningful Arabic–Islamic names that are also used as acronyms for English phrase names.

The first of these organizations is named AMILA, which means "work" in Arabic and stands for "American Muslims Intent on Learning and Activism."[16] Founded in 1992 by Muslims in the San Francisco Bay Area, AMILA's membership includes both first- and second-generation young Muslim professionals and students. Reflecting the ethnic patterns of the region, a large number of members are of South Asian origin, but Arabs and Americans also have a presence in the organization. Former members of AMILA have moved on to found other organizations; among them is Asifa Quraishi, who cofounded the Muslim Women Lawyer's Human Rights Group (KARAMAH, which means "dignity" in Arabic).[17] AMILA's activities include a regular lecture series, Qur'anic memorization and religious discussion, and community activism. AMILA's projects include outreach to prisoners in local institutions, support of a local soup kitchen, and tutoring needy children. Significantly, AMILA also works with Muslim refugees who have settled in the Bay Area. The assistance given to these refugees by Muslims who are religiously motivated but at the same time deeply engaged in American society helps break down a common new immigrant impression that America is hostile to Muslims. Immigrant social services by Muslims for Muslims, a relatively new aspect of Muslim immigration to America, will no doubt change the nature and speed of the integration of Muslim immigrants to American society.

While most members of AMILA are reaching out to needy Muslims and non-Muslims from a position of affluence—that is, their activities are in the realm of charity—a very different kind of activism emerged on the south side of Chicago in the mid-1990s. A kind of solidarity of the oppressed, with Islam as the proposed solution to oppression, was formed between African American Muslims and the children of Palestinian immigrants. This solidarity was expressed in the formation of an organization called IMAN, which means "faith" in Arabic and stands for "Inner-City Muslim Action Network." Most of the original members were students at DePaul University, where African American Muslim professor Amina McLeod helped them conceptualize the problem of racial division in Chicago generally and the Muslim community in particular. Many of the students were second- or third-generation Palestinian Muslims who had had little contact with the African Americans among whom they lived on the south side of the city. Indeed, there had been instances of explicitly hostile encounters between the two communities. Inspired by their belief in the true brotherhood of Islam, the members of IMAN decided to prove their faith through action. Their activities have expanded from an after-school tutoring program to the establishment of a mosque in a renovated liquor store owned by a former African American gang leader turned devout Muslim. Every two weeks, young Muslim men of Arab, South Asian, African, Latino, and European origin display their solidarity of faith in the "Bonds of Brotherhood" by studying and praying together all night in southside mosques. IMAN has women's and men's outreach programs geared to Muslim families and prisoners as well as a number of other programs. Significantly, IMAN has also formed multiple ties with non-Muslim grassroots activist organizations in Chicago. In the "Community Narrative" program, for example, IMAN invites members of other minority communities to share their struggles and experiences with the group. IMAN is a dynamic organization with a number of other programs and has served as a model for other Muslim communities situated in urban areas.

Community activism of the sort undertaken by the members of IMAN and AMILA does not necessitate engagement in local politics, but such a step is often inevitable, if only because of the need for project funding. Political engagement on the local level is also undertaken, often reluctantly at first, by Muslim parents trying to better their children's public school experience. At the most basic level, the accommodation of religious practices, such as prayer, dietary restrictions, and dress requirements, can bring parents to the school administration and local board. Parents may be drawn into a deeper engagement with the school system when they realize that their children are not affected only by "Muslim issues" but also by the quality of the school system as a whole.

Beyond the local level, engagement in the American political system has, until recently, been considered undesirable by many Muslims. The widespread cynicism about national politics held by Americans in general since the Nixon era has done little to reassure Muslims that they can participate politically at this level without violating their religious principles. However, the 2000 presidential election witnessed unprecedented efforts by various Islamic organizations to encourage Muslims to vote and even run for office. Increased political engagement was to be expected, given the growth of organizations such as the Muslim Public Affairs Council and the American Muslim Council, over the past decade. However, the responsiveness of the general Muslim community to calls for political engagement by these organizations seems to have been heightened by recent political pressure felt by Muslims, both domestically and internationally. Within America, the use of secret evidence to jail more than two dozen Palestinians frightened many Muslims who may have previously felt that they would be allowed to live freely in this country without being required to engage in the political system. Internationally, the intensity of the Israeli repression of Palestinians throughout the fall of 2000 catalyzed many Muslims to demonstrate their disapproval of American foreign policy.

Now, although many immigrant groups have come to believe that the interests of their communities will be served by engaging in national politics, the Muslim community is perhaps unique in demonstrating such concern for articulating the religious justification for this participation. This is necessitated by the fact that, as was shown previously, there are a number of religious paradigms that can be used to condemn any such participation by Muslims in non-Islamic political systems. One of the common religious justifications for political participation is a statement attributed to the Prophet Muhammad in which he explicitly approves of a pact made in the pre-Islamic period (and, hence, by non-Muslims) to punish any acts of theft committed in Mecca. The group who made this pact was known as the "Confederates of Fudul," and the

Prophet, who witnessed the agreement in his youth, said, "If I were invited to take part in it during Islam, I would do so."[18] This statement is taken as proof that Muslims may join with non-Muslims in political bodies to enforce a particular and limited social good.

Some who permit political participation by Muslims from a religious standpoint do so cautiously; others are more aggressive and enthusiastic. Among the prominent Muslim leaders who adopt a relatively cautious stance is Jamal Badawi, an Egyptian Canadian academic who is a widely respected Muslim speaker and leader in the Islamic Society of North America.[19] Cautious approval of political participation was also expressed at the Zaytuna Institute, a center for Islamic scholarship founded in California by American Muslim leader Hamza Yusuf. Visiting Mauritanian scholar Sheikh Abdullah Bin Bayyah, in a speech published on the Zaytuna website, urged Muslims to be guided by the principle of trying to ensure the greatest advantage for the community.[20] Interestingly, Bin Bayyah not only stressed the obligation of the Muslim community to be a positive force in society and protect its interests but also addressed the issue of the proper Islamic legal categorization of America. Correcting the notion that there were only two "abodes" in classical Islamic jurisprudence, Bin Bayyah says that beyond the abode of peace and the abode of war there is also an "abode of treaty," in which Muslims agree to respect the laws of a country if they are granted freedom and protection. America, Bin Bayyah argues, belongs to this category.

One of the strongest arguments for the participation of Muslims in national politics in 1999 came from Taha Jaber Al-Alwani, a traditionally trained Muslim jurist from Iraq who has been involved in American Islamic organizations for two decades and currently heads the North American *Fiqh* [Islamic Legal] Council. Al-Alwani argued in a legal verdict (*fatwa*) prepared for the American Muslim Council that participation in the American political system is not only permitted but also obligatory for Muslims in order to protect their interests and to correct societal evils.[21] Al-Alwani agrees with Bin Bayyah that America is not an abode of war but argues further that such categories are outdated in the contemporary world. Indeed, rather than categorizing America, Al-Alwani simply lists some of the "American particularities," such as religious and political freedom and legal equality for all people. The implication is that America simply does not fit any of the older Islamic paradigms for a non-Muslim political entity. If Al-Alwani's argument is convincing to Muslims, the result could be a far more profound integration of Muslims into American society than ever before.

In many cases, those Muslims who begin from a position of "selective embrace" of America move eventually to a position of "full embrace." When their efforts to effect positive change in society bear fruit, they may come to see advantages in the American political system that they did not see before. At this point, they may abandon the former paradigm they used to define America in favor of one that is more positive and comprehensive. The shift, however, is not inevitable. In some cases, Muslim activists, like their non-Muslim counterparts, become deeply disillusioned and highly skeptical of their ability to effect anything but superficial change within the parameters of the current American political system. In such cases, a reevaluation of the appropriate Islamic paradigm for America will lead to negative results.

No matter what happens within America, the deep connections between American Muslims and their brothers and sisters overseas means that American foreign policy will always have a profound effect on the way Muslims view this country. In the 1990s alone, the Persian Gulf War and ensuing sanctions against Iraq created great animosity toward America on the part of many Muslims, while American bombing of the former Yugoslavia to protect Kosovar Muslims resulted in a fair amount of goodwill toward America.

What this means is very simple: In both foreign and domestic affairs, the way Muslims define America will always depend a great deal on what America does. Although Muslims are certainly not immune to political ideology, most are unconvinced by claims to moral and political authority that are not backed up by action. Perhaps, then, the most powerful paradigm underlying all Muslim definitions of America is the dominant Islamic theological belief that one's true convictions will inevitably be made manifest by one's actions:

> They will offer their excuses to you (the Prophet) when you return to them. Say: "Offer no excuses; we will not believe you. Allah has already informed us of the true state of matters concerning you. It is your actions that Allah and His Messenger will observe. In the end will you be brought back to Him Who knows what is hidden and what is revealed. Then He will show you the truth of all that you did."[22]

NOTES

1. Farid Esack, *Qur'an Liberation and Pluralism: An Islamic Perspective of Interreligious Solidarity against Oppression* (Oxford: Oneworld, 1997); Abdullahi an-Naim, *Towards an Islamic Reformation: Civil Liberties, Human Rights and International Law* (Syracuse, N.Y.: Syracuse University Press, 1990); Sayyid Qutb, *Milestones,* translation of

Maᶜalim fiʾl-tariq (Cedar Rapids, Iowa: Unity Publishing, n.d.); Rashid Ghannouchi, *Huquq al-Muwatanah: Huquq ghair al-muslim fiʾ-mujtamaʾ al-Islami* (Herndon, Va.: International Institute of Islamic Thought, 1993); El Hassan Bin Talal, *Christianity in the Arab World* (New York: Continuum Publishing, 1998); Alija Izetbegovic, *Islam between East and West* (Indianapolis: American Trust Publications, 1989). For the most recent views of El-Affendi and Ghannouchi, consult various issues of the British journal *islam21* or its website at http://islam21.org.

2. For an analysis of these medieval juridical–political categories, see Majid Khadduri, *War and Peace in the Law of Islam* (Baltimore: The Johns Hopkins University Press, 1955).

3. Qutb, *Milestones*, 21.

4. Qurʾan 28:39.

5. Samory Rashid, "Blacks and the Law of Resistance in Islam," *Journal of Islamic Law* 4, no. 2 (fall/winter 1999): 87–124.

6. A primary source for the history of the life of the Prophet Muhammad and the first Muslim community is Ibn Ishaqʾs *Sirat Rasul Allah*, translated as *The Life of Muhammad* by A. Guillaume (Karachi: Oxford University Press, 1955). For the story of Bilal, see pp. 143–44 therein.

7. The groupʾs position is stated, among other places, on its website at www.khilafah.org.

8. Qurʾan 5:47.

9. Guillaume, *The Life of Muhammad*, 146–53.

10. Qurʾan 12:55–56.

11. Qurʾan 2:256.

12. Azizah Y. al-Hibri, "Islamic and American Constitutional Law: Borrowing Possibilities or a History of Borrowing?" www.law.upenn.edu/conlaw/issues/vol1/num3/alhibri.htm (accessed December 1999).

13. Qurʾan 3:104.

14. Qurʾan 9:71, 22:41, 31:17.

15. Ezzedin Ibrahim and Denys Johnson-Davies, trans., *An-Nawawiʾs Forty Hadith: An Anthology of the Sayings of the Prophet Muhammad* (Cambridge: Islamic Texts Society, 1997), 110.

16. For more information on AMILA, see its website at www.amila.org.

17. A further description of KARAMAH can be found on its website at www.karamah.org.

18. Guillaume, *The Life of Muhammad,* 57.

19. See his interview on the Soundvision website at www.soundvision.com/politics/badawi.html (accessed November 1999).

20. Speech found at www.zaytuna.org/sh_bin_bayyah.html (accessed November 1999).

21. *Fatwa* found at www.amconline.org/newamc/fatwa.html (accessed November 1999).

22. Qur'an 9:94.

12

Exploring the Religious Preferences of Recent Immigrants to the United States: Evidence from the New Immigrant Survey Pilot

GUILLERMINA JASSO, DOUGLAS S. MASSEY,
MARK R. ROSENZWEIG, AND JAMES P. SMITH

In the United States, immigration and religion are inextricably linked. Religious liberty—the freedom to practice any religion and, equally, to reject all religion—is a founding principle of the United States. Generations of immigrants have come to the United States in order to freely practice their religion or, alternatively, in order to free themselves from all religion, whether imposed legally or culturally. The religious composition of the U.S. population thus reflects the evolving history of infringements on religious liberty around the world and the steadfast American freedoms.

Although the religious composition of the native-born U.S. population has been studied in a systematic and rigorous way, owing principally to the General Social Survey (GSS), which since 1972 has collected data based on probability samples,[1] comparable studies of the foreign-born population have been hampered because of a lack of data based on probability samples of immigrants or foreign-born persons drawn from well-defined populations. Equally important, the lack of data has made it impossible to address major questions about the effects of living in the United States on the spiritual biography of immigrants and, reciprocally, the effects of immigration on the spiritual life of the United States.

The New Immigrant Survey (NIS), the first large-scale survey of a probability sample of new legal immigrants, which went into the field in late 2001, promises to remedy the situation by providing high-quality public-use data on the religious life of immigrants and their children, both at the start of their legal permanent residence and over time as they adjust to the United States. The New Immigrant Survey Pilot (NIS-P), based on a probability sample of persons admitted to permanent residence in July and August 1996, asked two questions on religion: one on religious preference and the other on frequency of attending services. This chapter utilizes the data on religious preference to paint a portrait of the religious composition of recent new legal immigrants.

We begin by reporting the percentage distribution of new adult immigrants by their religious preference. As will be seen, there are four major results: First, approximately two-thirds of the new immigrants are Christian, substantially below the 82 percent of the native born surveyed in the GSS of 1996. Second, the proportion of Catholics among the new immigrants is 42 percent, almost twice as large as among the native born (22 percent). Third, the proportion reporting themselves outside the Judeo-Christian fold is more than four times larger among recent immigrants than among the native born (17 vs. 4 percent). Fourth, 15 percent of the new immigrants report no religion, a larger fraction than among the native born (12 percent).

The composition of religious preference among recent immigrants reflects social and economic circumstances in both the United States and countries around the world, and it reflects the pathways for obtaining U.S. legal permanent residence. Accordingly, we explore the links between religious preference on the one hand and origin country and visa type on the other. The largest visa category is that for spouses of U.S. citizens, and because the NIS-P includes data on whether the couple has been married more than two years and on the sponsor's nativity, it is possible to examine patterns of religious preference by marital duration and sponsor nativity.

The schooling attainment of new immigrants is an important indicator of the skills and attributes they bring with them, and thus we also examine educational attainment among the new immigrants by religious preference. Moreover, the schooling differential between spouses is an important feature of the child-rearing environments provided by mixed-nativity and immigrant families; accordingly, we examine patterns of assortative mating among two types of couples (for which sample size permits closer scrutiny): those in which a U.S. citizen sponsored the immigration of a spouse and those who obtained employment-based visas.

The results presented here must be interpreted with caution, for they are based on a sample of not quite 1,000 immigrants, and thus results involving few cases are not robust. On the other hand, results involving categories in

utline

	Project
	Make contact with religious group and set up a time for an initial conversation
	Initial visit. Goals of initial visit: establishing rapport, coming to a preliminary agreement on what you will be producing as a result of your work there
	Hand in description of S-L project Observation visit #1 Identify Interviewee #1
8, 9	Work on S-L project Observation visit #2; Interview #1 Identify Interviewee #2
11 eserve)	Work on S-L project Interview #2; Identify Interviewee #3
7	Hand in S-L project progress report Interview #3
reserve)	Show S-L project preliminary product to key contact and get feedback
6	Draft of paper turned in
	Final paper due Friday
	Hand in completed S-L project, and also give final product to organization 15-minute class presentations on S-L projects

Week	Topic	Readings
1	Defining Culture, Religion, and Nationality	Appadurai Geertz RI, Intro
2	Studying Culture, Religion and Nationality	RAB, ch.1 RI, ch. 1, 12
3	Understanding the dynamics of Transnationalism, Immigration, and Globalization & how they play out in religious communities	Levitt (onlir RAB, ch. 3 RNI, ch. 3,
4	" (Continued)	RNI, ch. 6, RAB, ch. 4
5	Case Study: Islam	**RI, ch. 9, 1** Berridge (or
6	Case Studies: Judaism & Buddhism	**RI, ch. 6 an**
7	Case Studies: Hinduism & Sikhism	**RNI, ch. 10** **Williams (o**
8	Case Studies: Immigrant Christian Congregations: Greek, Latvian, and Hispanic	**RNI, ch. 14** **RI, ch. 4**
9	Case Studies: Immigrant Christian Congregations: Chinese & Korean	**RNI, ch. 12** **RAB, ch. 7**
10	Summing up: Culture, religion and nationality in U.S. diasporic religious communities	

which respondents are numerous—such as immigrants from Mexico or the Philippines, Catholics, or the employment and spouse-of-U.S.-citizen visa types—are more robust. The full NIS will have a sample size of 10,000, ample enough to support very fine distinctions and relationships in the data. For now, many of the results linking religious preference to visa type or schooling are best regarded as suggestive.

Finally, we emphasize that all these results pertain to a point near the beginning of the immigrant's new life as a permanent resident of the United States. Much will change with the passage of time—schooling attainment among both immigrants and their spouses, perhaps religious preference itself. Twenty years later, the results may be quite different.

DATA SOURCE: THE NEW IMMIGRANT SURVEY PILOT (NIS-P)

Efforts to describe and understand the religious experience of immigrants to the United States—both at admission and over time as they adjust to their new surroundings—have long been stymied by the lack of appropriate data. There are several fundamental problems with existing data on immigrants, including the failure to distinguish between legal immigrants, illegal immigrants, temporary migrants, and other foreign born; the lack of information on the provisions of U.S. immigration law by which immigrants obtain visas (family reunification, job skills, refugee status, and diversity); sampling designs that yield unrepresentative samples; small sample sizes, especially damaging given the considerable heterogeneity among different immigrant groups; and, finally, the inability to study immigrants and their children over time. Given that many immigrants subsequently return to their home countries (or leave for new countries), existing surveys include only those who decide to remain—a very selective subsample of those who originally migrated to the United States.

Over the past twenty to twenty-five years, as awareness grew of the severe deficiencies in the available data, a new vision for collecting data began to emerge. With contributions from many scholars, policymakers, and panels assembled in both the public and the private sectors (e.g., panels of the National Academy of Sciences, the National Institutes of Health, and the Rockefeller Foundation), a new plan was formulated for collecting immigrant data that would enable research that substantially advances understanding of the social and economic characteristics of immigrants and the effects of immigration in the United States. This new plan—the NIS—has a prospective–retrospective design in which large probability samples are drawn from new cohorts of legal permanent resident aliens, using the administrative records of the Immigration and Naturalization Service (INS). Sampled immigrants will be interviewed immediately after admission to permanent resident status and reinterviewed periodically thereafter; information will be collected on the sampled immigrants' spouses and family and household members, including their children—both the immigrant children they brought with them and the U.S.-citizen children born to them in the United States.[2]

Because such a design had never been tried before, a pilot—the NIS-P—was carried out with support from the National Institutes of Health, the National Science Foundation, and the INS. The pilot survey confirmed the soundness of the design, highlighted the importance of contacting sampled immigrants immediately after admission to permanent residence, and provided new information on immigrants never before available.

The data used in this chapter are drawn from the NIS-P, which is based on a random sample of all immigrants admitted to legal permanent residence in July and August 1996. The survey cycle consisted of a baseline interview and interviews after six and twelve months (with a randomly chosen subset also interviewed at three months after the baseline interview). The sampling design, procedures for locating sampled immigrants, and further details about response rates and information collected are described elsewhere.[3]

The NIS-P included two religion questions: one on religious preference and the other on frequency of attending services. The two questions are similar to those in the GSS. The response categories, however, were more refined in the NIS-P than in the (pre-1998) GSS; for example, the NIS-P question on religious preference added Muslim, Buddhist, and Hindu to the (pre-1998) GSS response categories (Catholic, Protestant, Jewish, and no religion). The religion questions were asked at the twelve-month round; the number of adult immigrants interviewed at that round was 985.[4]

RELIGIOUS PREFERENCE AMONG NEW IMMIGRANTS

Overview of Religious Preference

Table 12.1 reports religious preference among new immigrants aged eighteen or over at admission to permanent residence.[5] As shown, almost two-thirds (64.7 percent) expressed a preference for a Christian religion. Not surprisingly, given the immigrant concentrations from Mexico, Latin America, and the Philippines,

Table 12.1. Percentage Distributions of Religious Preference by Sex: NIS-P Adult Immigrants

Religious preference	Men	Women	All
Jewish	2.4	2.8	2.6
Christian—Catholic	40.7	42.9	41.9
Christian—Orthodox	4.2	4.1	4.2
Christian—Protestant	18.2	18.8	18.6
Muslim	8.1	7.8	8.0
Buddhist	4.1	4.02	4.04
Hindu	3.8	3.0	3.4
Other	2.1	0.8	1.4
No religion	15.1	14.8	15.0
No response	1.3	1.0	1.2
Total	100.0	100.0	100.0
N	457	519	976

Note: Estimates are for adults aged 18 and older and are based on weighted data. The Protestant category includes persons who identified their religion as "Other" and who provided a specific affiliation that is Christian but neither Catholic nor Orthodox; see text for details.

the largest contingent expressed a preference for Catholicism (42 percent). The proportions reporting a preference for an Orthodox or a Protestant religion were 4.2 and 18.6 percent, respectively. The next largest religious grouping was Muslim, preferred by 8 percent of the immigrants. Immigrants reporting themselves as Muslim, Buddhist, or Hindu together constitute 15 percent. Another 15 percent of the sample reported a preference for no religion.[6]

Overall, the figures in table 12.1 signal the continuing attractiveness of the United States as a place of tolerance for both diversity of religious expression and freedom from religion.

Comparison of Recent Immigrants with the U.S. Native-Born and Foreign-Born Population

To compare the NIS-P recent immigrants with both the native-born population and the foreign-born population in the United States, we use data from the 1996 GSS.[7] The GSS public-use microdata include the responses to the response categories separately identified in the question (Protestant, Catholic, Jew) but not the specific religion specified by the 4 percent of respondents who declared a preference for an "Other" religion.[8] The frequency distribution for these "Other" religions, kindly made available by the GSS office, includes the three religions separately identified in the NIS-P (Muslim, Buddhist, Hindu), plus some Eastern Orthodox and Protestant affiliations (including

the category with the largest number of responses—"Christian," with 37 responses out of 143) as well as some Native American religions. The GSS office
was unable to provide this information in such a way that we could incorporate it into the microdata file. Therefore, to establish comparability between
the NIS-P and the 1996 GSS, we combine the NIS-P Muslim, Buddhist, and
Hindu categories with the "Other" to form an expanded "Other" category.
Note that the Protestant category is underestimated in the GSS, as some
Protestants are included in the "Other" category; note also that Eastern Orthodox Christians in the GSS are included in the "Other" category.

Comparison with the native-born population in the United States suggests
that religious preference among recent immigrants is indeed distinctive (table
12.2).[9,10] First, the proportion Christian, which is 65 percent among the immigrants, is substantially larger among the native born—at least 82 percent.[11] Second, the proportion Catholic is almost twice as large among the immigrants as
among the native born—42 versus 22 percent. Third, the proportion reporting
themselves outside the classical Judeo-Christian fold is more than four times
greater among recent immigrants than among the native born—16.7 versus 4
percent.[12] Fourth, the proportion reporting no religion is somewhat larger
among the immigrants than among the native born—15 versus 11.6 percent.

If future immigrant cohorts display similar patterns of religious preference—
and if these patterns do not change significantly over the life course or if emigration is nonrandom with respect to religion—then the religious landscape in
the United States may be substantially altered, with larger fractions favoring
Catholicism and religions outside the Judeo-Christian fold and a nontrivial
no-religion contingent.

Table 12.2 also reports religious preference among the foreign born interviewed in the 1996 GSS. This group differs from the NIS-P immigrants in
three fundamental ways: 1) It is a group of undifferentiated foreign born, including not only permanent resident aliens but potentially also legal nonim-
migrants, former immigrants who naturalized, and illegal aliens; 2) it is heterogeneous in year of entry to the United States and of admission to a
particular visa status; and 3) given that the GSS interviews only in English, the
sample is sufficiently fluent in English that an interview can be carried out.
Nonetheless, despite the differences between the GSS foreign born and the
NIS-P samples, religious preference in the two samples is remarkably similar.
Only in the Protestant category is there a discrepancy, with the proportion

Table 12.2.   Religious Preference by Nativity and Sex: U.S. Native- and Foreign-Born Population in 1996 and NIS-P 1996 Immigrants

Religious preference	Native born, GSS 1996			Foreign born, GSS 1996			NIS-P 1996 immigrants			NIS-P 1996 immigrants interviewed in English		
	Men	Women	All	Men	Women	All	Men	Women	All	Men	Women	All
Jewish	1.7	2.4	2.1	2.7	2.7	2.7	2.4	2.8	2.6	1.8	1.8	1.8
Catholic	24.7	20.9	22.7	39.8	39.3	40.3	40.7	42.8	41.9	23.6	30.2	27.3
Orthodox	—	—	—	—	—	—	4.2	4.1	4.2	4.4	3.8	4.1
Protestant	54.9	63.2	59.4	21.8	32.3	26.6	18.2	18.8	18.6	28.9	25.5	27.0
Other	3.8	4.4	4.1	19.2	14.4	16.9	18.1	15.6	16.7	32.0	28.6	30.1
No religion	14.8	8.9	11.6	16.5	12.1	14.5	15.1	14.8	15.0	7.6	8.3	8.0
No response	0.2	0.1	0.1	0	0	0	1.3	1.0	1.2	1.6	1.8	1.7
Total	100	100	100	100	100	100	100	100	100	100	100	100
N	1,158	1,497	2,655	123	115	238	457	519	976	215	231	446

Note: All estimates are for persons aged 18 and older. Estimates are based on weighted data. Column percentages sum to 100.

Protestant in the foreign-born sample at least 8 percentage points larger than in the recent immigrant sample.

Interestingly, the 1996 GSS sample is substantially closer to the NIS-P sample than is the 1994 GSS sample.[13] If the difference in the composition of religious preference between the 1994 GSS and the 1996 GSS samples signals a trend, then this trend warrants scrutiny. At this time we may speculate that the same mechanisms that motivate persons to immigrate to the United States motivate previous immigrants to remain in the United States or that, given that 57 percent of the recent immigrants in the NIS-P's twelve-month round were already living in the United States and adjusting their status from a temporary to a permanent immigration status, the GSS and NIS-P samples would be predictably similar. Alternatively, we may speculate that the family-reunification character of U.S. law governing the selection of immigrants ensures similarities between recent and previous immigrants, although, of course, not all immigrants receive their visas by dint of kinship.

Table 12.2 also provides religious-preference estimates for the subset of NIS-P immigrants who were interviewed in English. At first blush, it would seem that this subset provides a better comparison to the GSS sample, given that the GSS interviews only in English. However, the English-interviewee subset of the NIS-P represents immigrants who *prefer* to be interviewed in English rather than immigrants who are fluent in English; that is, the NIS-P interview language is based on language preference rather than language ability. Thus, the comparison is less than ideal. Nonetheless, it is interesting that the proportion Catholic differs substantially between the NIS-P English interviewees and the GSS foreign-born sample—27.3 versus 40.3 percent. These figures are consistent with a number of mechanisms: 1) Catholics who do not speak English are more likely to leave the United States; 2) Catholics prefer to speak in their native language even if they know English; and 3) Catholics learn English as their stay lengthens. Whether these mechanisms are at work and the strength of their operation are matters that the NIS, with its large sample and longitudinal design, will be able to address.

Additional hints in table 12.2 point to a link between knowledge of English (or at least the preference to be interviewed in English) and the preference for no religion—while 15 percent of the sample report a preference for no religion, only 8 percent of those interviewed in English do so. It may be that becoming American means becoming religious (or, alternatively, becoming free to declare a religious preference), but further exploration of that link must await the larger sample size of the NIS.

RELIGIOUS PREFERENCE AND ORIGIN COUNTRY

Table 12.3 reports the top five origin countries for NIS-P immigrants in each religious grouping, including no religion.[14] The estimates in table 12.3 may be thought of as answers to the question, What is the likely origin country of recent immigrants of a specific religious preference? As shown, Mexico is the top provider of both Catholics (27.6 percent) and Protestants (12.4 percent), with Jamaica a close second as provider of Protestants (12 percent).[15] The Philippines is the second top provider of Catholics (12.6 percent) and the fourth provider of Protestants (5.5 percent). Jewish, Eastern Orthodox Christian, and Hindu immigrants are overwhelmingly single-source groups—70 percent of Jews and 57 percent of Eastern Orthodox Christians originating in countries of the former Soviet Union and 60 percent of Hindus originating in India. In contrast, only 12 percent of Protestant immigrants originate in the top origin country (Mexico). In an intermediate place are Buddhists, whose top origin countries (Taiwan and Thailand) send 21 and 19 percent, respectively, and Muslims, whose top origin country (Pakistan) contributes 18 percent.

Buddhists are also drawn from Vietnam, China, and, to a lesser extent, Japan; and Muslims are also drawn from Bangladesh (10.6 percent) and Jordan (9.4 percent), with Iran and India each providing around 6 percent. Interestingly, Iran is the source for almost equal percentages of Jews and Muslims (though not equal numbers). Finally, the former Soviet Union, besides providing most of the Jewish and Eastern Orthodox Christian immigrants, also provides the top share of immigrants with no religion (23 percent), although it is closely followed by China (22 percent) and, more distantly, by Vietnam (7.2 percent), which also provides 5.5 percent of Catholics, and Mexico (6.6 percent), which also provides the largest proportions of Catholics and Protestants.

Table 12.4 provides a complementary view, presenting, for selected countries, the percentage distributions across religious group. The estimates in table 12.4 may be thought of as answers to the question, What is the likely religious preference of immigrants from a specific origin country? As shown, the country with the largest proportion Catholic among its immigrants is Poland (92 percent), followed by Peru (86.8 percent), the Dominican Republic (86.4 percent), the Philippines (82.1 percent), and Mexico (77.8 percent).

Table 12.3. Top Five Origin Countries of Each Religious-Preference Group, with Percentage from Each Country: NIS-P 1996 Adult Immigrants

Religious preference							
Jewish	*Catholic*	*Orthodox*	*Protestant*	*Muslim*	*Buddhist*	*Hindu*	*No religion*
Former Soviet Union 70.4	Mexico 27.6	Former Soviet Union 56.9	Mexico 12.4	Pakistan 18.4	Taiwan 21.4	India 59.8	Former Soviet Union 23.0
Argentina 6.7	Philippines 12.6	Ethiopia 9.7	Jamaica 12.0	Bangladesh 10.6	Thailand 19.5	Guyana 12.1	China 22.1
Israel 6.7	Poland 7.4	Romania 7.4	Former Soviet Union 6.2	Jordan 9.4	Vietnam 16.7	Trinidad 9.2	Vietnam 7.2
Iran 5.2	Dominican Republic 6.1	Yugoslavia 7.4	Philippines 5.5	Iran 6.0	China 11.0	Nepal 6.3	Mexico 6.6
		Lebanon 4.2				Kenya 4.0	
Nigeria 5.2	Vietnam 5.5	Turkey 4.2	Ghana 4.4	India 5.6	Japan 5.2	Suriname 4.0	Taiwan 5.0
25	376	38	197	74	40	32	166

Note: Estimates are for adults aged 18 and older and are based on weighted data. Sample sizes appear in bottom row.

Table 12.4. Religious Preference among NIS-P Adult Immigrants by Country of Birth

Country of birth	Religious preference									N
	Jewish	Catholic	Orthodox	Protestant	Muslim	Buddhist	Hindu	Other	No religion	
China	0	5.9	0	12.6	0	8.5	0	9.6	63.5	73
Taiwan	0	0	0	6.2	0	46.9	0	6.2	40.6	23
India	0	11.4	0	11.4	12.4	3.8	56.2	4.9	0	30
Korea	0	37.7	0	52.5	0	0	0	0	9.8	18
Philippines	0	82.1	0	15.8	0	0	0	0	2.1	70
Vietnam	0	53.1	0	3.1	0	15.6	0	3.1	25.0	32
Mexico	0	77.8	0	15.5	0	0	0	0	6.6	116
Dominican Republic	0	86.4	0	4.6	0	0	0	0	9.1	22
Poland	0	92.0	4.0	0	0	0	0	0	4.0	35
Former Soviet Union	19.6	3.7	25.4	12.4	0	1.4	0	0.4	37.0	80
Canada	0	43.3	0	32.2	0	0	0	0	24.4	30
El Salvador	0	62.9	0	17.2	0	0	0	0	19.8	23
Jamaica	0	11.5	0	83.4	0	0	0	0	5.0	21
United Kingdom	0	18.7	0	54.7	0	0	0	0	26.7	25
Pakistan	0	0	0	0	91.6	0	0	8.4	0	19
Peru	0	86.8	0	6.6	0	6.6	0	0	0	18
Other	2.3	32.5	4.9	23.2	17.7	4.9	4.0	0.8	9.8	322
All immigrants	2.6	42.4	4.2	18.8	8.0	4.1	3.4	1.4	15.1	957

Note: Estimates are for adults aged 18 and older and are based on weighted data. Row percentages sum to 100.

The country with the largest proportion Protestant among its immigrants is Jamaica (83.4 percent), followed by the United Kingdom (54.7 percent) and Korea (52.5 percent). At the other extreme, the country with the largest percentage of no-religion immigrants is China (63.5 percent), followed more than 20 percentage points behind by Taiwan (40.6 percent) and the former Soviet Union (37 percent), with the United Kingdom, Vietnam, Canada, and El Salvador each registering 20 to 27 percent of their immigrants in the no-religion group.

Deeper insight into these figures requires additional questions and longitudinal tracking, as will be provided by the full NIS. Such data will shed light on both response effects and changes over the life course. For example, among immigrants from China, the former Soviet Union, and Vietnam, the no-religion statement may be accurate or instead may reflect the lifelong habit of keeping religion a secret; moreover, even if accurate, it may change over time. Similarly, those immigrants declaring a preference for Catholicism may change their religion or even reject religion altogether.

Overall, table 12.4 provides dramatic evidence of the universality of the Christian religions—whose Catholic and Protestant versions are represented among immigrants from almost all countries—and of the no-religion option, which is also exercised universally.

RELIGIOUS PREFERENCE AND VISA CLASS OF ADMISSION

As noted earlier, the observed configuration of religious preference also reflects the pathways by which persons gain legal permanent residence in the United States. The NIS-P respondents hold a total of seventy-eight distinct visa types. Here, we group the visas into nine major visa classes, plus a residual category. The nine visa classes include the two major numerically unlimited visa types available to adults—spouse of U.S. citizen and parent of U.S. citizen—and include as well the major numerically limited family-reunification classes—spouse of permanent resident alien and sibling of U.S. citizen—and the employment-based classes, plus the refugee class and the diversity-based category (whose visas are also known as "lottery" visas).[16] The oversampling of employment-based immigrants makes it possible to further subdivide employment-based immigrants according to whether the respondent is the principal immigrant (the immigrant who qualified on the basis of job skills) or the spouse of the principal immigrant.

Additionally, the visa type makes it possible to subdivide the spouses of U.S. citizens according to whether they have been married less than or more than two years;[17] longer-married immigrants in this group may be the spouses of persons who were legalized under the provisions of the Immigrant Reform and Control Act of 1986 (IRCA) and who have become naturalized citizens. Thus, the religious composition of the longer-married couples may be less representative of current trends. All the spouses of permanent resident aliens in the cohort have been married for more than two years and, like the longer-married spouses of U.S. citizens, may include spouses of IRCA-amnestied immigrants.[18]

Religious Preference by Visa Class of Admission
Table 12.5 reports the top five major visa classes for each religious preference group, including the no-religion group. The estimates in table 12.5 may be thought of as answers to the question, What is the likely visa class of recent immigrants of a specific religious preference? As shown, the answer is unambiguous. The two top visa classes represented in all the religion groups are newly married spouse of U.S. citizen and refugee/asylee. The proportion holding the newlywed spouse-of-U.S.-citizen visa is in the range of 22 to 29 percent among Catholics, Protestants, Muslims, Buddhists, and Hindus and exceeds that number among Eastern Orthodox Christians, 42 percent of whom are among the newlywed spouses. Meanwhile, more than two-thirds of the Jewish immigrants hold refugee/asylee visas, and 20 percent of the no-religion immigrants also hold refugee/asylee visas. Note, however, that combining the newlywed and longer-married spouses of U.S. citizens makes the spouse-of-U.S.-citizen visa the top category for the no-religion immigrants.

The newlywed–spouse category is also in second place among the no-religion immigrants and in third place among the Jewish immigrants. These figures underscore the well-known fact that the spouse-of-U.S.-citizen visa is the "workhorse" of U.S. immigration (29 percent of the adult immigrants in the NIS-P are spouses of U.S. citizens). Other results worth noting in table 12.5 include the nontrivial fractions of employment-based principals in several categories and the dominance of Catholic immigration by spouses (not only spouses of U.S. citizens but also spouses of permanent resident aliens). In addition, the estimates in table 12.5 raise further questions that cannot be answered without larger sample sizes (again, the full NIS will enable such further

Table 12.5. Top Five Major Visa Classes for Each Religious-Preference Group, with Percent from Each Visa Class: NIS-P Adult Immigrants

	Religious preference							
	Jewish	Catholic	Orthodox	Protestant	Muslim	Buddhist	Hindu	No religion
	Ref 67.4	Sp-Citz (<2) 22.2	Sp-Citz (<2) 42.1	Sp-Citz (<2) 23.2	Sp-Citz (<2) 28.8	Sp-Citz (<2) 23.3	Sp-Citz (<2) 24.1	Ref 19.8
	Emp-Prin 5.9	Sp-C5itz (>2) 11.6	Div 29.2	Emp-Prin 10.6	Div 18.6	Sib-Citz 20.0	Par-Citz 16.1	Sp-Citz (<2) 14.4
	Sp-Citz (<2) 5.2	Sp-PRA 11.6	Ref 9.7	Sp-Citz (>2) 9.4	Par-Citz 13.6	Ref 13.3	Sib-Citz 12.1	Emp-Prin 11.1
						Emp-Prin 6.7		
	Sp-PRA 5.2	Par-Citz 9.0	Emp-Prin 6.5	Ref 8.0	Sp-PRA 6.8	Emp-Sp 6.7	Sp-PRA 8.0	Sp-Citz (>2) 8.1
				Par-Citz 7.3		Sp-PRA 6.7		
	Div 5.2	Ref 6.8	Par-Citz 3.2	Sp-PRA 7.3	Emp-Prin 6.3	Div 6.7	Emp-Sp 8.0	Sib-Citz 8.1
	25	376	38	197	74	40	32	166

Note: Estimates are for adults aged 18 and older and are based on weighted data. Sample sizes appear in bottom row. Key: Ref = refugee; EmpPrin = employment principal; Sp-Citz (<2) = spouse of U.S. citizen, married less than 2 years; Sp-Citz (>2) = spouse of U.S. citizen, married more than 2 years; Sp-PRA = spouse of permanent resident alien; DIV = diversity; Par-Citz = parent of U.S. citizen; Sib-Citz = sibling of U.S. citizen; Emp-Sp = spouse of employment principal.

research). For example, it is curious that only one religious grouping—Buddhist—includes both employment-based principals and employment-based spouses among the top five visa classes; other groupings including only employment-based principals (Jewish, Eastern Orthodox Christian, Protestant, Muslim, and the no-religious group) or only employment-based spouses (Hindu). Mechanisms that may be operating include a correlation between marital status and religious preference—such that single employment-based principals are over- or underrepresented among certain religious groups—and mixed-religion marriages. Finally, note the dearth of employment-based visas among Catholics. This could be due to their hyperattractiveness in the marriage market and/or to their hypoattractiveness in the job market.

Table 12.6 provides a complementary view, reporting, for each of the major visa classes, the proportions in each religious-preference group. As shown, the proportion Catholic within visa classes ranges from 11.6 percent among diversity-based immigrants to 60 percent among spouses of permanent resident aliens; the proportion Catholic among newly married spouses of U.S. citizens is 42 percent and among parents of U.S. citizens 47.5 percent. These figures suggest that residents and citizens of the United States who marry and sponsor the immigration of foreign-born spouses are either themselves Catholic or choose mates who are Catholic and that, among former immigrants who naturalize, Catholics are likely to seek to bring their parents to the United States. While these figures are suggestive, they raise new questions that cannot yet be answered. For example, it would be important to learn whether among immigrants, and ceteris paribus, Catholics are more likely to naturalize than persons of other or no religion and whether among naturalized immigrants, again ceteris paribus, Catholics are more likely to sponsor the immigration of their parents. Note that as the NIS becomes institutionalized and information is collected five, ten, and fifteen years after immigration, it will be possible to answer these questions for sampled immigrant cohorts. Similarly, it would be important to learn whether among the native born, Catholics are more likely to marry foreign-born persons or whether U.S. native born who marry foreign-born persons are more likely to marry Catholics. These questions go to the heart of both family values and the universality of Catholicism.

A different way to approach table 12.6 is to look closely at the visa classes in which selected religious-preference groupings—those with abundant sample size—are over- or underrepresented relative to their proportion in the

Table 12.6.   Religious Preference among New Immigrants Aged 18 Years and Over by Visa Class of Admission: NIS-P 1996 Cohort Sample

Class of admission	Jewish	Catholic	Orthodox	Protestant	Muslim	Buddhist	Hindu	Other	No religion	N
Spouse of U.S. citizen, married <2 years	0.6	42.3	8.0	19.6	10.4	4.3	3.7	1.2	9.8	163
Spouse of U.S. citizen, married >2 years	0	59.0	0	21.3	3.3	1.6	0	0	14.8	61
Spouse of permanent resident alien	1.7	60.0	0	16.7	6.7	3.3	3.3	1.7	6.7	60
Parent of U.S. citizen	0	47.5	1.7	17.0	13.6	1.7	6.8	0	11.9	59
Sibling of U.S. citizen, principal and spouse	0	34.4	0	3.1	3.1	18.8	9.4	3.1	28.1	32
Employment based, principal	2.1	30.2	3.7	27.0	6.9	3.7	1.6	2.1	22.8	189
Employment based, spouse	2.6	20.9	2.6	24.4	5.2	6.1	6.1	5.2	27.0	115
Refugee/asylee, principal and spouse	16.9	27.3	3.9	14.3	3.9	5.2	0	0	28.6	77
Diversity based, principal and spouse	2.3	11.6	20.9	20.9	25.6	4.6	0	2.3	11.6	43
Other	1.2	53.3	1.2	19.2	5.4	1.8	4.2	1.8	12.0	167
All immigrants	2.6	42.4	4.2	18.8	8.0	4.1	3.4	1.4	15.1	966

Religious preference

Note: Row percentages sum to 100. Estimates for "All immigrants" based on weighted data.

whole sample. Accordingly, we examine the four groups with the largest sample sizes—Catholics, Protestants, Muslims, and no-religion immigrants. The proportion Catholic is lower than in the whole sample—lower, that is, than 42 percent—in all the separately identified major visa classes except the spouses of U.S. citizens and permanent resident aliens and the parents of U.S. citizens. Protestants, who constitute 18.6 percent of the whole sample, are overrepresented among the employment-based (27 percent among principals and 24 percent among spouses of principals) and diversity immigrants (21 percent) and underrepresented among the siblings of U.S. citizens (3.1 percent). Muslims, who are 8 percent of the sample, are overrepresented among diversity immigrants (25.6 percent) and parents of U.S. citizens (13.6 percent) and underrepresented among longer-married spouses of U.S. citizens (3.3 percent) and refugees (3.9 percent). Finally, no-religion immigrants, who constitute 15 percent of the sample, are overrepresented among refugee, sibling, and employment-based immigrants and underrepresented among spouses of permanent resident aliens and newlywed spouses of U.S. citizens.

Thus, among employment-based principals, the largest proportions are Catholic, Protestant, and of no religion, but of these only the Protestant and no-religion immigrants are overrepresented.

Finally, note the differences between newlywed and longer-married spouses of U.S. citizens. The newlywed group, which constitutes 72.8 percent of the spouses, is substantially less Catholic than is the longer-married group (42 vs. 59 percent), more Muslim (10.4 vs. 3.3 percent), and somewhat less likely to be in the no-religion group (9.8 vs. 14.8 percent).

To further explore the relationships between religious preference and visa type, we report in tables 12.7 and 12.8, the visa-specific proportions separately for men and women. Except among employment immigrants and Catholics, the sample sizes are small, and caution should be exercised in discussing and interpreting these figures.

Among recently married spouses of U.S. citizens, immigrant bridegrooms are substantially more likely than immigrant brides to be Catholic—52 versus 37 percent. This large difference of 15 percentage points suggests that the pool of U.S. women who marry foreign-born mates differs importantly from the pool of U.S. men who marry foreign-born mates. This is consistent with the finding[19] that the two subsets differ significantly in educational attainment, with U.S.-citizen men (and their immigrant brides) averaging 2.4 more years

Table 12.7. Religious Preference among Immigrant Men Aged 18 Years and Over by Visa Class of Admission: NIS-P 1996 Cohort Sample

Class of admission	Religious preference									N
	Jewish	Catholic	Orthodox	Protestant	Muslim	Buddhist	Hindu	Other	No religion	
Spouse of U.S. citizen, married <2 years	0	51.6	4.8	17.7	11.3	3.2	3.2	1.6	6.4	62
Spouse of U.S. citizen, married >2 years	0	56.2	0	21.9	0	3.1	0	0	18.8	32
Spouse of permanent resident alien	0	30.0	0	20.0	0	10.0	20.0	0	20.0	10
Parent of U.S. citizen	0	52.6	0	15.8	10.5	0	15.8	0	5.3	19
Sibling of U.S. citizen, principal and spouse	0	23.5	0	5.9	0	29.4	5.9	5.9	29.4	17
Employment based, principal	2.2	26.5	4.4	27.9	9.6	2.9	2.2	2.9	21.3	136
Employment based, spouse	0	25.7	0	40.0	2.9	11.4	5.7	5.7	8.6	35
Refugee/asylee, principal and spouse	15.8	34.2	2.6	15.8	2.6	2.6	0	0	26.3	38
Diversity based, principal and spouse	4.0	8.0	28.0	16.0	32.0	4.0	0	4.0	4.0	25
Other	0	52.6	1.3	15.4	7.7	0	3.8	3.8	15.4	78
All immigrants	2.4	41.2	4.2	18.4	8.2	4.1	3.8	2.2	15.3	452

Note: Row percentages sum to 100. Estimates for "All immigrants" based on weighted data.

Table 12.8. Religious Preference among Immigrant Women Aged 18 Years and Over by Visa Class of Admission: NIS-P 1996 Cohort Sample

Class of admission	Religious preference									N
	Jewish	Catholic	Orthodox	Protestant	Muslim	Buddhist	Hindu	Other	No religion	
Spouse of U.S. citizen, married <2 years	1.0	36.6	9.9	20.8	9.9	5.0	4.0	1.0	11.9	101
Spouse of U.S. citizen, married >2 years	0	62.1	0	20.7	6.9	0	0	0	10.3	29
Spouse of permanent resident alien	2.0	66.0	0	16.0	8.0	2.0	0	2.0	4.0	50
Parent of U.S. citizen	0	45.0	2.5	17.5	15.0	2.5	2.5	0	15.0	40
Sibling of U.S. citizen, principal and spouse	0	46.7	0	0	6.7	6.7	13.3	0	26.7	15
Employment based, principal	1.9	39.6	1.9	24.5	0	5.7	0	0	26.4	53
Employment based, spouse	3.8	18.8	3.8	17.5	6.2	3.8	6.2	5.0	35.0	80
Refugee/asylee, principal and spouse	18.0	20.5	5.1	12.8	5.1	7.7	0	0	30.8	39
Diversity based, principal and spouse	0	16.7	11.1	27.8	16.7	5.6	0	0	22.2	18
Other	2.2	53.9	1.1	22.5	3.4	3.4	4.5	0	9.0	89
All immigrants	2.8	43.3	4.2	19.0	7.9	4.1	3.0	0.8	15.0	514

Note: Row percentages sum to 100. Estimates for "All immigrants" based on weighted data.

of schooling than U.S.-citizen women (and their immigrant bridegrooms). The new information on religion suggests that the profile of U.S.-citizen women who marry foreign-born mates is a more Catholic one and one with lower schooling attainment than that of U.S.-citizen men who marry foreign-born mates.

In contrast, among longer-married couples, including both spouses of U.S. citizens and those of permanent resident aliens, the proportion Catholic is larger among immigrant women than among immigrant men. However, the sample sizes are smaller, and we refrain from discussing them here, except to say that the full NIS, with its large sample, will make it possible to explore the questions raised by this result, for example, whether it reflects the continuing effects of IRCA and so on.

Immigrants with employment-based visas also display interesting gender-related patterns of religious preference. While among principals (those who qualified for the visa on the basis of their job or job skills) the proportion Catholic is 13 percentage points higher among women than among men (39.6 vs. 26.5 percent), the opposite is true for spouses of employment-based principals, with the proportion Catholic among men exceeding that among women by 7 percentage points (25.7 vs. 18.8 percent). Restricting attention to married principals does not alter the results; the proportion Catholic among married male principals is 27 percent and among married female principals 44 percent.

To gain additional insight, we contrast the proportion female among the Catholic and non-Catholic subsets within the set of all employment-based principals. While women constitute over one-third (36.8 percent) of the Catholic employment-based principals, they do not reach a quarter (24.1 percent) of the non-Catholic ones. Again, incorporating marital status does not alter the Catholic/non-Catholic differential. Among married employment-based principals, the proportion female is 16 and 29 percent, respectively, in the non-Catholic and Catholic subsets; among the nonmarried, the corresponding figures are 40 and 53 percent.

Meanwhile, among the spouses of employment-based principals, the proportion female is lower among Catholics (60.9 percent) than among non-Catholics (72 percent), and the proportion Catholic is lower among women (17.3 percent) than among men (25.7 percent).

Thus, there are two unanswered questions: one concerning the religious preference of employment-based immigrants and the other concerning the possibility that religiously mixed marriages may be more common among employment-based immigrants. Again, the full NIS, which will collect information from spouses of sampled respondents as well as from the respondents themselves, will enable exploring these marriage and religion patterns.

Finally, tables 12.7 and 12.8 indicate that, of the Catholic parents sponsored, almost two-thirds (64.3 percent) are mothers. Thus, if parents and children have the same religion, Catholics are more likely to sponsor mothers than fathers. Of course, this may be due to the greater longevity of mothers relative to fathers or to a propensity to sponsor widowed parents, who, again because of differential life expectancy, are more likely to be mothers.

Nativity of the Sponsors of Immigrant Spouses

The NIS-P collected information on the nativity of the sampled immigrant's visa sponsor. Thus, among the immigrant spouses of U.S. citizens, it is possible to contrast religious preference not only between newlywed and longer-married couples but also between couples in which the sponsor is a native-born U.S. citizen and couples in which the sponsor is a naturalized immigrant. The sample sizes are substantially smaller, and in this section, though we present full tabulations, we discuss only the results for newlywed couples, which are based on a generous sample size.

Table 12.9 reports the religious-preference distributions for the four duration/ nativity subsets. As shown, among newlywed couples, the proportion Catholic among the immigrant spouses is substantially larger for native-born sponsors than for foreign-born sponsors. Thus, native-born U.S. citizens who marry foreign-born persons and come to live in the United States soon after their marriage are more likely to choose a Catholic mate than are naturalized U.S. citizens in a similar situation.

Tables 12.10 and 12.11 report the same information separately by sex. A fortiori, we restrict attention to the newlywed group. The major findings are 1) that U.S.-citizen women are more likely to choose a Catholic mate than are their male U.S.-citizen counterparts (57.5 vs. 40.4 percent among native born and 44.4 vs. 25.6 percent among foreign born) and 2) that native-born U.S. citizens are more likely to choose a Catholic mate than naturalized U.S. citizens (57.5 vs. 44.4 percent among women and 40.4 vs. 25.6 percent among men). There are other hints in tables 12.10 and 12.11 (e.g., involving Muslim and no-religion immigrants), but sample size does not support further discussion.

Table 12.9. Religious Preference among Immigrant Spouses of U.S. Citizens by Marital Duration and Sponsor Nativity: NIS-P 1996 Cohort Sample

Marital duration/sponsor nativity	Religious preference									N
	Jewish	Catholic	Orthodox	Protestant	Muslim	Buddhist	Hindu	Other	No religion	
A. Married <2 years										
U.S. citizen sponsor native born	1.0	47.8	6.5	19.6	7.6	5.4	1.1	0	10.9	92
U.S. citizen sponsor foreign born	0	31.6	8.8	21.0	15.8	3.5	8.8	3.5	7.0	57
B. Married >2 Years										
U.S. citizen sponsor native born	0	52.2	0	26.1	0	0	0	0	21.7	23
U.S. citizen sponsor foreign born	0	65.6	0	18.8	6.2	3.1	0	0	6.2	32

Note: Row percentages sum to 100. The proportions with native-born spouses are 61.7 percent among the newly married and 41.8 percent among the longer-married couples.

Table 12.10. Religious Preference among Immigrant Husbands of U.S. Citizens by Marital Duration and Sponsor Nativity: NIS-P 1996 Cohort Sample

Marital duration/sponsor nativity	Religious preference									N
	Jewish	Catholic	Orthodox	Protestant	Muslim	Buddhist	Hindu	Other	No religion	
A. Married <2 years										
U.S. citizen sponsor (wife) native born	0	57.5	5.0	17.5	10.0	2.5	2.5	0	5.0	40
U.S. citizen sponsor (wife) foreign born	0	44.4	5.6	16.7	11.1	5.6	5.6	5.6	5.6	18
B. Married >2 Years										
U.S. citizen sponsor (wife) native born	0	58.8	0	17.6	0	0	0	0	23.5	17
U.S. citizen sponsor (wife) foreign born	0	50.0	0	30.0	0	10.0	0	0	10.0	10

Note: Row percentages sum to 100. Immigrant husbands represent 41.7 percent of the immigrant spouses of U.S. citizens. Among these immigrant husbands, the proportions with native-born spouses are 69 percent among the newly married and 63 percent among the longer married.

Table 12.11. Religious Preference among Immigrant Wives of U.S. Citizens by Marital Duration and Sponsor Nativity: NIS-P 1996 Cohort Sample

Marital duration/sponsor nativity	Jewish	Catholic	Orthodox	Protestant	Muslim	Buddhist	Hindu	Other	No religion	N
					Religious preference					
A. Married <2 years										
U.S. citizen sponsor (husband) native born	1.9	40.4	7.7	21.2	5.8	7.7	0	0	15.4	52
U.S. citizen sponsor (husband) foreign born	0	25.6	10.3	23.1	18.0	2.6	5.6	2.6	7.7	39
B. Married >2 years										
U.S. citizen sponsor (husband) native born	0	33.3	0	50.0	0	0	0	0	16.7	6
U.S. citizen sponsor (husband) foreign born	0	72.7	0	13.6	9.1	0	0	0	4.6	22

Note: Row percentages sum to 100. Immigrant wives represent 58.3 percent of the immigrant spouses of U.S. citizens. Among these immigrant wives, the proportions with native-born spouses are 57.1 percent among the newly married and 21.4 percent among the longer married.

RELIGIOUS PREFERENCE AND EDUCATIONAL ATTAINMENT

Schooling among New Legal Immigrants

Table 12.12 reports the average years of schooling completed among recent immigrants aged twenty-five and over by religious preference. Among men, the figures range from 12.1 years (among Catholics) to 16.4 years (among Buddhists); among women, the span is from 10.8 (among Muslims) to 15.4 (among Hindus). Thus, the schooling differential across religious-preference groups is more than four years among men and approximately the difference between high school and college graduation. Among women, the schooling differential is slightly larger (4.6 years) and approximately one year lower on the schooling continuum.

The most educated immigrants are, among men, Buddhists and Muslims, with 16.4 and 15.1 average years of schooling, respectively, while among women, the most educated are Hindus, Orthodox Christians, and those of no

Table 12.12.   Average Years of Schooling among New Immigrants Aged 25 Years and Over by Religious Preference: NIS-P 1996 Cohort Sample

	Men		Women		All	
Religious preference	Mean (SD)	N	Mean (SD)	N	Mean (SD)	N
Jewish	13.1 (2.7)	10	14.4 (2.0)	12	13.8 (2.4)	22
Christian—Catholic	12.1 (4.9)	125	11.4 (5.7)	161	11.7 (5.4)	286
Christian—Orthodox	14.8 (3.0)	18	15.0 (3.7)	17	14.9 (3.3)	35
Christian—Protestant	13.6 (4.2)	86	12.1 (5.0)	76	12.8 (4.7)	162
Muslim	15.1 (6.9)	32	10.8 (5.7)	26	12.9 (6.6)	58
Buddhist	16.4 (2.8)	19	12.5 (3.5)	19	14.4 (3.7)	38
Hindu	12.2 (5.7)	13	15.4 (2.9)	13	13.7 (4.8)	26
Other	15.2 (6.9)	10	14.4 (3.6)	6	15.0 (5.8)	16
No religion	14.2 (4.3)	60	14.8 (4.7)	83	14.6 (4.6)	143
All immigrants	13.5 (4.9)	373	12.5 (5.3)	413	12.9 (5.1)	786
N		373		413		786

Note: Estimates are based on weighted data.

religion, with 15.4, 15, and 14.8 average years of schooling, respectively. Those with the lowest schooling are, among men, Catholics (12.1 years), followed closely by Hindus (12.2 years) and, at almost a year more of schooling, on average, Jews (13.1 years). Among women, those with the least schooling are Muslims (10.8 years), followed by Catholics (11.4 years) and Protestants (12.1 years).

Although sample sizes are small in several cases (see table 12.12), the figures suggest an overall pattern in which Catholics and Protestant women have relatively low schooling, as do Muslim women, and the most educated immigrants are from newer religions on the American landscape—men of Buddhist, Muslim, and other Eastern religions and women of Hindu and Christian Orthodox religions as well as no-religion women.

A further interesting result in table 12.12, but again one whose analysis requires a larger sample size, involves the possible assortative mating effects. While Orthodox and Catholic Christians and no-religion immigrants have a small sex differential in schooling (e.g., two-tenths of one year among the Orthodox), immigrants of Muslim, Buddhist, and Hindu religion have larger sex differentials in schooling, ranging from 4.3 years between Muslim men and women to 3.2 years between Hindu men and women. Interestingly, the direction of the differential differs, with Muslim and Buddhist men outschooling women but Hindu women outschooling men.

Schooling Attainment by Visa Category

To further explore educational attainment among recent immigrants, we report, in table 12.13, the average schooling completed by visa class and, in tables 12.14 and 12.15, the same information for men and women separately. Table 12.13 presents, in the right-most column, labeled "All," the average years of schooling completed by visa class. The most educated immigrants tend to be employment-based principals, their spouses, the spouses of U.S. citizens, and diversity-based immigrants. The high schooling of the spouses of employment-based principals and of the newlywed spouses of U.S. citizens reflects assortative mating mechanisms, given the high average schooling of employment-based principals and also of U.S. citizens. The high schooling of diversity-based immigrants reflects the educational requirement for diversity-based principals (a high school diploma or its equivalent, or two years of work experience, within the past five years, in an occupation requiring at least two years of training or experience) and, again, assortative mating.[20]

Table 12.13. Average Years of Schooling among New Immigrants Aged 25 Years and Over by Religious Preference and Visa Class of Admission: NIS-P 1996 Cohort Sample

Class of admission	Religious preference									All
	Jewish	Catholic	Orthodox	Protestant	Muslim	Buddhist	Hindu	Other	No religion	
Spouse of U.S. citizen, married <2 years	18.0	13.8	15.1	13.4	15.0	13.7	13.0	7.5	15.7	14.0
Spouse of U.S. citizen, married >2 years	—	11.8	—	13.8	19.0	21.0	—	—	14.0	12.9
Spouse of permanent resident alien	16.0	9.2	—	8.0	13.8	15.0	14.0	16.0	10.8	10.1
Parent of U.S. citizen	—	5.7	7.0	7.4	5.5	10.0	13.5	—	10.6	7.2
Sibling of U.S. citizen, principal and spouse	—	13.4	—	12.0	12.0	16.2	15.0	12.0	12.7	13.7
Employment based, principal	14.2	15.5	17.1	16.3	17.6	14.6	16.7	24.0	18.8	16.8
Employment based, spouse	14.3	14.5	16.7	14.9	14.5	14.3	16.0	17.0	16.5	15.4
Refugee/asylee, principal and spouse	13.0	13.7	15.7	10.8	6.0	12.5	—	—	14.5	13.1
Diversity based, principal and spouse	16.0	15.3	13.3	13.8	15.5	17.0	—	18.0	15.4	14.7
Other	—	11.8	21.0	13.4	13.2	10.5	11.7	15.0	11.6	12.5
All immigrants	13.8	11.7	14.9	13.8	13.3	14.4	13.7	12.9	14.6	12.9

Note: Estimates for "All immigrants" based on weighted data.

Table 12.14. Average Years of Schooling among Immigrant Men Aged 25 Years and Over by Religious Preference and Visa Class of Admission: NIS-P 1996 Cohort Sample

Class of admission	Religious preference									
	Jewish	Catholic	Orthodox	Protestant	Muslim	Buddhist	Hindu	Other	No religion	All
Spouse of U.S. citizen, married <2 years	—	13.1	14.3	11.9	17.3	17.5	5.0	5.0	13.5	13.2
Spouse of U.S. citizen, married >2 years	—	9.8	—	12.6	—	21.0	—	—	15.0	11.8
Spouse of permanent resident alien	—	14.7	—	9.5	—	15.0	14.0	—	10.0	12.6
Parent of U.S. citizen	—	5.2	—	13.7	3.0	—	14.0	—	16.0	8.3
Sibling of U.S. citizen, principal and spouse	—	15.8	—	12.0	—	16.2	19.0	12.0	11.2	14.3
Employment based, principal	14.0	14.8	16.8	16.8	17.6	16.2	16.7	24.0	17.9	16.8
Employment based, spouse	—	14.6	—	15.7	19.0	15.8	18.0	17.0	15.0	15.6
Refugee/asylee, principal and spouse	12.5	13.3	16.0	9.8	12.0	12.0	—	—	14.4	12.9
Diversity based, principal and spouse	16.0	14.0	13.6	13.2	16.5	18.0	—	18.0	13.0	14.8
Other	—	13.0	20.0	16.0	13.7	—	5.0	15.0	11.8	13.4
All immigrants	13.1	12.1	14.8	13.6	15.1	16.4	12.2	15.2	14.2	13.5

Note: Estimates for "All immigrants" based on weighted data.

Table 12.15. Average Years of Schooling among Immigrant Women Aged 25 Years and Over by Religious Preference and Visa Class of Admission: NIS-P 1996 Cohort Sample

Class of admission	Religious preference									All
	Jewish	Catholic	Orthodox	Protestant	Muslim	Buddhist	Hindu	Other	No religion	
Spouse of U.S. citizen, married <2 years	18.0	14.5	15.4	14.4	12.2	11.8	18.3	10.0	16.2	14.6
Spouse of U.S. citizen, married >2 years	—	13.9	—	15.2	19.0	—	—	—	12.3	14.2
Spouse of permanent resident alien	16.0	8.7	—	7.4	13.8	15.0	—	16.0	11.5	9.5
Parent of U.S. citizen	—	5.9	7.0	4.7	6.3	10.0	12.0	—	9.7	6.2
Sibling of U.S. citizen, principal and spouse	—	12.0	—	—	12.0	16.0	13.0	—	14.5	13.1
Employment based, principal	15.0	16.7	19.0	14.8	—	12.3	—	—	20.5	17.0
Employment based, spouse	14.3	14.5	16.7	14.1	13.6	12.3	15.6	17.0	16.7	15.3
Refugee/asylee, principal and spouse	13.5	14.2	15.5	11.6	0.0	12.7	—	—	14.5	13.3
Diversity based, principal and spouse	—	18.0	12.5	14.2	12.5	16.0	—	—	16.0	14.6
Other	—	10.9	22.0	11.6	12.0	10.5	15.0	—	11.0	11.7
All immigrants	14.4	11.4	15.0	12.1	10.8	12.5	15.4	14.4	14.8	12.5

Note: Estimates for "All immigrants" based on weighted data.

Given the gender differences in table 12.12 as well as the earlier finding of a sex differential in schooling among the spouses of U.S. citizens, we do not discuss table 12.13 but move immediately to the two sex-specific tables. Again, we begin with the right-most column, labeled "All." Immigrant women (table 12.15) display the expected patterns exactly: The most educated immigrant women are employment-based principals (17 years), employment-based spouses (15.3 years), newlywed spouses of U.S. citizens (14.6 years), and diversity-based immigrants (14.6 years). Immigrant men, however, deviate from the pattern in that spouses of U.S. citizens are not in the top group (newlywed or otherwise); among men, the most educated are employment-based principals (16.8 years), employment-based spouses (15.6 years), diversity-based immigrants (14.8 years), and sibling immigrants (14.3 years). This is not surprising, given the earlier finding of sex-specific pools of U.S. citizens sponsoring immigrant spouses.

Next we examine differences across religious-preference groups. We restrict attention to religious-preference groups with at least fifteen respondents; among both women and men, the religious-preference groups satisfying this criterion are all three Christian groups, Muslims, Buddhists, and the no-religion group (table 12.12). Table 12.14 indicates that 1) employment-based principals and spouses are among the top four best-educated visa classes among all six religion-based groups except Buddhists; 2) newlywed spouses of U.S. citizens are among the top four among Orthodox Christian, Muslim, and Buddhist immigrants; and 3) diversity-based immigrants are among the top four only among Muslims and Buddhists. Among women (table 12.15), 1) employment-based principals are among the top four best-educated visa classes among all the religion groups except Buddhists; 2) employment-based spouses are among the top four among all religion groups except Protestants and Buddhists; 3) newlywed spouses of U.S. citizens are among the top four only among Catholics, Protestants, and the no-religion group; and 4) diversity-based immigrants are among the top four best-educated visa classes among all religion groupings except Orthodox Christians.

There is also substantial variability in schooling within visa categories, even within the employment-based principal group. Here we focus on visa classes with large sample sizes, especially the employment based (who were oversampled) and spouses of U.S. citizens. For example, average schooling attainment of employment-based principals ranges from 14 to 24 years among men (a span of 10 years of completed schooling, from Jewish men to other-religion men), and from 12.3 to 20.5 years among women (a range of more than 8 years, from Buddhist women to no-religion women). The schooling of newlywed spouses of U.S. citizens also ranges substantially among both immigrant brides and immigrant bridegrooms. Among newlywed immigrant bridegrooms (table 12.14), schooling ranges from 5 years for the Hindu and the other-religion groups to 17.5 in the Buddhist group; among newlywed immigrant brides (table 12.15), schooling ranges from 10 years for the other-religion group to 18.3 among Hindus.

Assortative Mating by Schooling within Religious-Preference Subsets

A final question concerns assortative mating. Tables 12.14 and 12.15 provide hints about assortative mating among employment-based immigrants under the assumptions that single and married principals are similar and that husbands and wives have the same religion. Those assumptions, however, may be unrealistic. A more direct way to explore assortative mating in schooling across religious-preference groups is to look at married couples, given that the NIS-P obtained information on the schooling of the respondent's spouse, although religious preference is available only for the sampled immigrant.

We restrict attention to married couples in which both the sampled immigrant and his or her spouse are aged twenty-five or older and in which there at least fifteen couples in each subset of couples defined by the sampled immigrant's visa type and religious preference. Four sets of married couples are obtained in this way, comprising Catholic and Protestant employment-based immigrants, separately by whether the wife or husband is the principal immigrant.[21]

Table 12.16 reports the average schooling completed by the husbands and wives in these couples. The information for each set of couples is contained in the diagonals. For example, in couples in which the sampled immigrant is Catholic and the wife is the principal immigrant, the average schooling is 16.3 years for the wife principals and 14.9 years for the husband accompanying spouses.

As shown, the spousal schooling differential is about 1.5 years among these couples, tending to almost two years only in one subset, that involving Protestant wife principals. The direction of the differential is interesting: While among Catholics the principal is the more highly schooled, regardless of gender, among Protestants the husband is always the more highly schooled, on

Table 12.16.   Average Years of Schooling among Married Employment-
Based NIS-P 1996 Immigrants Aged 25 Years and Over, by Religious
Preference and Whether Wife or Husband Is Principal Immigrant

	Wives	Husbands
A. Catholic		
Principal	16.3	16.1
Accompanying spouse	14.5	14.9
B. Protestant		
Principal	13.3	16.4
Accompanying spouse	14.9	15.2

Note: Married couples appear in the diagonals. Sample sizes for the four subsets
of married couples are Catholic employment-based/wife-principal, 15; Catholic
employment-based/husband-principal, 36; Protestant employment-based/
wife-principal, 19; Protestant employment-based/husband-principal, 37.

average, regardless of immigration status. In the entire set of couples with
employment-based visas, average schooling is higher among husbands than
among wives, regardless of which spouse is the principal, but the differential
is attenuated when the wife is the principal.[22] Our new results suggest that the
attenuation in the schooling differential may be due to Catholic couples.

This type of analysis, sharpened still further by looking at the distribution
of couple-specific schooling differentials and incorporating information
about the religious preference of both spouses, will be made possible by the
large sample size of the NIS.

The NIS-P makes it possible, for the first time, to examine religious preference among a probability sample of new legal immigrants. The data suggest
that recent new immigrants, early in the immigrant career, have a distinctive
religious-preference profile, a profile different from that among the native
born. First, approximately two-thirds of the new immigrants are Christian,
substantially below the 82 percent of the native born surveyed in the GSS of
1996. Second, the proportion Catholic among the new immigrants is 42 percent, almost twice as large as among the native born (22 percent). Third, the
proportion reporting themselves outside the Judeo-Christian fold is more
than four times larger among recent immigrants than among the native born
(17 vs. 4 percent). Fourth, 15 percent of the new immigrants report no religion, a larger fraction than among the native born (12 percent).

Examination of religious preference by country of origin underscores the
universality of Christian religions—Catholic and Protestant versions are rep-

EXPLORING THE RELIGIOUS PREFERENCES OF RECENT IMMIGRANTS   249

resented among immigrants from almost all countries—and the preference for no religion is also exercised universally. In contrast, Jewish and Hindu immigrants are overwhelmingly single-source groups, with 70 percent of the Jewish immigrants originating in countries of the former Soviet Union and 60 percent of Hindu immigrants in India. While the largest subset of Catholics come from Mexico (nearly 28 percent), Mexico ranks only fifth in the proportion Catholic among a country's immigrants, after Poland (92 percent), Peru (87 percent), the Dominican Republic (86 percent), and the Philippines (82 percent).

For all religious-preference groups except the Jewish one, the most widely used visa type is marriage to a U.S. citizen. This is not surprising, given this visa's role as the workhorse of U.S. immigration. The NIS-P data also suggest the possibility of gender and visa patterns within religious-preference groups, but the sample sizes are small, and thus sharp analysis must await the full NIS data. For example, U.S.-citizen women are substantially more likely to choose a Catholic mate than are their male U.S.-citizen counterparts (58 vs. 40 percent), and native-born U.S. citizens are more likely to choose a Catholic mate than are naturalized U.S. citizens (58 vs. 44 percent among women and 40 vs. 26 percent among men).

With respect to educational attainment, the data indicate that, among recent new immigrants, Catholics of both sexes, Hindu men, and Protestant and Muslim women have relatively low schooling. The best-educated immigrants are men of Buddhist, Muslim, and other Eastern religions and women who are Hindu or Christian Orthodox or prefer no religion.

A closer look at educational attainment by visa category suggests wide variation within visa category, by gender, and across religious-preference subsets. For example, the average years of schooling completed among employment-based principals range from 14 to 24 years among men (from Jewish men to other-religion men) and from 12 to 21 years among women (from Buddhist women to no-religion women).

Finally, the data enable a preliminary look at the schooling differential between spouses among Catholic and Protestant employment-based immigrants. We find that among Catholics, the principal who qualified for the employment-based visa is more highly schooled than the accompanying spouse regardless of gender, while among Protestants, the husband is more highly schooled than the wife regardless of which spouse is the principal.

Whether and how these results change over time—as some immigrants leave, others find that their religious propensities need not be kept secret, and still others change their religious preference—are a matter that only longitudinal data, of the sort to be collected in the full NIS, can illuminate.

NOTES

The New Immigrant Survey Pilot research was supported by the National Institutes of Health (NICHD and NIA) under grant HD33843, with partial support from the Immigration and Naturalization Service and the National Science Foundation.

1. James A. Davis and Tom W. Smith, *The NORC General Social Survey: A User's Guide* (Newbury Park, Calif.: Sage Publications, 1992); James A. Davis, Tom W. Smith, and Peter V. Marsden, *General Social Surveys, 1972–1998: Cumulative Codebook* (Chicago: National Opinion Research Center, 1999); Tom W. Smith "Counting Flocks and Lost Sheep: Trends in Religious Preference since World War II," *GSS Social Change Report*, no. 26 (Chicago: National Opinion Research Center, 1988).

2. The first cohort to be surveyed in the NIS is the fiscal year 2002 cohort, which includes persons who become legal permanent resident aliens in the period from October 1, 2001, to September 30, 2002. The sample to be drawn consists of 10,000 adult immigrants (drawn from among both "principal" immigrants—those who qualify for an immigrant visa under U.S. law—and immigrants who obtained their visas as accompanying spouses of principal immigrants) and 1,000 children who are principal immigrants (and therefore would not be covered in the households of sampled adult immigrants). Information will be obtained about both the sampled immigrant and members of the immigrant's family and household.

3. Guillermina Jasso, Douglas S. Massey, Mark R. Rosenzweig, and James P. Smith, "Assortative Mating among Married New Legal Immigrants to the United States: Evidence from the New Immigrant Survey Pilot," *International Migration Review* 34 (2000): 443–59; "Family, Schooling, Religiosity, and Mobility among New Legal Immigrants to the United States: Evidence from the New Immigrant Survey Pilot," in *Immigration Today: Pastoral and Research Challenges*, ed. Lydio F. Tomasi and Mary G. Powers (Staten Island, N.Y.: Center for Migration Studies, 2000); "The New Immigrant Survey Pilot (NIS-P): Overview and New Findings about U.S. Legal Immigrants at Admission," *Demography* 37 (2000): 127–38.

4. The religious preference question asked, "What is your religious preference? Is it Catholic, Protestant, Muslim, Jewish, Buddhist, Hindu, some other religion, or no religion?" Respondents who replied "Other" were asked to specify the religion. The

attendance question asked, "How often do you attend religious services?" There were ten response categories, ranging from "Never" to "Every day."

5. The NIS-P sample oversampled immigrants with employment-based visas, who represent a small subset of the cohort (approximately 11 percent of adult immigrants) but one in which there is great interest. Accordingly, all estimates for cross-visa groupings are based on weighted data.

6. These data sharpen the preliminary description in Jasso et al., "Family, Schooling, Religiosity, and Mobility among New Legal Immigrants to the United States." That earlier report was based on the respondents' declared preferences among the response categories and included approximately 15 percent in the "Other" category. The specific religions named by respondents in the "Other" category recently became available, and we coded them. The overwhelming majority consisted of denominations usually classified as Protestant (that is, post-Reformation Christian) plus some Eastern Orthodox religions and a sprinkling of other religions. The specific religious preference with the largest number of responses was "Christian," named by 34 out of 140 respondents who declared "Other." The new information resulted in the separate Orthodox category in table 12.1, which numbers 4 percent, and a substantial increase in the Protestant category, from 8.8 percent in the earlier research report to 18.6 percent in table 12.1. The proportion in the "Other" category shrank from 15 to 1.4 percent. An important question for future research involves the behavioral mechanisms by which individuals declare a preference for a grouping such as "Protestant" or instead declare "Other." Such research requires asking the traditional question with response categories as well as asking everyone a follow-up question about the specific religion they prefer.

7. Thus, we update the comparison reported in Jasso et al., "Family, Schooling, Religiosity, and Mobility among New Legal Immigrants to the United States," which was based on the then-most-recent GSS data, namely, the data for 1994.

8. The GSS data also provide further detail on the specific denomination or affiliation of Protestant and Jewish respondents, but we do not make use of those data here, as the NIS-P does not provide comparable detail (except for those Christians who declared themselves "Other").

9. In the sampling design of the 1996 GSS, the probability of selection varies inversely with the number of adults in sampled households. Accordingly, we report estimates based on weighted data.

10. The GSS interviews only persons living in noninstitutionalized settings, and thus the probability of selection for college students depends on their living arrangements. We recalculated all estimates reported in this section for the subset of respondents in both the NIS-P and the GSS who are twenty-five years of age and older. The results

do not differ appreciably, and, given that all the other analyses are based on respondents eighteen and older, we report in table 12.2 the results for the eighteen-and-older groups. A version of table 12.2 based on the twenty-five-and-older group is available from the authors.

11. This figure of 82 percent is an underestimate, as some cases in the GSS "Other" category involve Christian religions.

12. This is a conservative estimate, given that the NIS-P figures in the "Other" column contain only persons who are neither Christian nor Jewish, while the GSS figures include some Christians.

13. Jasso et al., "Family, Schooling, Religiosity, and Mobility among New Legal Immigrants to the United States," 70, table 8.

14. Caution is necessary in interpreting these figures because of the small sample size in some cases.

15. We may say, for example, that there is a 28 percent chance that a recent Catholic immigrant is from Mexico and a 12 percent chance that a recent Protestant immigrant is from Mexico.

16. For further information on U.S. immigration law, see the *Statistical Yearbook of the Immigration and Naturalization Service* and the websites of the U.S. Immigration and Naturalization Service and of the U.S. Department of State Visa Office. For further detail on visa class of admission in the NIS and the NIS-P, see the Jasso et al. works cited in note 3.

17. This reflects the conditional immigrant visas awarded to spouses married less than two years under the provisions of the Immigration Marriage Fraud Amendments of 1986.

18. This visa category usually has large backlogs, and thus new immigrants admitted with this visa type are seldom newlyweds. For example, in June 2001, the most recent priority date for which visas are being issued to spouses of permanent resident aliens is September 1996.

19. Jasso et al., "Assortative Mating among Married New Legal Immigrants to the United States," and "Family, Schooling, Religiosity, and Mobility among New Legal Immigrants to the United States."

20. For further detail on the schooling of recent new immigrants, see the Jasso et al. works cited in note 3. Because public-use census/CPS data do not provide information

on visa status or date of admission to current visa status and, meanwhile, public-use INS data do not provide the schooling of new legal immigrants, the NIS-P provides the first data ever collected on the schooling of a probability sample drawn from a cohort of legal immigrants.

21. This procedure is described in detail in Jasso et al., "Assortative Mating among Married New Legal Immigrants to the United States," 455. Note that the couple is classified by the religious preference of the sampled immigrant, who can be either the principal or the accompanying spouse and either male or female.

22. Jasso et al., "Assortative Mating among Married New Legal Immigrants to the United States," 456.

Bibliography

Abdul Hadi, Fahhim. "Protecting the Future of Islam in America." *Islamic Horizons,* January/February 1998, 22.

Abrams, Jeanne Lichtman. "Chasing the Cure: A History of the Jewish Consumptives' Relief Society." Ph.D. diss., University of Colorado, 1983.

———. "'For a Child's Sake': The Denver Sheltering Home for Jewish Children in the Progressive Era." *American Jewish History* 79 (winter 1989–1990): 181–202.

———. "*Unsere Leit* ('Our People'): Anna Hillkowitz and the Development of the East European Jewish Woman Professional in America." *American Jewish Archives* 37 (November 1985): 275–89.

Abu, Sameer. "Some Milestones in Islamic Education in North America." *The Message,* May 2000, 23.

Acuña, Rodolfo. *Occupied America.* San Francisco: Canfield Press, 1972.

Ahmed, Gutbi Mahdi. "Muslim Organizations in the United States." In *The Muslims of America.* New York: Oxford University Press, 1991.

Ali-Akbar, Nassir. "Challenges Faced by Islamic Schools." *The Message,* May 2000, 25.

Allen, Barbara. *Tocqueville on Covenant and the American Republic: Harmonizing Heaven and Earth.* Baltimore: The Johns Hopkins University Press, 2000.

Altalib, Omar. "Muslims in America: Challenges and Prospects." *American Muslim Quarterly* 2, no. 1 (spring 1998): 39–49.

American Jewish Year Book 97 (1997).

American Jewish Year Book 99 (1999).

Ammerman, Nancy. "Whose Story Is It? Who Says Churches Are in Trouble?" *Ethics and Policy* (newsletter of the Graduate Theological Union, Berkeley, California), fall 1997, 4–7.

Andreu Iglesias, Cesar. *Memorias de Bernardo Vega*. Rio Piedras: Editorial Coquí, 1977.

An-Naim, Abdullahi. *Towards an Islamic Reformation: Civil Liberties, Human Rights and International Law*. Syracuse, N.Y.: Syracuse University Press, 1990.

An-Nawawi's Forty Hadith: An Anthology of the Sayings of the Prophet Muhammad. Translated by Ezzedin Ibrahim and Denys Johnson-Davies. Cambridge: Islamic Texts Society, 1997.

Anson, Robert, Marshall Berges, Sandra Burton, and Susan J. Diamond. "The Little Strike That Grew to La Causa." *Time* 94, no. 1 (July 4, 1969): 16–21.

Baer, Hans. *The Black Spiritual Movement: A Religious Response to Racism*. Knoxville: University of Tennessee Press, 1984.

Bailey, Ronald, and Guillermo V. Flores. "Internal Colonialism and Racial Minorities." In *Structures of Dependency*, edited by Frank Bonilla and Robert Girling. Palo Alto, Calif.: Nairobi Press, 1973, 151–53.

Balmer, Randall. *Mine Eyes Have Seen the Glory: A Journey into the Evangelical Subculture in America*. 3rd ed. New York: Oxford University Press, 2000.

Bancroft, Frederick. *Slave-Trading in the Old South*. Baltimore: J. H. Furst, 1931.

Barazinji, Jamal. "History of Islamization of Knowledge and Contributions of the International Institute of Islamic Thought." In *Muslims and Islamization in North America: Problems and Prospects*, edited by Amber Haque. Beltsville, Md.: Amana Publications, 1999, 13–32.

Baron, Jeremy Hugh. "The Mount Sinai Hospital: A Brief History." *Mount Sinai Journal of Medicine* 67 (January 2000): 3–5.

Barrera, Mario. *Beyond Aztlán*. Notre Dame, Ind.: University of Notre Dame Press, 1988.

Barrera, Mario, Carlos Muñoz, and Charles Ornelas. "The Barrio as an Internal Colony." In *La Causa Política: A Chicano Politics Reader*, edited by F. Chris Garcia. Notre Dame, Ind.: University of Notre Dame Press, 1972. Reprinted from Harlan Han, ed., *Urban Affairs Annual Reviews*. Vol. 6. Beverly Hills, Calif.: Sage, 1972, 465–98.

Basit, Abdul. "How to Integrate without Losing Muslim Identity." *Islamic Horizons*, March/April 1998, 32–33.

Bates, Barbara. *Bargaining for Life: A Social History of Tuberculosis, 1876–1938*. Philadelphia: University of Pennsylvania Press, 1992.

Beirne, Charles J. *The Problem of Americanization in the Catholic Schools of Puerto Rico*. Río Piedras: Editorial Universitaria de la Universidad de Puerto Rico, 1975.

Bellah, Robert N. *The Broken Covenant: American Civil Religion in a Time of Trial*. New York: Subarea Press, 1975.

Berger, Peter. *The Sacred Canopy*. Garden City, N.Y.: Doubleday, 1967.

Besalga, Edward. "Cultural Change and Protestantism in Puerto Rico: 1945–1966." Ph.D. diss., New York University, 1970.

Birt, Robert. "Existence, Identity, and Liberation." In *Existence in Black: An Anthology of Black Existential Philosophy*, edited by Lewis L. Gordon. New York: Routledge, 1997, 205–13.

Blauner, Robert. "Internal Colonialism and Ghetto Revolt." *Social Problems*, spring 1969, 393–408.

———, ed. *On Racial Oppression in America*. New York: Harper & Row, 1972.

Blaut, James M. "Assimilation vs. Ghettoization." *Antipode* 15, no. 1 (1983): 35–41.

Bogen, Boris D. *Jewish Philanthropy: An Exposition of Principles and Methods of Jewish Social Service in the United States*. New York: Macmillan, 1917. Reprint, Montclair, N.J.: Patterson Smith Publishing, 1969.

Bogen, Hyman. *The Luckiest Orphans: A History of the Hebrew Orphan Asylum of New York*. Urbana: University of Illinois Press, 1992.

Bolkosky, Sidney. *Harmony and Dissonance: Voices of Jewish Identity in Detroit, 1914–1917*. Detroit: Wayne State University Press, 1991.

Brandon, George. *Santeria from Africa to the New World: The Dead Sell Memories*. Bloomington: Indiana University Press, 1993.

Bridge, Ethan. "The Rise and Development of the Jewish Hospital in America." Rabbinical thesis, Hebrew Union College, 1985.

Brieger, Gert H. "Classics and Character: Medicine and Gentility." *Bulletin of the History of Medicine* 65 (spring 1991): 88–109.

Burdick, John. "Struggling against the Devil: Pentecostalism and Social Movements in Urban Brazil." In *Rethinking Protestantism in Latin America,* edited by Virginia Garrard-Burnett and David Stoll. Philadelphia: Temple University Press, 1993, 20–44.

Burnham, Kenneth. *God Comes to America.* Boston: Lambeth Press, 1979.

Burns, Jeffrey M. "Mexican Americans and the Catholic Church in California, 1910–1965." In *Mexican Americans and the Catholic Church, 1900–1965,* edited by Jay P. Dolan and Gilberto M. Hinojosa. Vol. 1. Notre Dame Series on Hispanic Catholics in the U.S. Notre Dame, Ind.: University of Notre Dame Press, 1994, 9–125.

Cabot, Richard C. *Social Service and the Art of Healing.* 2nd ed. New York: Dodd, Mead, 1931.

Calhoun, Craig, ed. *Social Theory and the Politics of Identity.* Cambridge, Mass.: Blackwell Publishers, 1994.

Carrette, Jeremy R., ed. "Prologue to a Confession of the Flesh." In *Religion and Culture: Michel Foucault.* New York: Routledge, 1999.

Carter, Stephen L. *The Dissent of the Governed: A Meditation of Law, Religion and Loyalty.* Cambridge, Mass.: Harvard University Press, 1998.

Casterline, Gail Farr. "St. Joseph's and St. Mary's: The Origins of Catholic Hospitals in Philadelphia." *Pennsylvania Magazine of History and Biography* 108 (July 1984): 289–314.

Cetina, Judith G. "In Times of Immigration." In *Pioneer Healers: The History of Women Religious in American Health Care,* edited by Ursula Stepsis and Delores Liptak. New York: Crossroad, 1989, 86–117.

Chadwick, John. "American Muslims Gain a Political Voice." *The Record,* September 24, 2000, 27.

Chavez, Linda. *Out of the Barrio: Towards a New Politics of Hispanic Assimilation.* New York: Basic Books, 1991.

Cheever, Susan. *Treetops: A Family Memoir.* New York: Bantam, Doubleday Dell, 1991.

Chenault, Lawrence R. *The Puerto Rican Migrant in New York City.* New York: Columbia University Press, 1938.

Chilcote, Ronald H., and Joel C. Edelstein, eds. *Latin America: The Struggle with Dependency and Beyond.* New York: John Wiley & Sons, 1974.

Clark, Margaret. *Health in the Mexican-American Community: A Community Study.* Berkeley: University of California Press, 1970.

Clegg, Claude Andrew III. *An Original Man: The Life and Times of Elijah Muhammad.* New York: St. Martin's Press, 1997.

Cohen, Steven M. *Religious Stability and Ethnic Decline: Emerging Patterns of Jewish Identity in the United States.* New York: Florence G. Heller–Jewish Community Centers Association Research Center, 1998.

———. "Why Intermarriage May Not Threaten Jewish Continuity." *Moment* 19 (December 1994): 54–57.

Coleman, Will. *Tribal Talk: Black Theology, Hermeneutics, and African/American Ways of "Telling the Story."* University Park: Pennsylvania State University Press, 2000.

Cone, James H. *The Spirituals and the Blues.* Maryknoll, N.Y.: Orbis Books, 1991.

Cox, Harvey. *Fire from Heaven: The Rise of Pentecostal Spirituality and the Reshaping of Religion in the Twenty-First Century.* New York: Addison-Wesley, 1996.

Creel, Margaret Washington. *"A Peculiar People": Slave Religion and Community-Culture among the Gullah.* New York: New York University Press, 1988.

Curray, Mary Elaine. "Making the Gods in New York: The Yoruba Religion in the Black Community." Ph.D. diss., City University of New York, 1991.

Davis, James A., and Tom W. Smith. *The NORC General Social Survey: A User's Guide.* Newbury Park, Calif.: Sage Publications, 1992.

Davis, James A., Tom W. Smith, and Peter V. Marsden. *General Social Surveys, 1972–1998: Cumulative Codebook.* Chicago: National Opinion Research Center, 1999.

De la Garza, Rudolfo O., Louis DeSipio, F. Chris García, John García, and Angelo Falcón. *Latino Voices: Mexican, Puerto Rican and Cuban Perspectives on American Politics.* Boulder, Colo.: Westview Press, 1992.

Deck, Allan Figueroa. "The Challenge of Evangelical/Pentecostal Christianity to Hispanic Catholicism." In *Hispanic Catholic Culture in the U.S.: Issues and Concerns*, edited by Jay Dolan and Allan Figueroa. Notre Dame, Ind.: University of Notre Dame Press, 1994, 409–39.

———. "The Crisis of Hispanic Ministry: Multiculturalism as an Ideology." *America* 163, no. 2 (July 14–21, 1990): 33–36.

———. *The Second Wave*. Mahwah, N.J.: Paulist Press, 1989.

Deedy, John. *American Catholicism: And Now Where?* New York: Plenum Press, 1987.

DellaPergola, Sergio. "Changing Cores and Peripheries: Fifty Years in Socio-Demographic Perspective." In *Terms of Survival: The Jewish World since 1945*, edited by Robert S. Wistrich. London: Routledge, 1995, 13–43.

Delorenzo, Yusuf Talal. "The Fiqh Councilor in North America." In *Muslims on the Americanization Path?*, edited by Yvonne Haddad and John L. Esposito. London: Oxford University Press, 1998, 65–86.

Deren, Maya. *Divine Horsemen: The Living Gods of Haiti*. New York: McPherson, 1953.

Desmangles, Leslie G. *The Faces of the Gods: Vodou and Roman Catholicism in Haiti*. Chapel Hill: University of North Carolina Press, 1992.

Deutsch, Sarah. *No Separate Refuge: Culture, Class and Gender on an Anglo-Hispanic Frontier in the American Southwest, 1880–1940*. New York: Oxford University Press, 1987.

Díaz-Stevens, Ana María. *Oxcart Catholicism on Fifth Avenue: The Impact of the Puerto Rican Migration upon the Archdiocese of New York*. Notre Dame, Ind.: University of Notre Dame Press, 1993.

———. "The Saving Grace: The Matriarchal Core of Latino Catholicism." *Latino Studies Journal* 4, no. 3 (September 1993): 60–78.

Díaz-Stevens, Ana María, and Anthony M. Stevens-Arroyo. *Recognizing the Latino Resurgence in U.S. Religion: The Emmaus Paradigm*. Boulder, Colo.: Westview Press; Oxford: HarperCollins, 1998.

Dinges, William D. "'We Are What You Were': Roman Catholic Traditionalism in America." In *Being Right: Conservative Catholics in America*, edited by Mary Jo Weaver and R. Scott Appleby. Bloomington: Indiana University Press, 1995, 241–69.

Diouf, Sylvaine. *Servants of Allah: African Muslims Enslaved in the Americas.* New York: New York University Press, 1998.

Donnan, Elizabeth. *Documents Illustrative of the History of the Slave Trade to America.* Vols. 1 and 2. New York: Octagon Books, 1969.

Douglas, Mary. "Introduction." *Natural Symbols: Explorations in Cosmology.* New York: Routledge, 1996.

Du Bois, W. E. B. *The Suppression of the African Slave-Trade to the United States of America, 1638–1870.* New York: Longmans, Green, 1896.

Dubos, Rene, and Jean Dubos. *The White Plague, Tuberculosis, Man, and Society.* 1952. Reprint, New Brunswick, N.J.: Rutgers University Press, 1987.

El Hassan, Sarvath. "Educating Women in the Muslim World." *Islamic Horizons,* March/April 1999, 27.

Elizondo, Virgil. *Christianity and Culture.* Huntington, Ind.: Our Sunday Visitor Press, 1975.

———. *The Future Is Mestizo.* New York: Crossroad, 1992.

Esack, Farid. *Qur'an Liberation and Pluralism: An Islamic Perspective of Interreligious Solidarity against Oppression.* Oxford: Oneworld, 1997.

Espín, Orlando. "Pentecostalism and Popular Catholicism: The Poor and Tradition." *Journal of Hispanic/Latino Theology* 3, no. 2 (November 1995): 14–43.

Essien-Udom, E. U. *Black Nationalism: A Search for an Identity in America.* Chicago: University of Chicago Press, 1962.

Faber, Eli. *A Time for Planting: The First Migration, 1654–1820.* Baltimore: The Johns Hopkins University Press, 1992.

Fauset, Arthur Huff. *Black Gods of the Metropolis: Negro Religious Cults of the Urban North.* New York: Octagon Books, 1970.

Fifty-First Annual Report of the St. Vincent's Hospital of the City of New York for the Year 1900. New York: Meany Printing, 1901.

First Annual Report of Saint Vincent's Hospital under the Charge of the Sisters of Charity for the Year Ending January First, 1859. New York: D. & J. Sadlier, 1859.

Fitzpatrick, Joseph P. *Puerto Rican Americans: The Meaning of Migration to the Mainland.* Englewood Cliffs, N.J.: Prentice Hall, 1971.

Forster, Brenda, and Joseph Tabachnik. *Jews by Choice: A Study of Converts to Reform and Conservative Judaism.* New York: Ktav, 1991.

Freeman's Journal and Catholic Register, February 20, 1847.

Froehle, Bryan T., and Mary L. Gautier. *Catholicism USA: A Portrait of the Catholic Church in the United States.* Maryknoll, N.Y.: Orbis Books, 2000.

Fruton, Joseph S. *Eighty Years.* New Haven, Conn.: Yale University Press, 1994.

Fry, Gladys-Marie. *Stitched from the Soul: Slave Quilts from the Ante-Bellum South.* New York: Dutton Studio Books/Museum of American Folk Art, 1990.

Gallup, George, and Jim Castelli. *The People's Religion: American Faith in the 90s.* Princeton, N.J.: Princeton Research Center, 1989.

García, Gabriel Márquez. *One Hundred Years of Solitude.* New York: HarperPerennial, 1991.

Gargani, Aldo. "Religious Experience as Event and Interpretation." In *Religion,* edited by Jacques Derrida and Gianni Vattimo. Stanford, Calif.: Stanford University Press, 1998, 111–35.

Ghannouchi, Rashid. *Huquq al-Muwatanah: Huquq ghair al-muslim fi' al-mujtama' al-Islami.* Herndon, Va.: International Institute of Islamic Thought, 1993.

Ghorab, Ahmad. *Subverting Islam: The Role of Orientalist Centers.* London: Minerva Books, 1996.

Giese, James Richard. "Tuberculosis and the Growth of Denver's Eastern European Jewish Community: The Accommodation of an Immigrant Group to a Medium-Sized Western City, 1900–1920." Ph.D. diss., University of Colorado, 1979.

Gillis, Chester. *Roman Catholicism in America.* New York: Columbia University Press, 1999.

Glazer, Nathan, and Daniel P. Moynihan. *Beyond the Melting Pot: The Negroes, Puerto Ricans, Jews, Italians, and Irish of New York City.* Cambridge, Mass.: MIT Press, 1963; London: MIT Press, 1970.

Glazier, Jack. *Dispersing the Ghetto: The Relocation of Jewish Immigrants across America.* Ithaca, N.Y.: Cornell University Press, 1998.

Goldstein, Sidney. "Profile of American Jewry: Insights from the 1990 National Jewish Population Survey." *American Jewish Year Book* 92 (1992): 77–173.

Gómez, David F. *Somos Chicanos: Strangers in Our Own Land.* Boston: Beacon Press, 1973.

González, Rudolfo. "Corky." "I Am Joaquín." Copyright of poem, 1967. New York: Bantam Books, 1972. (Reproduced with permission in Antonio M. Stevens-Arroyo. *Prophets Denied Honor: An Anthology on the Hispano Church of the United States.* Maryknoll, N.Y.: Orbis Books, 1980, 15-20.)

Gordon, Milton. *Assimilation in American Life: The Role of Race, Religion and National Origins.* New York: Oxford University Press, 1974.

Griswold del Castillo, Richard. *The Los Angeles Barrio, 1850–1890: A Social History.* Berkeley: University of California Press, 1979.

Grossman, Cathy Lynn. "In Search of Faith." *USA Today,* December 23–26, 1999, A1–A2.

Guillaume, A. *The Life of Muhammad.* Karachi: Oxford University Press, 1955.

Haddad, Yvonne. "The Dynamics of Islamic Identity in North America." In *Muslims on the Americanization Path?,* edited by Yvonne Haddad and John L. Esposito. London: Oxford University Press, 1998, 19–46.

Haddad, Yvonne, and John L. Esposito, eds. *Muslims on the Americanization Path?* London: Oxford University Press, 1998.

Haddad, Yvonne, and Adair Lummis. *Islamic Values in the United States: A Comparative Study.* New York: Oxford University Press, 1987.

Hadhrami, Abu Amal. "Muslims Gain Political Rights." *Islamic Horizons,* January/February 1999, 24–25.

Hall, Stuart, and Paul Du Gay. *Questions of Cultural Identity.* London: Sage Publications, 1996.

Henry, Paget. "African and Afro-Caribbean Existential Philosophies." In *Existence in Black: An Anthology of Black Existential Philosophy,* edited by Lewis R. Gordon. New York: Routledge, 1997, 11–36.

Herberg, Will. *Protestant, Catholic, Jew: An Essay in American Religious Sociology.* New York: Doubleday, 1955.

———. *Protestant, Catholic, Jew: An Essay in American Religious Sociology.* Rev. ed. New York: Anchor, 1960.

Hernandez, Jos. "Hispanics Blend Diversity." In *Handbook of Hispanic Cultures in the United States: Sociology,* edited by Felix Padilla. Houston: Arte Público Press, 1994, 17–34.

Hertzberg, Arthur. *The Jews in America, Four Centuries of an Uneasy Encounter: A History.* New York: Simon & Schuster, 1989.

Hirsh, Joseph, and Beka Doherty. *The First Hundred Years of the History of Mount Sinai Hospital of New York, 1852–1952.* New York: Random House, 1952.

Hooper, Ibrahim. "Media Relations Tips for Muslim Activists." In *Muslims and Islamization in North America: Problems and Prospects,* edited by Amber Haque. Beltsville, Md.: Amana Publications, 1999, 231–58.

Hospital Situation in Greater New York: Report of a Survey of Hospitals in New York City by the Public Health Committee of the New York Academy of Medicine. New York: G. P. Putnam's Sons, 1924.

Howe, Irving. *World of Our Fathers: The Journey of the East European Jews to America and the Life They Found and Made.* New York: Harcourt Brace Jovanovich, 1976.

Hughes, Philip. *A Popular History of the Catholic Church.* New York: Macmillan, 1949.

Hussain, Altaf. "Youth and the Emerging Islamic Identity." *The Message,* June/July 1999, 21–22.

Hyatt, Harry Middleton. *Hoodoo-Conjuration-Witchcraft-Rootwork: Beliefs Accepted by Many Negroes and White Persons These Being Orally Recorded among Blacks and Whites.* Vol. 1. Hannibal, Mo.: Western Publishing, 1970; distributed by American University Bookstore, Washington, D.C.

Inikori, J. E., ed. *Forced Migration: The Impact of the Export Slave Trade on African Societies.* New York: Africana Publishing, 1982.

Ismail, Mohamed. "Islamic Education in the Weekend and Full-Time Islamic Schools." *The Message,* May 2000, 35.

Israel, Sherry R. *Comprehensive Report on the 1995 CJP Demographic Study.* Boston: Combined Jewish Philanthropies, 1997.

Izetbegovic, Alija. *Islam between East and West.* Indianapolis: American Trust Publications, 1989.

Jacobs, Claude F., and Andrew J. Kaslow. *The Spirituals Churches of New Orleans: Origins, Beliefs, and Rituals of an African-American Religion.* Knoxville: University of Tennessee Press, 1991.

Jasso, Guillermina, Douglas S. Massey, Mark R. Rosenzweig, and James P. Smith. "Assortative Mating among Married New Legal Immigrants to the United States:

Evidence from the New Immigrant Survey Pilot." *International Migration Review* 34 (2000): 443–59.

———. "Family, Schooling, Religiosity, and Mobility among New Legal Immigrants to the United States: Evidence from the New Immigrant Survey Pilot." In *Immigration Today: Pastoral and Research Challenges,* edited by Lydio F. Tomasi and Mary G. Powers. Staten Island, N.Y.: Center for Migration Studies, 2000, 52–81.

———. "The New Immigrant Survey Pilot (NIS-P): Overview and New Findings about U.S. Legal Immigrants at Admission." *Demography* 37 (2000): 127–38.

Johnson, Paul E. *A Shopkeeper's Millennium: Society and Revivals in Rochester, New York, 1815–1837.* New York: Hill & Wang, 1979.

Jordan, Winthrop D. *White over Black: American Attitudes toward the Negro, 1550–1812.* Durham: University of North Carolina Press, 1968.

Joyner, Charles. "'Believer I Know': The Emergence of African-American Christianity." In *Religion and American Culture: A Reader,* edited by David G. Hackett. New York: Routledge, 1995, 186–207.

Kelly, George Armstrong. *Politics and Religious Consciousness in America.* New Brunswick, N.J.: Transaction Press, 1984.

Kent, Christina. "Jewish Hospitals: Staying When the Getting Gets Tough." *Faulkner & Gray's Medicine & Health* 46 (September 14, 1992): 1–4.

Khadduri, Majid. *War and Peace in the Law of Islam.* Baltimore: The Johns Hopkins University Press, 1955.

Khan, M. A. Muqtedar. "Barriers to American Muslim's Political Cohesiveness Is Largely Internal." *Washington Report on Middle East Affairs* 19, no. 5 (July 2000): 70.

———. "The Case for an American Muslim Identity," www.beliefnet.com/story/35/story_3508_1.html (accessed September 20, 2002).

———. "Collective Identity and Collective Action: Case of Muslim Politics in America." In *Muslims and Islamization in North America: Problems and Prospects,* edited by Amber Haque. Beltsville, Md.: Amana Publications, 1999, 147–60.

———. "Islamic Identity and the Two Faces of the West." *Washington Report on Middle East Affairs* 19, no. 6 (August/September 2000): 71.

————. "The Manifest Destiny of American Muslims." *Washington Report on Middle East Affairs* 19, no. 8 (December 2000): 68.

————. "Public Face of Bigotry." *Washington Report on Middle East Affairs* 20, no. 1 (January/February 2001): 73.

————. "Rationality and Identity in International Relations: A Constructivist Theory of Agency and Choice." Ph.D. diss., Georgetown University, 2000.

————. "What Is the American Muslim Perspective?" *Washington Report on Middle East Affairs* 19, no. 10 (December 1999): 82.

Klor de Alva, J. Jorge. "Aztlán, Borinquen and Hispanic Nationalism in the United States." In *Aztlán: Essays on the Chicano Homeland,* edited by Francisco Anaya and Rodolfo Lomeli. Albuquerque: University of New Mexico Press, 1991, 135–71.

Kosmin, Barry A. *The National Survey of Religious Identification 1989–1990.* New York: City University of New York, 1991.

Kosmin, Barry A., and Seymour P. Lachman. *One Nation under God: Religion in Contemporary American Society.* New York: Harmony Books, 1993.

Kottak, Conrad P., and Katherine Kozaitis. *On Being Different: Diversity and Multiculturalism in the North American Mainstream.* New York: McGraw-Hill, 1998.

Kottek, Samuel S. "The Hospital in Jewish History." *Review of Infectious Diseases* 3 (July–August 1981): 636–39.

Kraut, Alan M. *Silent Travelers: Germs, Genes, and the "Immigrant Menace."* New York: Basic Books, 1994.

Lazarus, Barry A. "The Practice of Medicine and Prejudice in a New England Town: The Founding of Mount Sinai Hospital, Hartford Connecticut." *Journal of American Ethnic History* 10 (spring 1991): 21.

Letter of the Right Rev. John Dubois, D.D., Bishop of New York, the Secretary of the Association for the Propagation of the Faith, Lyons, March 16, 1830. In United States Catholic Historical Society, *Historical Records and Studies.* Vol. 5, pt. 1. New York: United States Catholic Historical Society, 1907, 228.

Levenson, Dorothy. *Montefiore: The Hospital as Social Instrument, 1884–1984.* New York: Farrar, Straus & Giroux, 1984.

Levi, Solomon, to Jacob Furth, October 22, 1878, as quoted in David A. Gee, *216 S.K.: A History of the Jewish Hospital of St. Louis*. St. Louis, Mo.: Jewish Hospital of St. Louis, 1981.

Limerick, Patricia Nelson. *The Legacy of Conquest: The Unbroken Past of the American West*. New York: W. W. Norton, 1987.

Lincoln, C. Eric. *The Black Muslims in America*. Boston: Beacon Press, 1961.

Linenthal, Arthur J. *The History of Boston's Jewish Hospitals, 1896 to 1928*. Boston: Beth Israel Hospital in association with the Francis A. Countway Library of Medicine, 1990.

Long, Charles. "The Oppressive Elements in Religion and the Religions of the Oppressed." In *Significations*. Philadelphia: Fortress Press, 1986, 165–71.

López, Alfredo. *The Puerto Rican Papers: Notes on the Re-Emergence of a Nation*. Indianapolis: Bobbs-Merrill, 1973.

Lovin, Robin. "Social Contract or a Public Covenant?" In *Religion and American Public Life*, edited by Robin Lovin. Mahwah, N.J.: Paulist Press, 1987, 132–45.

Ludmerer, Kenneth M. *Time to Heal: American Medical Education from the Turn of the Century to the Era of Managed Care*. New York: Oxford University Press, 1999.

Martin, David. "The People's Church: The Global Evangelical Upsurge and Its Political Consequences." *Books & Culture*, January/February 2000, 13.

———. *Tongues of Fire: The Explosion of Protestantism in Latin America*. London: Blackwell, 1990.

Massa, Mark S. *Catholics and American Culture: Fulton Sheen, Dorothy Day, and the Notre Dame Football Team*. New York: Crossroad, 1999.

Matthews, Donald H. *Honoring the Ancestors: An African Cultural Interpretation of Black Religion and Literature*. New York: Oxford University Press, 1999.

Mayer, Brantz. *Captain Canot, an African Slaver*. New York: Arno Press and the New York Times, 1968.

McCarthy Brown, Karen. *Mama Lola: A Vodou Priestess in Brooklyn*. Berkeley: University of California Press, 1991.

McGreevy, John T. *Parish Boundaries: The Catholic Encounter with Race in the Twentieth-Century Urban North*. Chicago: University of Chicago Press, 1996.

Melton, J. Gordon, ed. *The Encyclopedia of American Religions.* 3rd ed. Detroit: Gale Research, 1989.

Merton, Thomas. *Conjecture of a Guilty Bystander.* New York: Doubleday, 1968.

Miller, John J. *The Unmaking of Americans: How Multiculturalism Has Undermined America's Assimilation Ethic.* New York: Free Press, 1998.

Mills, Samuel A. "Parochiaid and the Abortion Decisions: Supreme Court Justice William J. Brennan, Jr. versus the U.S. Catholic Hierarchy." *Journal of Church and State* 34, no. 4 (1992): 753.

Mine Eyes Have Seen the Glory. Three-part PBS documentary (Chicago: WTTW, 1993).

Mirza, Ambereen. "Muslim Women and American Choices." *Islamic Horizons,* May/June 1999, 50–51.

Moore, Kathleen. *Al-Mughtaribun.* Albany: State University of New York Press, 1995.

———. "The Hijab and Religious Liberty: Anti-Discrimination Law and Muslim Women in the United States." In *Muslims on the Americanization Path?,* edited by Yvonne Haddad and John L. Esposito. London: Oxford University Press, 1998, 105–28.

Morgan, Thomas B. "The Vanishing American Jew." *Look* 28 (May 5, 1964): 42–46.

Morris, Charles. *American Catholic: The Saints and Sinners Who Built America's Most Powerful Church.* New York: Times Books, 1997.

Morrison, Toni. "The Site of Memory." In *Out There: Marginalization and Contemporary Cultures,* edited by Russell Ferguson, Martha Gever, Trinh T. Minh-ha, and Cornel West. New York: New Museum of Contemporary Art; Cambridge, Mass.: MIT Press, 1990.

Mother Divine. *The Peace Mission Movement.* Philadelphia: Imperial Press/Palace Mission, Inc., 1982.

Mulira, Jessie Gaston. "The Case of Voodoo in New Orleans." In *Africanisms in American Culture,* edited by Joseph E. Holloway. Bloomington: Indiana University Press, 1990.

Munir, Ghazala. "Muslim Women in Dialogue: Breaking Walls, Building Bridges." In *Muslims and Islamization in North America: Problems and Prospects,* edited by Amber Haque. Beltsville, Md.: Amana Publications, 1999, 337–42.

Murphy, Dean E. "For American Muslims Influence in American Politics Comes Hard." *New York Times,* October 27, 2000, A1.

"Muslim in the West Serving Muslim Worldwide." *Islamic Horizons,* January/February 1998, 3.

Myers, Ernest R. *Challenges for Changing America: Perspectives on Immigration and Multiculturalism in United States.* New York: Austin & Winfield, 1995.

Myers, J. Arthur. *Captain of All These Men of Death: Tuberculosis Historical Highlights.* St. Louis, Mo.: Warren H. Green, 1977.

Negrón Montilla, Aida. *Americanization in Puerto Rico and the Public School System, 1900–1930.* Río Piedras: Editorial Edil.

Nizamuddin, Azam. "What Muslims Can Offer America." *Islamic Horizons,* March/April 1998, 35.

Numan, Fareed H. *The Muslim Population in the United States.* Washington, D.C.: American Muslim Council, 1992.

Nyang, Sulayman S. "Islam in America: A Historical Perspective." *American Muslim Quarterly* 2, no. 1 (spring 1998): 7–38.

O'Brien, David J. *Isaac Hecker: An American Catholic.* Mahwah, N.J.: Paulist Press, 1992.

Oren, Dan. *Joining the Club: A History of Jews at Yale.* New Haven, Conn.: Yale University Press, 1986.

Origins. April 27, 2000.

Ott, Katherine. *Fevered Lives: Tuberculosis in American Culture since 1870.* Cambridge, Mass.: Harvard University Press, 1996.

Padilla, Felix. *Latino Ethnic Consciousness: The Case of Mexican Americans and Puerto Ricans in Chicago.* Notre Dame, Ind.: University of Notre Dame Press, 1985.

———. *Puerto Rican Chicago.* Notre Dame, Ind.: University of Notre Dame Press, 1987.

Paulson, Michael. "Muslims Eye Role at US Polls." *Boston Globe,* October 23, 2000, A1.

Perez y Mena, Andres I. *Speaking with the Dead: Development of Afro-Latin Religion among Puerto Ricans in the United States.* New York: AMS Press, 1991.

Pinn, Anthony. *Varieties of African American Religious Experience.* Minneapolis: Fortress Press, 1998.

———, ed. *Making the Gospel Plain: The Writings of Bishop Reverdy C. Ransom.* Harrisburg, Pa.: Trinity Press International, 1999.

Piven, Frances Fox, and Richard A. Cloward. *Poor People's Movements*. New York: Vintage Books, 1979.

Poblete, Renato, and Thomas O'Dea. "Anomie and the 'Quest for Community': The Formation of Sects among the Puerto Ricans of New York." *American Catholic Sociological Review* 21 (spring 1960): 18–36.

Portes, Alejandro, and Robert L. Bach. *Latino Journey: Cuban and Mexican Immigrants in the United States*. Berkeley: University of California Press, 1985.

Pritchard, James B., ed. *The Ancient Near East: An Anthology of Texts and Pictures*. Princeton, N.J.: Princeton University Press, 1958.

Privett, Stephen A. *The United States Catholic Church and Its Hispanic Members: The Pastoral Vision of Archbishop Robert E. Lucey*. San Antonio, Tex.: Trinity University Press, 1988.

Qutb, Sayed. *Milestones*. Translation of *Ma'alim fi'l-tariq*. Cedar Rapids, Iowa: Unity Publishing, n.d.

Ransom, Reverdy C. *The Pilgrimage of Harriet Ransom's Son*. Nashville: A.M.E. Sunday School Union, 1949.

Rashid, Samory. "Blacks and the Law of Resistance in Islam." *Journal of Islamic Law* 4, no. 2 (fall/winter 1999): 87–124.

Rawidowicz, Simon. "Israel: The Ever-Dying People." In *Studies in Jewish Thought*, edited by Nahum N. Glatzer. Philadelphia: Jewish Publication Society, 1974, 210–24.

Rendón, Armando. *Chicano Manifesto*. New York: Collier Books, 1971.

Reynolds, Edward. *Stand the Storm: A History of the Atlantic Slave Trade*. New York: Allison & Busby, 1985.

Rischin, Moses. *The Promised City: New York's Jews, 1870–1914*. Cambridge, Mass.: Harvard University Press, 1962.

Roof, Wade Clark, and Cristel Manning. "Cultural Conflicts and Identity: Second-Generation Hispanic Catholics in the United States." *Social Compass* 41, no. 1 (1994): 171–84.

Rosen, Jonathan. "Abraham's Drifting Children." *New York Review of Books*, March 30, 1997, A19.

Rosenberg, Charles E. *The Care of Strangers: The Rise of America's Hospital System.* New York: Basic, 1987.

Rosner, David. *A Once Charitable Enterprise: Hospitals and Health Care in Brooklyn and New York, 1885–1915.* Princeton, N.J.: Princeton University Press, 1982.

Ross, Edward Alsworth. *The Old World in the New: The Significance of Past and Present Immigration to the American People.* New York: Century, 1914.

Rothman, Sheila M. *Living in the Shadow of Death: Tuberculosis and the Social Experience of Illlness in American History.* New York: Basic Books, 1994.

Sachar, Howard M. *A History of the Jews in America.* New York: Alfred A. Knopf, 1992.

Sackheim, Eric, comp. *The Blues Line: A Collection of Blues Lyrics.* Hopewell, N.J.: Ecco Press, 1993.

Said, Edward. *Covering Islam: How the Media and the Experts Determine How We See the Rest of the World.* New York: Pantheon Books, 1981.

The Sanatorium 12 (May–August 1918): 54–55. (Jewish Consumptive Relief Society publication located in the JCRS papers in the collection of the Rocky Mountain Jewish Historical Society, University of Denver.)

Sarna, Jonathan D. *The American Jewish Community's Crisis of Confidence.* Policy Forum No. 10. Jerusalem: World Jewish Congress, 1996.

———. *The American Jewish Experience.* 2nd ed. New York: Holmes & Meier, 1997.

———. "Interreligious Marriage in America." In *The Intermarriage Crisis: Jewish Communal Perspectives and Responses.* New York: American Jewish Committee, 1991, 1–6.

———. *Jacksonian Jew: The Two Worlds of Mordecai Noah.* New York: Holmes & Meier, 1981.

Sernett, Milton C. *Bound for the Promised Land: African American Religion and the Great Migration.* Durham, N.C.: Duke University Press, 1997.

Shaheen, Jack. "Hollywood's Reel Arabs and Muslims." In *Muslims and Islamization in North America: Problems and Prospects,* edited by Amber Haque. Beltsville, Md.: Amana Publications, 1999, 179–202.

Shils, Edward. *Tradition.* Chicago: University of Chicago Press, 1981.

Siddiqi, Shamim A. "Islamic Movement in America—Why?" In *Muslims and Islamization in North America: Problems and Prospects,* edited by Amber Haque. Beltsville, Md.: Amana Publications, 1999, 355–62.

Siddiqui, Ahmadullah. "Islam, Muslims and the American Media." In *Muslims and Islamization in North America: Problems and Prospects,* edited by Amber Haque. Beltsville, Md.: Amana Publications, 1999, 203–30.

Silk, Mark. *Spiritual Politics: Religion and America since World War I.* New York: Simon & Schuster, 1988.

Simons, Manly H. "The Origin and Condition of the Peoples Who Make Up the Bulk of Our Immigrants at the Present Time and the Probable Effect of the Absorption upon Our Population." *The Military Surgeon* 23 (December 1908): 433.

Skerry, Peter. "Do We Really Want Immigrants to Assimilate?" *Society* 37, no. 3 (March/April 2000): 57–62.

Sklare, Marshall. "American Jewry: The Ever-Dying People." In *Observing America's Jews,* edited by Jonathan D. Sarna. Hanover, N.H.: University Press of New England, 1993, 262–74.

Smith, Abbot Emerson. *Colonists in Bondage: White Servitude and Convict Labor in America, 1607–1776.* Chapel Hill: University of North Carolina Press, 1947.

Smith, Christian. "The Spirit and Democracy: Base Communities, Protestantism, and Democratization in Latin America." *Sociology of Religion* 99 (summer 1994): 119–43.

Smith, James P., and Barry Edmonston, eds. *The Immigration Debate: Studies on the Economic, Demographic, and Fiscal Effects of Immigration.* Washington, D.C.: National Academy Press, 1998.

———. *The New Americans: Economic, Demographic, and Fiscal Effects of Immigration.* Washington, D.C.: National Academy Press, 1997.

Smith, Jane I. *Islam in America.* New York: Columbia University Press, 1999.

Smith, Timothy L. "Religion and Ethnicity in America." *American Historical Review* 83 (1978): 1155–85.

Smith, Tom W. "Counting Flocks and Lost Sheep: Trends in Religious Preference since World War II." *GSS Social Change Report,* no. 26. Chicago: National Opinion Research Center, 1988.

Sokoloff, Leon. "The Question of Antisemitism in American Medical Faculties, 1900–1945." *Patterns of Prejudice* 31 (1997): 43–54.

———. "The Rise and Decline of the Jewish Quota in Medical School Admissions." *Bulletin of the New York Academy of Medicine* 68 (November 1992): 498.

Solomons, Adolphus S. "Some Scraps of History Concerning Mount Sinai Hospital." *Jewish Messenger* 3 (December 17, 1875): 1.

Soyer, Daniel. *Jewish Immigrant Associations and American Identity in New York, 1880–1939.* Cambridge, Mass.: Harvard University Press, 1997.

Spickard, Paul R. *Mixed Blood: Intermarriage and Ethnic Identity in Twentieth Century America.* Madison: University of Wisconsin Press, 1989.

Stevens-Arroyo, Anthony. "Ill programma Latino: Deamericanizzare e recattolicizzare il Cattolicesimo Americano." *Religioni e Societa: Rivista di Scienze Sociali Della Religione* 21, no. 10 (March–April 1995): 10–29.

Stevens-Arroyo, Anthony M., and Ana María Díaz-Stevens. "Religious Faith and Institutions in the Forging of Latino Identities." In *Handbook of Hispanic Cultures in the United States: Sociology,* edited by Félix Padilla. Houston: University of Houston/Arte Público Press, 1994, 257–91.

Stoll, David. *Is Latin America Turning Protestant?: The Politics of Evangelical Growth.* Stanford, Calif.: Stanford University Press, 1990.

Stone, Carol L. "Estimate of Muslims Living in America." In *The Muslims of America,* edited by Yvonne Yazbeck Haddad. New York: Oxford University Press, 1991, 25–36.

Stuckey, Sterling. *Going through the Storm: The Influence of African American Art in History.* New York: Oxford University Press, 1994.

Sullivan, James A. "Catholics United for Faith: Dissent and the Laity." In *Being Right: Conservative Catholics in America,* edited by Mary Jo Weaver and R. Scott Appleby. Bloomington: Indiana University Press, 1995, 132.

Talal, El Hassan Bin. *Christianity in the Arab World.* New York: Continuum, 1998.

Tenenbaum, Shelley. *A Credit to Their Community: Jewish Loan Societies in the United States, 1880–1945.* Detroit: Wayne State University Press, 1993.

Tipton, Steven M. *Getting Saved from the Sixties: Moral Meaning in Conversion and Cultural Change.* Berkeley: University of California Press, 1982.

Tobin, Jacqueline L., and Raymond G. Dobard. *Hidden in Plain View: A Secret Story of Quilts and the Underground Railroad*. New York: Anchor Books, 2000.

Tocqueville, Alexis de. *Democracy in America*. Translated by George Lawrence. New York: Harper & Row, 1969.

Turner, Bryan S. "The Body in Western Society: Social Theory and Its Perspectives." In *Religion and the Body*, edited by Sarah Coakley. New York: Cambridge University Press, 1998, 19–20.

U.S. Bureau of the Census. *Population Projections of the U.S. by Age, Sex, Race and Hispanic Origin, 1995 to 2050*. Series P25-1130. Washington, D.C.: U.S. Government Printing Office, February 1996.

U.S. Immigration and Naturalization Service. *Statistical Yearbook of the Immigration and Naturalization Service*. Washington, D.C.: U.S. Government Printing Office, various years.

Vogel, Morris J. *The Invention of the Modern Hospital, Boston, 1870–1930*. Chicago: University of Chicago Press, 1980.

Wagner, Mary. "Jewish Hospitals Yesterday and Today." *Modern Healthcare* 21 (February 14, 1991): 33.

Walsh, Marie De Lourdes. *With a Great Heart: The Story of St. Vincent's Hospital and Medical Center of New York, 1849–1964*. New York: St. Vincent's Hospital, 1965.

Warner, R. Stephen, and Judith G. Wittner, eds. *Gatherings in Diaspora: Religious Communities and the New Immigration*. Philadelphia: Temple University Press, 1998.

Washington, Joseph. "How Black Is Black Religion?" In *Quest for a Black Theology*, edited by James J. Gardiner and J. Deotis Roberts. Eric Lincoln Series on Black Religion. Philadelphia: Pilgrim Press, 1971, 28.

Wasserstein, Bernard. *Vanishing Diaspora: The Jews in Europe since 1945*. Cambridge, Mass.: Harvard University Press, 1996.

Weaver, Mary Jo. "Self-Consciously Countercultural: Alternative Catholic Colleges." In *Being Right: Conservative Catholics in America*, edited by Mary Jo Weaver and R. Scott Appleby. Bloomington: Indiana University Press, 1995, 300–24.

Webster, Ann Kathryn. "The Impact of Catholic Hospitals in St. Louis." Ph.D. diss., St. Louis University, 1968.

Weisbrot, Robert. *Father Divine and the Struggle for Racial Equality.* Urbana: University of Illinois Press, 1983.

Wellmeier, Nancy. "Marimbas for the Saints: Culture and Religion in a Maya Refugee Association." Paper presented at the RRA-SSSR Conference, St. Louis, Mo., October 1995.

Wertheimer, Jack. *A People Divided: Judaism in Contemporary America.* New York: Basic Books, 1993.

West, Cornel. *Prophesy Deliverance! An Afro-American Revolutionary Christianity.* Philadelphia: Westminster Press, 1982.

White, Shane, and Graham White. *Stylin': African American Expressive Culture from Its Beginnings to the Zoot Suit.* Ithaca, N.Y.: Cornell University Press, 1998.

Whittemore, Henry. *Progressive, Patriotic, and Philanthropic Hebrews of the New World.* New York: Henry Whittemore and Company, 1907.

Williams, Raymond Brady. *Religions of Immigrants from India and Pakistan.* New York: Cambridge University Press, 1988.

Wilmore, Gayraud. *Black Religion and Black Radicalism: An Interpretation of the Religious History of Afro-American People.* Maryknoll, N.Y.: Orbis Books, 1983.

Witte, John, Jr. *Religion in the American Constitutional Experiment: Essential Rights and Liberties.* Boulder, Colo.: Westview Press, 2000.

Wong, Dennis. "Adversarial Identities and Multiculturalism." *Society* 37, no. 2 (January/February 2000): 10–14.

Woodward, Kathryn, ed. *Identity and Difference.* London: Sage Publications, 1997.

Wuthnow, Robert. *Christianity in the 21st Century.* New York: Oxford University Press, 1993.

Youmans, Guy P. *Tuberculosis.* Philadelphia: W. B. Saunders, 1979.

Zederbaum, Adolph. "Kosher Meat in Jewish Hospitals and Sanatoria." *The Sanatorium* 2 (November 1908): 275.

Zoller, Michael. *Washington and Rome: Catholicism and American Culture.* Translated by Steven Rendall and Albert Wimmer. Notre Dame, Ind.: University of Notre Dame Press, 1999.

Index

About the Contributors

Randall Balmer is Ann Whitney Olin Professor of American Religion at Barnard College, Columbia University. Balmer has published widely both in academic and scholarly journals and in the popular press. He is a senior writer for *Christianity Today,* and his commentaries on religion in America, distributed by the New York Times Syndicate, have appeared in newspapers across the country. *Mine Eyes Have Seen the Glory: A Journey into the Evangelical Subculture in America,* in its third edition, was made into an award-winning documentary for PBS. His latest book is *Blessed Assurance: A History of Evangelicalism in America.* He recently completed the *Encyclopedia of Evangelicalism* and is currently working on a history of religion in North America for Oxford University Press.

Ana María Díaz-Stevens is professor of church and society at Union Theological Seminary. Her research interests include sociology, particularly as it relates to the religious experiences of Hispanics and women; the study of institutions and processes, with special emphasis on the churches, education, and the family; and the analysis of religious and literary production of migrating peoples. Díaz-Stevens's book, *Oxcart: Catholicism on Fifth Avenue: The Impact of Puerto Rican Migration upon the Archdiocese of New York* (1993), received the annual award of the Cushwa Center for the Study of American Catholicism in 1991. She has recently published *An Enduring Flame: Studies of Popular Religiosity among Latinos* (coedited with Antonio M. Stevens-Arroyo) and *Recognizing the Latino*

Resurgence in U.S. Religion: The Emmaus Paradigm (coauthored with Stevens-Arroyo). The latter publication recently received the Outstanding Academic Book Award from *Choice Magazine.* Díaz-Stevens is the recipient of a fellowship on sociological research from the National Institute of Mental Health and is a co-founder of two national organizations: Program for the Analysis of Religion Among Latinos (PARAL) and the Puerto Rican Studies Association. She is coinvestigator of a national survey on Hispanic/Latino religious leadership funded by the Eli Lily Endowment, the Ford Foundation, and the Casey Foundation.

John L. Esposito is university professor and director of the Center for Muslim-Christian Understanding: History and International Affairs at the Edmund Walsh School of Foreign Service at Georgetown University. He is a past president of the Middle East Studies Association. His publications include the *Oxford Encyclopedia of the Modern Islamic World, The Oxford History of Islam, Islam: The Straight Path, The Islamic Threat: Myth or Reality?, The Islamic Revival since 1988, Islam and Politics, Women in Muslim Family Law, Islam and Democracy, Islam and Christian-Muslim Relations, Unholy War: Terror in the Name of Islam,* and the forthcoming *Islam 101: What Everybody Needs to Know.*

Chester Gillis is professor and chair of theology at Georgetown University. His varied research interests include comparative religion, feminist theology, and contemporary Roman Catholicism. He is the author of *A Question of Final Belief: John Hick's Pluralistic Theory of Salvation* and *Pluralism: A New Paradigm for Theology.* In 1999, his book *Roman Catholicism in America* was published by Columbia University Press in the Columbia Contemporary American Religion series. He is currently at work on a book about the social and theological implications of interfaith marriage.

Yvonne Yazbeck Haddad is professor of history of Islam and Christian–Muslim relations at the Center for Muslim-Christian Understanding at the Edmund Walsh School of Foreign Service at Georgetown University. She has taught Middle East history and Islamic studies at the University of Massachusetts, Amherst; Hartford Seminary; and Colgate University. She is a past president of the Middle East Studies Association. Haddad's research interest has focused on twentieth-century Islamic thought and Muslims in the West. Her numerous publications include *Contemporary Islam and the Challenge of History; Muslim Communities in North America; The Islamic Revival; The Muslims of America; Women, Religion and Social Change; Muslims on the Americanization Path?; Muslims in the West: From Sojourners to Citizens;* and *Muslim Minorities in the West: "Visible" and "Invisible."*

Guillermina Jasso is professor of sociology at New York University. Her major research interests are justice analysis, international migration, mathematical methods for theory building, and factorial survey methods for empirical analysis. Jasso served as special assistant to the commissioner of the U.S. Immigration and Naturalization Service from 1977 to 1979 and as director of research for the U.S. Select Commission on Immigration and Refugee Policy from 1979 to 1980. She has written numerous articles that have appeared in journals such as *American Sociological Review, Demography,* and *International Migration Review.* She is coauthor of *The New Chosen People: Immigrants in the United States.* Jasso was a member of the National Academy of Sciences Panel on the Demographic and Economic Consequences of Immigration and of the Core Research Group of the Binational Study of Migration between Mexico and the United States. She has also served as chair of the Theory Section and the International Migration Section of the American Sociological Association and currently serves as chair of the Rational Choice Section. Jasso was elected to the Johns Hopkins Society of Scholars and to the Sociological Research Association and during 1999–2000 was a fellow at the Center for Advanced Study and Behavioral Sciences. Currently, with support from the National Institutes of Health, Jasso, Douglas Massey, Mark Rosenzweig, and James Smith are designing and directing a new program of national longitudinal studies of entering cohorts of immigrants to the United States.

M. A. Muqtedar Khan is assistant professor of political science at Adrian College in Michigan. He is on the board of the Center for the Study of Islam and Democracy and the Center for Balanced Development and on the Executive Committee of the Association of Muslim Social Scientists. He is also on the editorial board of the *American Journal of Islamic Social Sciences.* Khan writes the "Islam in America" column for *Washington Report on Middle East Affairs* and is active both as a scholar and as a public intellectual within the American Muslim community. He has published extensively in academic and popular journals and provides Islamic advice in his web page.

Alan M. Kraut is professor of history at American University. He has published a wide array of books, articles, chapters, and reports concerning immigrants, refugees, and ethnic communities in the United States. His book *Silent Travelers: Germs, Genes, and the "Immigrant Menace"* received two awards: the Theodore Saloutos Prize for the Outstanding Book in Immigration and Ethnic History and the Phi Alpha Theta Book Award for the Best Book in History by an established author. His most recent publication, *Deadly Deficiencies: Dr. Joseph Goldberger's War on Disease and Depravation*, was released in April 2002. Kraut's forthcoming publications are *Landmarks of American Immigration* and an immigration history teaching guide to middle and high school students.

Douglas S. Massey is Dorothy Swaine Thomas Professor of Sociology and department chair at the University of Pennsylvania. He has published various books, articles, and chapters on migration, immigration, and race relations. His books include *American Apartheid: Segregation and the Making of the Underclass, Worlds in Motion: International Migration at the End of the Millennium*, and *Problem of the Century: Racial Stratification in the United States at Century's End*. Massey is currently working on *Smoke and Mirrors: U.S. Immigration Policy in the Age of Globalization*.

Ingrid Mattson is professor of Islamic studies at the Macdonald Center for the Study of Islam and Christian-Muslim Relations at Hartford Seminary and associate editor of *The Muslim World* journal. She specializes in Islamic law and society. Mattson has been a lecturer and teaching assistant at the University of Chicago. In 1995, she served as an adviser to the Afghan delegation at the UN Commission on the Status of Women in New York. Mattson has been active in Muslim–Christian dialogue in Chicago and in the greater Hartford area.

Aminah B. McCloud is associate professor of Islamic studies at DePaul University. She is the author of *African American Islam, Questions of Faith: A Guide for Muslim Prisoners*, and the forthcoming *Immigrant American Islam*.

Jacob Neusner is research professor of religion and theology at Bard College. He has published more than 800 books and innumerable articles, both scholarly and popular, and is the most published humanities scholar in the world. Neusner has been the recipient of numerous academic and scholarly awards in both the United States and Europe. His most recent contributions include his editorship of *Academic Studies in the History of Judaism, Academic Studies on Religion and the Social Order, International Studies in Formative Christianity and Judaism, Encyclopaedia of Judaism* (vols. 1–3), *The Brill Reference Library of Judaism,* and *Studies in Ancient Judaism.* Neusner now acts as the editor for "Judaism" in the forthcoming revision of *Encyclopaedia Britannica.*

David J. O'Brien is Loyola Professor of Roman Catholic Studies and director of the Center for Religion, Ethics and Culture at Holy Cross College. He is the author of numerous publications about Catholics and Catholicism in America, including *Catholic Social Thought: The Documentary Heritage* (1992) and *Isaac Hecker: An American Catholic* (1992), for which he won the John Gimary Shea Prize of the American Catholic Historical Association for the best book on the history of Catholicism and the Alpha Sigma Nu Award for the best book in the humanities. Articles and reviews written by O'Brien have appeared in such journals as the *Catholic Historical Review, Church History, Cross Currents,* and the *Journal of the American Academy of Religion.* He has recently received an Honorary Doctor of Humanities from Rivier College in 1999 and from Loyola University in 1998.

Anthony Pinn is associate professor of religious studies and coordinator of the African American Studies Program at Macalester College. His research and teaching interests include liberation theologies, religion and popular culture, African American religious history, and comparative African American religious experience. His publications include *Why Lord?: Suffering and Evil in Black Theology* (1995), *Varieties of African American Religious Experience* (1998), *Making the Gospel Plain: The Writings of Bishop Reverdy C. Ransom* (1999), and *By These Hands: A Documentary History of African American Humanism.*

Mark R. Rosenzweig is Walter H. Annenberg Professor in the Social Sciences and professor of economics at the University of Pennsylvania. He has written extensively on the family in developed and developing countries and was coauthor with Guillermina Jasso of the Census Monograph on immigration *The New Chosen People.* In 1980, Rosenzweig served as research director of the Select Commission on Immigration and Refugee Policy. He is a fellow of the Econometrics Society and coeditor of the *Journal of Development*

Economics. He, along with Guillermina Jasso, Douglas Massey, and James Smith, are designing and directing a new program of national longitudinal studies of entering cohorts of immigrants to the United States.

Jonathan D. Sarna is Joseph H. and Belle R. Braun Professor of American Jewish History at Brandeis University. He also serves as chair of the Department of Near Eastern and Judaic Studies and is on the academic advisory and editorial board of the Jacob Rader Marcus Center of the American Jewish Archives, where he serves as consulting scholar. Holder of fellowships from the American Council of Learned Societies, he is the author, editor, or coeditor of sixteen books, including *Minority Faiths and the American Protestant Mainstream* (1997) and *Religion and State in the American Jewish Experience,* with David Dalin (1997). Sarna is now working on a new history of American Judaism to be published by Yale University Press.

James P. Smith holds the Rand chair in labor markets and demographic studies. He has conducted extensive research on immigration, the economics of aging, racial and ethnic differences in wages and employment, economic development, wealth accumulation and savings behavior, and the interrelation of health and economic status. He is currently a co–principal investigator of the New Immigrant Survey and has received the National Institute of Health's MERIT award, its most distinguished honor awarded to a researcher.

Jane I. Smith is professor of Islamic studies and codirector of the Macdonald Center for Christian-Muslim Relations at Hartford Seminary. She has worked extensively on Muslim communities in the United States, Christian theology in relation to Islam, historical relations between Christians and Muslims, and the role and status of women in Islam. Smith is currently the coeditor of *The Muslim World,* editor of the "Islam" section in the new *Encyclopedia of Women in World Religions,* and area editor of *Women in Islamic Cultures.* She has frequently traveled to various regions of the Muslim world and speaks to academic and community groups about Islam and its relationship to the West. Among Smith's most recent publications are *Islam in America, Muslim Minorities in the West: "Visible" and "Invisible,"* and "Islam and Christendom" in *The Oxford History of Islam.* She is codirector of the Henry Luce Forum in Abrahamic Religions, cosponsored with the Greenberg Center of the University of Hartford.